To David Bau[...]

Thank you for your [...]
of my dream — and for your
service to our Nation during
this difficult period in our history

Best wishes for victory
and personal success.
Sincerely,
James Scott
Korea
October 2005

The
Iran Contradictions

JAMES A. SCOTT

The cover-up and the truth hide a deeper secret!

First Edition 2005
Cover design by Dawn M. Budd, Dorothy Ford-Carlton, and J.A. Scott.

Library of Congress Cataloging-in-Publication Data
Scott, James A., 1938-
    The Iran contradictions / James A. Scott.
    p. cm.
    LCCN 2004106880
    ISBN 0-9639250-9-1

    1. Iran-Contra Affair, 1985-1990--Fiction.
    2. Vietnamese Conflict, 1961-1975--Fiction. 3. Military assistance, American--Fiction. 4. Banks and banking--Switzerland--Fiction. I. Title.

PS3619.C665T73 2005   813'.6
                     QBI04-700240

For information and to place orders:
AAFTON Research and Media, Inc.
73 Greentree Drive, Suite 47, Dover, Delaware 19904
E-mail:AAFTON4201@yahoo.com

This book is a product of the writer's imagination. With the exception of historical events and personalities included to create an air of reality, similarities to persons living or dead, or events past or ongoing, are coincidental. Where actions and personality attributes are ascribed to historical figures, they are consistent with testimony before the Congress of the United States and with reports in responsible news media of the period. The sole exception of which the writer is aware is the inclusion of the President of the United States and the First Lady. To the writer's knowledge they were not involved in events described in this work or any similar events.

To
Dorothy
Two Dellas, Two Hazels,
and
James Henry Arnold
wherever you are.

Time will tell, but Silence is
The Code of the Village Triflers

"[P]erhaps the most serious revelation
to have taken place during the course of these proceedings
is that of a plan
proposed by or conceived by high ranking officials
to create a contingency fund
for the intended purpose
of carrying out other covert operations
at some time in the future—
with or without...notice to Congress....
[I]f Members of Congress are not disturbed about that revelation,
then I think the American people should be...."

From a statement by Senator William S. Cohen,
*Joint Hearing on the Iran-Contra Investigation—
Testimony of Oliver L. North*, 100-7, vol. I
(Washington, DC: Government Printing Office, 1988), p. 323.

The
Iran Contradictions

Prologue

In the mid-1980s, the United States Government imposed upon itself two foreign policy constraints that were to have dramatic consequences: it would not negotiate with terrorists, especially for the release of hostages, and it would not provide lethal support to the Contra rebels fighting the communist regime in Nicaragua. At the same time, members of the White House staff, by their own admission, took part in illegal covert activities designed to circumvent or directly violate these policies. They managed the sale of U.S. weapons to Iran at exorbitant prices in return for Iranian efforts to influence the release of American hostages held in Lebanon. Staff members then channeled the "profits" from these weapons sales through Swiss banks to provide lethal aid to the Contras and took part in other questionable fundraising activities to support the rebels. These activities and the subsequent failed attempt to cover them up became known as the "Iran-Contra scandal." Investigations by the Tower Commission, the Congress, and the media left questions at the heart of the scandal unanswered. Chief among them was, "Who was ultimately responsible for Iran-Contra?"

This is a story of the men and women who knew and who kept the secret.

CHAPTER 1

January 1987, Washington, D.C.

Jack Slayton stood in the shadows of the Forrestal Building, nervously anticipating his clandestine meeting with the wife of the President of the United States. Slayton, a former member of the National Security Council staff, was no longer welcome at the White House. This meeting would probably be his only chance to do what had to be done. He ignored the wind whipping about him. Night had descended on the city like a cold, angry animal, but it didn't matter. Slayton had fortified himself with a heavy cashmere coat, several Beefeater martinis, and a .357 Colt revolver.

Down the block and across the street at the Hirschhorn Museum, an unseen watcher lowered the infrared binoculars and picked up his radio. "Fly, this is Walker." Walker was the code name for ground surveillance. "Our man is at the corner of Independence Avenue and 10th Street. He's waiting."

A helicopter with police markings circled lazily near Capitol Hill. The copilot, code name Fly, acknowledged Walker's call. "Roger." Neither the helicopter nor its two occupants had anything to do with the police department.

At 7:45, Walker spoke into his radio again. "Fly, a black Chrysler just turned off Independence and stopped in front of our man." Walker read the license number while Fly wrote on a pad.

Two men got out of the Chrysler and walked briskly toward Slayton. He tensed as they approached and his sweaty fist tightened around the butt of the gun in his pocket. One of the men held up his credentials and said, "Secret Service, Mr. Slayton. We're here to take you to your appointment."

Slayton recognized them as members of the First Lady's security detail.

"We'll have to search you."

"I have a license to carry a gun," Slayton said defensively.

Both agents stopped in their tracks. The one nearest Slayton asked, "Do you have a weapon on your person now?"

"It's in the right pocket of my overcoat." Slayton moved his hands away from his sides to show that he was not a threat.

The agents were on him in a flash, removing the gun and going over him expertly with a metal detector. Slayton had to offer up his gold pens and cigarette case for inspection before they were satisfied. They hustled him into the car, and the Chrysler made a quick U-turn and entered the flow of traffic.

"Fly, this is Walker. The Chrysler made the pickup. It's headed west on Independence."

"Roger, Walker. We see them. Go over to Constitution and drive west. We'll keep you on their tail, but stay well back. We don't want to spook these people."

The Secret Service agents took turns making conversation with their passenger. Slayton tried to relax and joke with them. He knew that if he showed the slightest agitation, he would not get within a block of the First Lady. As they neared Kennedy Center, the small talk ceased and one of the agents turned to Slayton. "We'll be meeting the First Lady shortly. Please remain in this car until I give you clearance to move to hers. You will accompany her as far as Bethesda Medical Center. We'll follow along and bring you back to Washington."

Kennedy Center was bathed in floodlights, but deserted. The Chrysler parked near the front entrance, motor running. Seconds later, a black limousine with opaque rear windows drew close and stopped, its motor also running. The agent who had last talked to Slayton got out of the Chrysler and walked over to the limousine, looking carefully in all directions as he went. The front door of the limo opened as he approached. Slayton could see two men seated inside. The agent said something to them. Slayton guessed it was about the gun. The focus of attention shifted to the rear seat for an extended conference. Perhaps they were trying to convince the First Lady that Slayton was dangerous. He was.

The agent nodded, walked back to the Chrysler and said, "Please come with me." Slayton got out and they walked to the limo. The agent opened the rear door and Slayton slid into the seat next to a smartly dressed woman in her sixties.

The First Lady took his hand and smiled sympathetically. "Jack, how are you?"

"Fine. Just fine," he lied and tried to force a smile that didn't quite come off. The limousine roared off and headed up Rock Creek Parkway.

How is Miriam taking all of this?" the First Lady inquired about Slayton's wife.

"She's not taking it at all. She went back to Kansas," he answered bitterly. "She just got tired of the harassing calls, the hate mail, and the reporters camped out on our lawn day and night. Miriam couldn't take anymore of it and I'm not sure that I can either."

"Maybe you should join her."

"No," Slayton said thoughtfully. "I have business here." He checked to be sure the glass partition separating them from the two Secret Service men in the front seat was closed before he spoke. "I apologize for contacting you in such a roundabout way, but the palace guard won't let me or my messages into the White House anymore."

The First Lady squeezed his hand. "I know, Jack. I am sorry."

Slayton sank back into the soft leather seat. His mental and physical exhaustion were obvious from the lines in his face and the dark circles under his eyes. "I have to talk to the President about a very important matter."

"I'll be glad to give him a message, Jack, but you must know that a meeting between you and the President is impossible. This Iran-Contra thing is out of control and, quite frankly, you are a political liability. That's why he had to let you go."

"That's what I have to talk to him about." There was urgency in Slayton's voice. "He can pick the time and place. I'll even talk to him on a secure phone, as long as he's alone. I don't want the palace guard around. He must talk to me and I don't have much time."

"Jack, why don't you just tell me? I promise to give the President your message word-for-word."

Slayton knew that he was not going to get through. No one ever got past the First Lady to the President unless she wanted them to. He leaned forward in the seat and covered his face with his hands. The Secret Service man in the front seat watched Slayton through a wide-angle rearview mirror and, remembering Slayton's gun, grew uneasy at his passenger's apparent stress level.

The First Lady leaned forward and put her hand on Slayton's shoulder. "Jack, it's alright. You can tell me."

Slayton looked at her with tired eyes. "No. I can't tell you. What I have to say is only for the President." In a barely audible whisper, he added, "Besides, he's the only one who can save me. I've got to look out for myself now."

The First Lady was about to ask a question, but Slayton spoke first. "Tell the President that he must stop the Iran-Contra inquiry. If he doesn't, it will destroy his presidency. Tell him not to trust anybody. If he wants to know the real story of what happened, he'll have to talk to me."

The First Lady was alarmed. "What do you mean, 'destroy his presidency'?"

"What I mean is, the investigation is going to drag on and nobody is going to get close to the truth. And even if someone does, these people will ruin the President's reputation. That's how they plan to save themselves, if they think they're going to be exposed." Slayton was emphasizing his points with hand gestures that betrayed a controlled fury . . . or controlled fear. "They've got money! They've got power! They've got plans! These people are not crackpots. They're practical men with a lot to lose."

The First Lady had been relaxed and sympathetic to her old friend. Now, she sat erect and distanced herself from Slayton's personal agony. This was a matter of the President's survival. Her voice took on a cold and distant quality. "What people have what plans, Jack?"

Slayton knew that he had said too much. His hands trembled ever so slightly. If he didn't get his foot out of his mouth, the First Lady would have him hauled in for a grilling by the Secret Service. That was the last thing he wanted. "No one will harm the President, physically. It won't come to that, but he *must* stop the investigation."

The First Lady said, "No. Congress is involved. He couldn't stop the investigation if he wanted to. That's why you have to give me the message so the President can protect himself."

"Then my message to him is to lie. Tell him to say that he authorized the arms sales to Iran and diversion of the profits to the Contras. He can say that he did it in the hope of freeing the hostages and preserving democracy in Central America. People understand goals like that. They'll support him. His admission of guilt will take the issue away from Congress and the investigation will be over."

But not the impeachment proceedings, thought the First Lady. They would drag on forever. She had no intention of letting her husband suffer the humiliation that Nixon endured. She would beg Slayton, if necessary. She took one of his hands and looked pleadingly into his troubled face. "Jack, you obviously know something of great value to the President." She squeezed his hand. "Please tell me what it is. I promise you the President's support."

Her plea came too late. Slayton realized that he would never talk to the President and he resented the First Lady for blocking him. He was the one who was distant now and desperate. "Tell the President that I'm his John Dean. I know where the cancer is and it's in his bosom. I won't say anymore, except that if he wants to talk, he had better contact me soon." The Secret Service man's heart stopped when Slayton reached inside his coat for a pen and business card. Slayton scribbled a phone number on the back of the card and gave it to the First Lady. "I'll be at this number for a couple of days. I've rented a place in Virginia to get away from the reporters. They're camped outside my house in Georgetown. Ask the President to call me."

Slayton looked out of the window to get his bearings. "Let me out here, please."

While the Secret Service men drove Slayton back to Washington, his meeting with the First Lady was being reported to persons elsewhere in Washington. Decisions were made.

* * *

The intruder picked the lock on the door of Jack Slayton's apartment and made a quick, thorough search of the premises. The place was empty. He took stock of the layout to decide how to set up the action. There was one piece of furniture in the entrance hall: a high, glass-topped table holding a vase of flowers. A half-bath opened off the right side of the hall and a bedroom off the left. The living room was straight ahead. At the living room entrance, the hall took a turn to the right toward the back of the apartment, where the bathroom, den, and kitchen were located. The intruder noted that there was a balcony off the kitchen.

His first order of business was to arrange for an alternate escape route, a precaution against the odd chance that Slayton might bring guests home with him. The intruder went to the kitchen and unlocked the balcony door. Then he looked for a good position for himself during the action. He picked the point where the entrance hall turned right to the kitchen and den. This would put him out of sight when Slayton opened the door and the light from the hallway spilled into the apartment. One final touch remained. He turned on his small flashlight, found the circuit breaker box, and flipped all switches to the "off" position.

Next, the intruder went to the living room and selected a chair near one of the large windows that gave him a view of the parking lot three floors below. On the table next to the chair, he placed a rolled newspaper with a rubber band around it. A blowgun—even a bean shooter—would have been more efficient, but either would be difficult to explain if he was apprehended near the scene. A newspaper, on the other hand, could be carried away inconspicuously or discarded in an emergency. The intruder took a blue capsule, the size of a common cold medication, from his pocket and placed it on the table next to the newspaper. Then he sat down in the darkness and waited.

The intruder would have gotten adequate warning of his prey's arrival, if Slayton had not been paranoid. Slayton should have driven into the housing complex and parked in the space designated with his apartment number. He didn't. Slayton was aware that every reporter in Washington knew or could get his license number and a description of his car. That had been true even before the Iran-Contra story became big news. He was not about to let his car expose his hideaway due to a chance sighting by some vigilant member of the Washington press corps. So, he parked in an undesignated space three buildings away and walked to the stone path leading to the door of his building. The intruder was not alerted until he saw Slayton pause under the street lamp at the curb to locate his door key.

Slayton's sudden appearance startled the intruder. In a rare moment of panic, he reached clumsily for the rolled newspaper and leaped to his feet. Remembering the capsule, he groped frantically for it in the dark, without success. Slayton unlocked the outside door downstairs. The intruder dropped to his knees and swept the rug with his hands, but could not find the capsule. He cursed quietly and gave up. Slayton was starting up the first flight of stairs. The intruder took a second capsule from his pocket, removed one end, and inhaled deeply several times. Then, he closed the capsule and returned it to his pocket. Slayton was at the landing between the second and third floors. The intruder hastily tore open the end of an envelope containing a fine powder and, holding the rolled newspaper in his left hand, with his forefinger over the down end of the aperture, he emptied the contents into the up end, like a soldier pouring powder into a muzzle-loading pistol. Slayton's key was in the door. The intruder flattened himself against the wall. Slayton opened the door and flicked the hall light switch. Nothing happened. He grumbled, closed the door, and walked into the apartment. When Slayton reached the point where the hall turned right, the intruder blew as hard as he could into the rolled newspaper and a jet of dust streamed out of the other end and into Slayton's face. Instantly, Slayton experienced the crushing pressure of an intense pain in his chest.

Slayton gasped and clawed at his shirtfront. He staggered backwards and fell against the hall table. The glass tabletop and flower vase crashed to the floor, shattering into a hundred pieces. The intruder winced at the noise. Slayton rolled away from what was left of the table. He was face up, still clutching his chest, and unconscious.

The intruder stuffed the newspaper into one pocket and from another extracted a small, but powerful, battery-operated vacuum cleaner and quickly ran it over Slayton's hair, face, coat, and the hall floor to remove any residue of the dust. The hit and clean-up had taken less than two minutes. Now, for the escape.

After the table crash, it was impossible for the intruder to leave by the front door. That might bring him face to face with a curious neighbor on the stairs. He dashed to the kitchen balcony at the back of the apartment, climbed over the railing, and shinnied down a balcony support column to the back yard.

The couple in the apartment below Slayton's didn't notice. Suspecting burglary, they were busy phoning the police. The intruder did not escape unseen. A Vietnamese man watched from his darkened window across the courtyard. He considered rushing out to follow the hit man, but he had no way of knowing that Slayton was dead and rejected the idea. The man making the unorthodox exit from Slayton's apartment would be on his guard and the Vietnamese had come too close to expose himself prematurely.

* * *

Baltimore, Maryland, the following evening

Rear Admiral Gordon Schaeffer paced the floor of his hideaway condominium overlooking Baltimore's Inner Harbor. Assistant Secretary of the Treasury, Jules Vaterman, sat on the couch sipping coffee. He wondered if the admiral's judgment was slipping under the pressure of current events. Schaeffer spun in mid-stride and jabbed a finger in Vaterman's direction. "Jules, you've got to come up with some kind of economic aid package for the Vietnamese. As soon as I got off the airplane yesterday, there was another note from the White House. The President wants to see movement on recovering those MIA remains from the Vietnamese Government."

Vaterman threw up his hands in a helpless gesture. "We've been over this before. The Vietnamese are playing stud poker with us and they're only holding one card that the American people care about: those MIA remains. In return, they want diplomatic recognition and three billion dollars in economic aid. The President refuses to make any concessions to the Vietnamese until they set up a system for locating and repatriating the MIA remains. We're deadlocked. End of conversation."

"Then why don't we arrange for some aid from the slush fund?"

"Too risky. If there was even a hint that the U.S. gave aid to the Vietnamese in exchange for MIA remains, we would have another hostage crisis on our hands. This administration can't survive two Iran-Contra scandals . . . and neither can we."

The admiral sat down on the couch beside Vaterman and spoke with a quiet urgency. "Jules, we can't let the Vietnamese go public with the information they have. If it's not practical to give them aid directly, why not move in one of our proprietary firms? The

Vietnamese can charge them three billion in taxes over some agreeable period. That way, they still get what they want and keep their mouths shut. We get the MIA remains. Everybody is happy. Who would know?"

"The world would know, Gordon." Vaterman let out a sigh before starting his tutorial on the politics of the Socialist Republic of Vietnam. "What you're proposing might be a good idea if we were dealing with another government, but it won't work with the Vietnamese. They have no reason to keep quiet about any aid that we give them. What the Vietnamese want most is legitimacy for their regime. They need it for support at home and it would give them new status in the international community. The best stamp of legitimacy they can get is recognition by the United States. Economic aid is a form of recognition. And mark my words, the day that the first dollar changes hands, the Vietnamese will stage a propaganda field day. They might turn over a few sets of MIA remains," conceded Vaterman, "but in the process, they'll tell the world how they beat us in the war and then made us pay damages. For those people, 'face' is the name of the game. You have to understand that, if you want to win. The other side of the coin is that we can't afford to drain that kind of money from our private sources for Vietnam."

"Well, what are we going to do?"

"Nothing, for the time being. Tell the White House that progress is impossible under the current guidelines. Say hopeful things to the MIA lobby. Give the action to some third echelon staff guy and move on to more important issues. Wait for circumstances to improve. The Vietnamese won't make trouble until they see what Colonel Can turns up. He may be an economic wizard, but he isn't going to find what he's looking for. When he comes up empty, we'll have another opportunity to bargain."

"And what happens if Can does turn up something?"

"We'll just have to rely on you to see that he doesn't."

When Vaterman had gone, Schaeffer sat down and took a folder from his desk drawer. The folder held a thick Defense Intelligence Agency report marked "TOP SECRET." Schaeffer turned to the first page and read again the final sentences of the executive summary. They were burned into his brain after months of fruitless negotiations with the Vietnamese.

*The evidence presented herein supports the inescapable
conclusion that the SRV (Socialist Republic of Vietnam)
is currently holding the remains of 400 dead Americans
in a warehouse in Hanoi. (See satellite photograph and
street map at Appendix K.) It is estimated that SRV
will neither acknowledge the existence of these remains
nor return them en masse, in spite of current U.S.
diplomatic initiatives. SRV will likely release sets of
remains at times which suit their propaganda or political
objectives.*

Schaeffer wondered, "How in the hell can you deal with these barbarians?"

Vaterman had been gone for over an hour. Schaeffer sat at the desk peering intently at the array of file cards describing the MIA problem and possible solutions. It was exasperating. He removed the reading glasses from his tired blue eyes and let his gaze drift through the large window into the darkness and the harbor lights below. Being there, above the crowds, watching the lights dance on the water usually generated serenity in him and a creativity that provided solutions to his problems. That was why he had become attached to the place. It was almost like being on a ship again. He smiled at the thought. The smile froze, then disappeared when the doorbell rang. Only a handful of people knew about this place and they rarely visited—for security reasons. Schaeffer pressed a button on his desk console and a television screen to his right flickered to life, revealing the image of a familiar face.

The man was in his forties. From the crown of his blond head to the tip of his straight nose, he had a refined, even regal, look about him. His mouth was the inharmonious part of his face. Beneath his thin upper lip sat a pouting, oversized lower one. It had a slightly bluish tint and angled to one side, imparting a debauched and cruel cast to his face. The total impression was one of a keen intelligence without scruples. That was an accurate reflection of the inner man. Schaeffer pressed the electronic lock release and watched the screen until the man entered and the door was secured. He switched channels and, minutes later, observed the man leave the elevator and approach the apartment. Schaeffer turned the monitor off and opened the door for his guest. Neither man spoke until both were inside the apartment. Schaeffer walked to a bank of stereo equipment and turned on two radios tuned to different stations, a minimum precaution against electronic eavesdropping. Then, he motioned his guest to a cul-de-sac of soft chairs. "Well, Ackerman, what brings you to the States? I hope you came to tell me that you found Dillworth."

"No."

The admiral was surprised. "Well, what the devil have you been doing over there? It's been three weeks. You people have been sitting on your duffs—and don't tell me that you don't have sufficient resources."

The visitor examined his nails just long enough to remind Schaeffer that he was dealing with an equal. He said gently, "We wouldn't be looking for Dillworth if you hadn't confronted him. We could have dealt with him quietly and avoided the manhunt."

Schaeffer glared, but said nothing. Ackerman was correct.

"We all have as much to lose as you do," continued Ackerman. "We'll get Dillworth." There was a grim determination in his voice.

"If you didn't come about Dillworth, why are you here?" asked Schaeffer.

"Slayton had a heart attack last night."

"You're late. I read about it in the paper this morning. I hope you didn't come all the way from Switzerland to deliver that news."

"No. I came to deliver Slayton's heart attack," he said coldly.

"Slayton's death was a hit?" The admiral jumped to his feet.

"Yes."

"For God's sake, why?"

"Slayton was trying to get an audience with the President to bare his soul. He came very close. He got to the First Lady."

"Why wasn't I consulted?"

"You were out of touch. The Embassy Man ordered the hit."

Schaeffer worked to contain his anger. He walked to the window and peered out at the lights dancing on the dark water below. The visitor joined him. Without turning, Schaeffer said, "I don't like it. You start hitting committee members and pretty soon everyone is looking over his shoulder. Trust evaporates." Schaeffer turned to the man. "We're a fragile organization. We can't exist without trust. Do you understand?"

Smirking, Ackerman observed, "You want Dillworth hit. He's a committee member."

"Damn it! That's different and you know it."

"I understand that. I even agree with you, but you have to draw the line somewhere. There are people you can trust and people you can't. We trust you, even though you've made some bad calls lately. Colonel Can is running around, looking under rocks. Then, there was Dillworth. That confrontation stuff might work for the Navy, but we're not in the Navy. All you did was warn him. Now, he's on the run. As for Slayton, we should have hit him when he first opposed our plan to cover ourselves if the Iran-Contra investigation came too close to home. You voted 'no.' So we end up hitting him after he talks to the First Lady. That tends to validate whatever he may have told her. That's not good. We couldn't trust Slayton, we can't trust Dillworth, and we sure as hell can't trust that little Vietnamese bastard, Can. So, we have to deal with them."

There was a long silence while both men stared out into the night. Finally, Ackerman spoke. "Three strikes and you're out, Gordon. It's the American way. We want you in. So, I'll take care of Dillworth. The committee agreed that Colonel Can is your problem." Ackerman turned and headed for the door, pausing at Schaeffer's desk to glance at some documents. He looked up smiling. "Well, I see you're already working on the Vietnamese issue. That's good."

Schaeffer continued to stare out into the night.

"No hard feelings, Admiral. Remember that we agreed a long time ago to tell it like it is . . . to maintain that trust you're so concerned about."

Schaeffer ignored the comment. "When do you go back to Geneva?"

"Tomorrow. I have an early flight out of BWI."

"Good hunting." Behind the remark was the hope that Ackerman would find Dillworth quickly and dispose of him. With Dillworth and Slayton dead, the committee could focus its energies on the Vietnamese.

CHAPTER 2

March 1975
Prisoner of War Interrogation Center, Vung Tau, South Vietnam

"You had better have some damn good intelligence to drag me out of the embassy at a time like this," said the blond man. He strode into the room and dropped his Swedish K submachinegun onto the battered field table that served as the captain's desk. "The North Vietnamese Army is kicking butt on all fronts. The South Vietnamese are in full retreat. Everybody who is anybody is trying to leave the country before the commies take over and my station chief wants a situation briefing every other minute. What the hell is so important? And tell me fast because I am going to get back on that helicopter in ten minutes." He looked at his watch to emphasize the fact that he was serious about the departure time. The embassy man took a handkerchief from the pocket of his meticulously pressed jungle fatigues, removed his gold-rimmed granny glasses, and mopped the perspiration from his handsome, tanned face.

The room was hot. Its small windows were high and barred. The walls were whitewashed cinderblock and the floor was bare concrete. Both were covered with a thin film of moisture. "Penal austere" was the motif. There were only five pieces of furniture in the place: a rusting file cabinet, the battered field table, two ancient folding chairs, one of which was occupied by the captain, and a small Japanese refrigerator. This last item was the only concession to comfort.

The captain sat behind the field table. It held a desk plate notifying visitors that he was the "U.S. Army Liaison Officer" to the Vietnamese interrogation center. He was tough, intelligent, barrel-gutted, and profane. The large ring on his left hand signified a better-than-average education, but he had emerged unrefined by the experience. Like many men who had survived more than one tour in Vietnam and considered themselves field soldiers, he held civilians in low esteem. The embassy man would normally have fallen into that category, CIA or not, but the captain recognized, beneath his polished veneer, cunning intelligence and ambition. On past occasions, that combination had driven the embassy man to quick, ruthless action. These traits attracted the captain. They also made him wary.

The captain tilted his chair back, opened the refrigerator, and took out his last two bottles of San Miguel beer. He pried off the tops and handed a bottle to the embassy man. "Put this in your mouth. It's cold and it'll keep you from saying anything stupid while I give you the freaking mother lode." He tilted his chair back again and took a long pull on his bottle.

"Three nights ago," began the captain, "the Vietnamese naval district operations center here reported that one of their radar stations had sighted a submarine about a mile off the coast." He used his weight to twist the chair toward the wall map behind him. "Right about here." He pointed to a spot on the map.

The embassy man frowned. "That should have been reported in one of the daily intelligence summaries. I don't remember reading anything about a submarine sighting." And he read everything.

"If the District had made an official report, someone would have had to sail out to the submarine and investigate. The Vietnamese naval commander did not want to do that."

"Why not?"

The captain smiled at the naive embassy man. "Because, no captain is going to risk having his ship torpedoed out from under him, considering how the war is going. It's his transportation out of the country if the NVA wins. Some of the navy officers already have their families on board."

"Well, did *anybody* try to find out what the sub was up to?" The embassy man set his beer down on the rusting file cabinet and took a writing pad and pen from the pocket of his fatigue jacket.

"Yeah, someone checked it out, but you might not want to put this on paper just yet."

In Vietnam, there were things that one had to know and to pass on, but a prudent man did not always write them down. The embassy man shoved the pen and pad back into his pocket.

After another pull on the beer, the captain picked up the story. "The navy people figured that if the sub wasn't friendly, it might be dropping off infiltrators. They passed the information to the local army commander, who sent out patrols to cover the beaches where infiltrators were likely to land. For the first couple of hours, it was just a stroll along the seashore for everybody. But at 2 a.m., one of the patrols spotted a rubber boat floating near the beach and hauled it in. Someone had blasted it full of holes and left it to sink."

"Sloppy work," noted the embassy man.

"Half an hour later," continued the captain, "another patrol stumbled into a second NVA landing party, trying to bury their rubber boat in a sand dune behind the beach. There was one hell of a firefight and when the smoke cleared, all of the NVA on the ground were dead."

"For crying out loud," said the embassy man. "Couldn't they have taken just one prisoner?"

"I said all of the NVA *on the ground* were dead. A sharp Vietnamese lieutenant pulled the rubber boat out of the hole to check it out and found one of the infiltrators hiding underneath. The man must have jumped into the hole during the firefight, figuring he could slip away before dawn. The patrol turned him over to us for interrogation."

"What did he tell you?"

"Nothing, yet."

The embassy man slammed down his beer bottle. "Well, what the hell did you bring me down here for?"

"Because you know him." The captain grinned.

"Who is he?"

"I don't know, but I saw him the last time I was in your office at the embassy. There was a chart on the wall near your desk that had a diagram of the North Vietnamese Ministry of Economics. You had photographs of the bigwigs stuck to the diagram and our prisoner's picture was one of them. I thought you might be able to help us ask him the right questions. He's been lying to us since they brought him in." The captain continued to smile his crooked, knowing smile.

The embassy man looked at his host incredulously. "You must be mistaken. The men on that chart are high civil servants. They don't hit beaches with raiding parties."

The captain's smile faded and his voice took on a hard edge. "Don't you bet the family jewels on it, my friend. This was no ordinary team of infiltrators. They were armed like no NVA soldiers I have ever seen—silencers on their automatic rifles and side arms, a sniper rifle with a laser scope, and enough explosives to blow up Saigon. One was a pilot, too, judging from the gear he was carrying." The captain paused to drink the last of his warm beer. "Oh, yeah. There is one other little detail that might interest you. One of the dead infiltrators looked Russian. Maybe the submarine was Russian, too."

The embassy man raised his eyebrows. "We had better have a serious talk with your prisoner. You say he's told you nothing so far?"

"Oh, he gave us his cover story . . . in Vietnamese, by the way. Says he doesn't understand or speak English. Claims he didn't come in on the sub with the others. Says he's a local Viet Cong guide. His job was to meet the infiltrators on the beach and take 'em to a rendezvous near the marketplace in Vung Tau. Another guide was supposed to take over at that point and lead the team to an unknown location."

"Why don't you believe him?"

"His story has too many holes. He said he was a farmer, but his hands and muscles are soft. A farmer works in the sun. He's not tanned. Got good teeth, too. You ever see a Vietnamese farmer over thirty with good teeth? The clincher was that I remembered seeing his picture in your office."

"Does he know that you recognized him?"

"No," replied the captain.

"Does he know what happened to the rest of his landing party?"

"No. Like I told you, it was dark when the firefight took place. The ARVNs"—he was referring to soldiers of the Army of the Republic of (South) Vietnam—"found him just after that, threw a bag over his head, and hustled him down here within thirty minutes. He'd have no way of knowing who got away and who didn't."

"Good." The embassy man rubbed his hands. "We have a lot to work with. What kind of shape is he in?"

The captain snorted. "He hasn't had any food or sleep to speak of since he got here and the ARVNs have been steady kicking his ass."

"I'm not concerned with the condition of his anatomy," said the embassy man, impatiently. "What about his mental state? How close is he to breaking? How much longer before he tells you just what the hell he's doing here?"

"It's hard to tell. He's a tough little sucker and well-briefed on resisting interrogation. He won't say anything until he can't stand the pain anymore. Then, he tells us his cover story, even though he knows it won't hold water." The captain rubbed his fingers thoughtfully over his cheek. "But the way he tells the cover story has changed. When we started interrogating him, he told it slow and deliberate. He was stalling for time. Now, he blurts it out like he can't wait to tell us, once he starts talking. His resistance is wearing thin. If we could just get him to tell the truth about any small aspect of his mission, I think he would spill his guts. We need some mental or physical leverage to make him start giving us the straight skinny."

The captain cocked his head to one side and said, mockingly, "Out of respect to your sensibilities with regard to the treatment of prisoners, I didn't use the more medieval physical techniques. Perhaps you could show us how to finesse the information out of him." The crooked smile played at the corners of the captain's mouth.

The embassy man considered the problem. "It's been three days since the infiltrators landed. Whatever they came to do could happen any day. Perhaps we should combine a little of the mental and the medieval to persuade the prisoner to speak candidly with us." He gave the captain a cold smile. "Is Ky here?"

"He's been kicked upstairs to administration. His methods were too medieval, even by Vietnamese standards."

"I want Ky for this interrogation. Make it happen."

The embassy man stood at the door and peered through the peephole into the interrogation room. Turning to the captain he said, "You've got a damn good memory. It's him. Let's get started."

The prisoner was seated in an uncomfortable metal chair under a battery of spotlights. His head hung forward and his eyes were closed. His small body was lost in the traditional black Vietnamese pajamas. A hand-cranked electric generator with two wire leads stood near the prisoner's chair. It was still warm. The room was just like the captain's office, except that it was windowless and manacles were attached to the walls and the floor so that a prisoner could be chained in any position imaginable and most of them uncomfortable. A South Vietnamese sergeant, wearing sunglasses, hovered over the prisoner, barking questions and denying the truth of his answers. Behind the spotlights, an American Army sergeant paced and chewed on a cigar.

The embassy man burst into the room with the captain at his heels. "Has he told you anything yet?"

The American sergeant said something in Vietnamese to the sergeant with the sunglasses. Both men shook their heads. The American sergeant said, "The sum-bitch is half dead and he ain't give us squat. We need to stop being nice and give him a real goingover."

The embassy man dismissed the suggestion with a wave of his hand. What he said next were mainly lies for the prisoner's ears. "You don't even know the right questions to ask this man. There's no need for anymore of this, anyway. I have all of the information I need."

The prisoner raised his head slowly and squinted into the lights, trying to get a look at the speaker.

"Get him some food and water," commanded the embassy man, "and prepare those papers for his transfer to Saigon. I want everybody out and knock before you bring the food in."

When the others had left, the embassy man turned off the spotlights. "What is your name?" he asked the prisoner, in English.

In a halting accent, the prisoner answered, "I-no-spee-En'lish."

"Really? Then you must have had a difficult time with your studies at the London School of Economics." The prisoner's eyes focused.

"What is your name and occupation?" This time the embassy man spoke in Vietnamese and his tone was gentle.

"Pham Van Minh. I am a farmer," said the prisoner.

"Please don't insult my intelligence, Dr. Nu. I know everything about you. I knew that you were coming here before you set foot aboard that submarine," the embassy man lied. "I knew your time and place of arrival. That's why we were waiting to ambush you on the beach. I know your target, time of attack, and the methods you planned to use. I know everything, thanks to our spies in Hanoi and the details that we were able to sweat out of your men."

Dr. Nu looked up at the embassy man with tired eyes.

The embassy man smiled. "Oh, yes. Several of them were persuaded to talk. But then, we couldn't expect all of them to be as brave as you, could we?"

The embassy man walked around behind the prisoner's chair. "We've pieced the entire plan together and alerted the American and Vietnamese authorities. I must admit that it would have been a brilliant stroke. Unfortunately for you, it's aborted." He paused to let his lie sink into the prisoner's consciousness. "But, that is the past. You need to start thinking about the future."

The embassy man walked back into the prisoner's field of vision and gave him a grave look. "You are a spy, Dr. Nu, and they shoot spies here. There's no trial, no delay. They just take spies out behind the building, stand them against the wall, and blow their brains out." He let that image sink in.

"You have some very good brains and it would be a shame to see them splattered all over the compound wall, especially with your army so close to victory over the South Vietnamese."

The prisoner's eyes widened.

"Oh, yes, Dr. Nu, you North Vietnamese will win the war. It's just a matter of weeks, maybe days. A united Vietnam will need people like you to bind the nation together and rebuild it. Killing someone of your ability would be a waste. With that in mind, I have requested that you be transferred to a detention center in Saigon. You will be relatively safe there until your army takes the city."

The embassy man could sense the prisoner's relief. "Dr. Nu, my profession is intelligence, not murder. I have no need to see you killed. However, these are violent times. People want to shoot spies." He raised his palms hopelessly. "And now that I know your plan, you have nothing to trade for your life. . . . Well, almost nothing." The embassy man left the prisoner to wonder what he meant and moved on, still conversing in fluent Vietnamese.

"You understand the concept of losing face and saving it. So, let me tell you about one of the interrogators here: Sergeant Ky. He is, in fact, one of the best interrogators in the South Vietnamese Army. Sergeant Ky is in a position of having to save face, to avoid embarrassment in front of his family and friends, because of you.

"Three nights ago, when you and your people came ashore and fell into the trap I had set for you, most of your men were killed or captured. Unfortunately, two of them slipped away in the darkness and confusion, and made their way to a military motor pool not far from the beach. There, they knifed a Vietnamese guard and stole a truck to make their getaway. That guard was Sergeant Ky's younger brother. You haven't had the pleasure of Sergeant Ky's company during your stay with us. He's been busy . . . mourning and burying his brother. But he is back at work today and he can't wait to get his hands on you. He wants to know the whereabouts of the two soldiers who killed his brother. And, frankly, that is the only information that you could trade for your life. If you don't give Sergeant Ky the address of the safe house where your men are hiding, he is going to lose face with the people here at the interrogation center. He is going to lose face with his friends. Most important of all, he is going to lose face with his family. All of these people know that you are here. They expect Sergeant Ky to find out from you where those two soldiers are hiding so that he can avenge his brother's death. If you don't give him that information—and quickly—he will torture you unmercifully and shoot you."

The prisoner began to sweat. The embassy man continued, "I don't want Sergeant Ky to kill you, but I have very limited influence over what goes on here. This compound is under South Vietnamese control. However, you have my word that if you give Sergeant Ky the information he wants, I will take you to Saigon today. I wouldn't give a piaster for your chances of survival here."

Nu's mouth started to work, but the embassy man shook his head. "No. You must give the information to Sergeant Ky. Otherwise, he will lose face."

Sergeant Ky wore tiger-striped fatigues, was bowlegged, and built like a fire plug. He entered Nu's interrogation room exuding a controlled fury. Randy, the American sergeant, was with him, whispering a loud reminder in Vietnamese that he was not to kill the prisoner. The Vietnamese sergeant with the sunglasses had also returned—to help with the "hands-on" part of the interrogation.

There was no need to tell Dr. Nu that the man advancing toward him was Ky. The terror in his eyes said it all and he began to blurt out his worthless cover story before anyone got near him. "My name is Pham Van—"

Ky cut the prisoner's lie short with a sharp blow to the head. He yanked Nu out of the chair by his pajama top and flung him into the arms of the other Vietnamese sergeant. Together, they manacled the prisoner to the floor. Ky reached down and tore away Nu's pajama top with a single yank. The prisoner's pants and underwear followed. Nu tensed his little body in anticipation of the pain that would follow. But nothing could have prepared him for what happened during the next ten minutes. Ky neither asked questions nor acknowledged the screams and worthless information that Nu voluntarily gave him to stop the pain. He was a man possessed as he committed unspeakable atrocities on the body of Dr. Nu. For everyone but Ky, those ten minutes were an eternity of pain and screams, against the constant background whir of the electric generator, overlaid with the sickening odors of burning butane and charred flesh. The horror continued until the embassy man signaled.

For a time the room was silent, except for Nu's fading sobs. Then, Ky knelt beside the prisoner and calmly told the embassy man's lie.

"Your men killed my brother. You will give me the location of their safe house." He paused. "In a minute, the pain is going to start again and it's not going to stop until you tell me everything I want to know. The pain will get worse if you lie and it will decrease if I believe you, but it will not stop until you have been completely truthful with me. Understand?"

Nu didn't respond. Ky jabbed one of the prisoner's wounds and the man's body recoiled violently in response to the pain.

"Do you understand?" Ky repeated.

There were tears in Nu's eyes when he whispered, "Yes."

The horror started again. The generator whirred and the butane burned and the prisoner screamed and Ky asked his questions.

"Where are your men? Where is their safe house located? What street? What address?"

Finally, Nu could stand the pain no longer and he gave Ky the safe house information. But the pain and the questions did not cease.

"Why did you and your men come here to kill my brother? If you didn't come to kill him, why did you come? What was your mission?"

The pain increased and Nu cursed and screamed. He went on screaming until finally the answers gushed out of him in a babble of Vietnamese, English, and French. He told them everything: the target, the date, and every detail he could remember or manufacture. When Nu finished, they all stood in stunned silence. The Vietnamese sergeants were afraid of the secrets that Nu had told them. They should have been because for the Americans in the room, it was a once-in-a-lifetime opportunity. They all had to make some quick decisions about what to do with the information—and each other.

The embassy man knew what had to be done. He turned to the captain and said, "Nobody leaves this room until I get back." Before anyone could react, he opened the door and was gone.

The captain hesitated for a moment and darted after him. He caught up with the embassy man halfway down the corridor and grabbed him by the arm. "Wait a minute. You ain't gonna tell those faggots in Saigon about this, are you? We've got an opportunity here. You tell Saigon and a bunch of Vietnamese generals are gonna get on that plane and fly off to their villas in France. You and me, we're gonna get screwed without gettin' kissed."

The embassy man's anger was cold and contained. "Take your hand off my arm." The captain did. "I know what's at stake. I need a couple of minutes to figure out what to do about it." In a more conciliatory tone, he added, "You and I are thinking the same thing; we could handle this ourselves."

"Damn right! I could go back to Saigon with you and put a team together in a couple of days."

"First things first. I need a few minutes to map this out. Meantime, I'm going to the helicopter to get my camera. I want a picture of Nu. You go back inside and don't let anybody leave." The embassy man strode off down the corridor.

The captain went back into the interrogation room and leaned against the door. The three sergeants looked at him with questions in their eyes, but considering what they had heard from Nu, they dared not ask them. After an uncomfortable silence, the American sergeant asked, "Is he gonna report this to Saigon?"

"No," answered the captain.

"I don't trust that embassy man, Cap'n. He ain't got the balls for this kinda action. He's probably calling Saigon on the helicopter radio right now. You better stop him before he blows this."

Before the captain could react to Randy's suggestion, the embassy man returned. His right hand hung loosely at his side and in it was an automatic with a long black silencer attached to the barrel.

Sergeant Ky was standing near the center room. The embassy man fired a bullet that hit him in the forehead. The impact carried Ky backwards while his feet worked furiously to keep his body upright. He went down when the second bullet hit him in the chest. The sergeant in the sunglasses knew that he was next. He opened his mouth to scream. Nothing came out because the first bullet tore his throat away and the second snapped his head back. He rolled away into the corner, dead.

Randy tried to get to the shoulder holster under his fatigue jacket, but the embassy man had him covered. "Take your gun out and put it on the floor. Then, step back."

Randy did as he was told. The embassy man picked up Randy's .45 with his left hand and asked, "Are you in or out?"

"In," said Randy, though not sure exactly what he was in*to*.

Without taking his eyes or gun off Randy, the embassy man addressed the captain. "He's your man. Can he be trusted with an operation of this magnitude?"

"Yeah."

"You better be sure of that because he's your responsibility. If he screws up, I'll be looking for both of you." Then, to Randy, he said, "Get the prisoner on his feet."

Randy took the manacles off Dr. Nu's wrists and ankles and helped him struggle painfully to his feet. Without warning, the embassy man raised Randy's .45 and fired two rounds into Dr. Nu's chest. The impact of the bullets flung the little man against the far wall of the room. While Randy was still in shock, the embassy man handed the smoking weapon back to him and tossed his own gun on the floor near Dr. Nu's body. Calmly, he surveyed the carnage and explained the situation to Randy and the captain.

"Now, the way I figure it, someone smuggled a gun in to Nu. Nu shot Ky and the other Vietnamese sergeant and Randy shot Nu. Any questions?" There were none. "Good. That's what we'll tell the Vietnamese."

"Let's get out of here," said the embassy man. "We've got to stop Nu's men before they make their move on Tan Son Nhut Airport. First, we'll take the safe house. Then, we figure out what to do about the plane."

CHAPTER 3

The secretary's voice purred reverently out of the intercom. "Dr. Eaton, the White House is on Line 2."

Ellis Eaton, graying, fiftyish, and regal, smiled. The word would spread through the grapevine like wildfire while his colleagues turned green with envy. When one was brilliant and had all the money one would ever need, access to the center of political power set one apart from the intelligentsia and the old money. To actually wield influence at that center was the ultimate ego trip—and Eaton relished that kind of journey. He was a man who secretly reveled in the appearance as well as the substance of power. Though many months had passed since he had tendered his resignation as a White House special adviser on national security matters—some said he left when he saw Iran-Contra coming—he still received personal calls from the President.

Eaton greeted the caller and listened attentively. "Yes, Mr. President. I can be there at two o'clock. You are quite welcome."

* * *

The President rose to greet Eaton as he was ushered into the Oval Office. "Welcome back, Ellis," smiled the President. "How are things in academia?"

"Very interesting, but without the challenge and excitement of the White House. How are you, Mr. President?"

"I've been better, but the rumor that I'm in a coma in the White House basement has been greatly exaggerated." Both men laughed.

"And the First Lady?" inquired Eaton.

"Fine, until she talked to Jack Slayton last night."

Eaton raised a disapproving eyebrow. "She met with Slayton?"

"Yes and she's worried about some of the things he said. To tell you the truth, I'm concerned too. That's why I asked you to come by." The President sat down at his desk and motioned Eaton to a chair.

Eaton said, "You know that Slayton was found dead last evening."

"I read about it in the newspaper. Slayton talked to my wife last night for about twenty minutes. He made some wild accusations about the White House staff." Eaton frowned, but said nothing. "That's probably not unusual for a man in his position. He's taken a lot of heat over this Iran-Contra mess. The problem is that he was scared and carrying a gun. Less than three hours later, he was dead. I'm having difficulty accepting that as a coincidence. "

"What accusations did he make?" asked Eaton.

"What he said is not important at this point, but the man was afraid for his life and now he's dead. For my own peace of mind and for my wife's, I need to know if Slayton died of natural causes."

"How may I be of service to you?"

"You've made discreet inquiries for me in the past, Ellis. I'd like you to have someone look into Slayton's death and confirm the cause. I don't want White House people involved. How about someone from your old team; that fellow I gave the medal to, What's-his-name?"

"Holloway."

*　*　*

Ed Holloway got out of his gunmetal gray 300ZX and walked up the stone path to the building where Jack Slayton had been murdered. It was a few minutes to four in the afternoon and one hour since he and Ellis Eaton had worked out the cover under which he would inquire into Slayton's death. A call from a friend in the Defense Investigative Service to the Alexandria Police Department had smoothed the way for a little intergovernmental cooperation.

The outside door was open. Holloway walked up the two flights of stairs to Slayton's apartment and knocked. A thin detective with bug eyes opened the door.

Holloway flashed his identification card and said, "Holloway. Defense Investigative Service. Your office authorized me to take a look at the apartment. They were supposed to call you."

"They did. I'm Hicks." The detective extended his hand while he compared Holloway's face to the picture on the identification card. "I thought you guys only did background investigations."

"That's close," replied Holloway with a shrug, "but when someone with a top security clearance dies, the Pentagon likes to make sure that nobody pulled out his fingernails before he cashed in. Slayton had access to a lot of classified information when he worked in the White House. That qualifies him for a look-see. Find any fingernails?" Before the detective could answer, Holloway jammed his hands into his pockets and began to examine a painting hanging in the hallway. His inattention was calculated to give the impression that he did not take the inquiry seriously. It worked.

Hicks closed the door, shaking his head in disgust. Here was another Pentagon bureaucrat wasting police time and the taxpayers' money. "Sorry to disappoint you. All of Slayton's fingernails were still connected to his hands. The coroner's preliminary diagnosis was that he died of a heart attack."

Holloway, still inspecting the painting, mused, "I'm not surprised. Slayton was under a lot of stress because of the Iran-Contra thing."

"Yeah," said Hicks, his tone reflecting Holloway's disinterest in the conversation. "Well, is there something specific I can do for you?"

Holloway reluctantly shifted his attention from the painting. "Give me a rundown on what's happened so far. Then, I'd like to have a look around the apartment and chat with the neighbors."

The detective ran through the key events in a bored monotone. "About 9:30 last night, Slayton came here, opened the door, and dropped dead. He knocked over some furniture when he fell. The noise alerted the family in the apartment below. They called the police. A patrol car got here at 9:42; that's when the body was found. The coroner arrived at 10:14 and pronounced Slayton dead. No signs of foul play. The body is at the morgue for an autopsy."

"For what it's worth," continued Hicks, "this apartment is leased by one of Slayton's friends. The friend is vacationing in California. We contacted him by phone last night. He said Slayton's been hiding out here for a few weeks to get away from the limelight. Now, you know as much as I do. You can look the place over, but don't touch. If the autopsy turns up anything strange, the fingerprint boys will come in and dust the place. Life might get interesting for you if they found your prints all over the art work." Hicks gave Holloway a cold smile.

"Thanks," said Holloway. "Looks like I won't have to waste a lot of time on this one. I'll have a quick look around and be on my way."

"You do that. I'll be in the den."

When Hicks had disappeared, Holloway surveyed the rooms opening off the entrance hall: a half-bath on the right and a bedroom on the left. Then he walked back to the living room and tried to visualize how a hit man, if indeed there had been one, would have prepared for Slayton. He tried to recall the methods that he himself had used in what seemed like another life. There would have been some early warning of Slayton's arrival. Holloway noted the chair near the window, overlooking Slayton's parking space. And there would have been an escape route; the back balcony, he noted, would do nicely for that purpose.

A hit man would have had to wait. Most hitters were careful during the wait. But if it was overly long, there was a danger of losing one's concentration, of doing something unprofessional. Holloway decided that a killer would have waited in the living room. The bathroom and bedroom offered no access to an escape route if something went wrong. The kitchen and den were too far away from where Slayton fell. Holloway walked through the living room carefully examining all surfaces where a hitter might have left some trace of his presence. Nothing. Methodically, he removed and replaced all of the chair and sofa cushions, collecting little treasures that had accumulated beneath them. He was replacing the last cushion when the detective's voice brought him up with a start.

"What the hell are you doing?"

Holloway looked up to see the man scowling at him from the doorway. "Just checking. You never can tell what will fall out of a person's pocket." Holloway hoped he sounded casual.

"What did you find?" Hicks moved in for a closer look.

"Thirty-five cents, a key, and a glass ball." The ball was one of those marble-size, cut glass globes that attach to the end of a key chain. As Holloway extended his hand so that Hicks could see the items, the ball rolled off Holloway's palm, hit the floor, and disappeared under the sofa. Hicks took the key and examined it while Holloway went down on all fours to find the glass ball. The first thing Holloway saw when he looked under the couch was a blue capsule with an orange stripe around it. He had seen a capsule like that once while attending a tradecraft course. Holloway palmed the capsule with one hand and collected the glass ball with the other.

The detective took an envelope from his pocket and dropped in the items that Holloway had collected from the couch. "I'll hang onto these, just to be on the safe side." He gave Holloway an appraising look. "You're pretty thorough. Let me know if you find anything else interesting. And next time, don't touch it. Call me." Hicks stuffed the envelope into his pocket and went back to the den.

Holloway wanted to leave immediately to check out the capsule, but that would have aroused suspicion. Instead, he followed Hicks to the den.

The room was large enough to accommodate a couch, several bookcases, two filing cabinets, and two desks, one under each of the windows. A computer and printer occupied one of the desks. Hicks was going through a stack of papers and mail on the other.

Trying hard not to sound serious, Holloway asked, "Find a suicide note?"

The detective smiled and grunted. "No, but that was the first thing we looked for."

"What about the computer?"

"We checked that too. He used it to write a couple of business letters and some 'I love you' stuff to his wife."

"Mind if I look?"

"Help yourself," Hicks said, as he rummaged through a desk drawer. Holloway sat down at the computer, turned it on, and pulled up the word processing directory. It was voluminous. Hicks told him what documents to look for. Holloway scanned Slayton's letters for signs of a code, but couldn't spot one. Two letters were addressed to business associates and concerned the sale of a house in Georgetown. Slayton's third letter was to his wife. Holloway made a mental note of Miriam Slayton's address in Kansas. "Any floppies around?" Holloway asked.

"A mountain of 'em." Hicks jerked a thumb toward the filing cabinets. "One of my men screened the labels for anything that might have been done by Slayton. Came up with a zero. All that stuff looks like it belongs to the lawyer who let Slayton use the apartment."

Holloway turned off the computer and wandered into the kitchen for a look at the balcony door. If Slayton had been murdered, Holloway knew that this was the killer's escape route. Slayton had made too much of a racket when he fell for a hit man to chance the front stairs in such a small apartment building. He looked across the courtyard at the apartment building facing Slayton's balcony and wondered if anyone there had seen someone sliding down the balcony poles last night. The answer, of course, was "yes." It was the same Vietnamese man who was watching Holloway through binoculars at that very moment.

Holloway left Detective Hicks to his desk drawers and headed for a small computer store in a mall south of Washington. He needed the expertise of Dan Vogle. Vogle was on retainer for Holloway Security Consultants. When Holloway entered the shop, Vogle excused himself from the sales pitch he was giving a customer and came over to greet his employer. Vogle was a tall redhead in his late twenties. The only conventional thing about him was his crew cut. Otherwise, his clothes were trendy, his orientation was antiestablishment, and his lifestyle erratic. He was a genius with computers and had a promising career at the CIA, until he scuttled it with several messy office romances and a disdain for regular working hours.

His impish smile revealed buckteeth. "Hello, Holloway. Got something for me?"

"I need a black bag job tonight, Dan." Black bag job was CIA code for burglary and theft. "I want you to dump a computer memory for me. It's a Zenith 248. Here's the address." He gave Vogle the address where Slayton was killed. "Meet me there at seven this evening. I can give you three hours with the computer. If you need more time, bring a look-alike and switch them, but make sure you get the original back into the apartment early tomorrow morning. Can you make that schedule?"

"No problem."

Holloway smiled and patted Vogle on the shoulder. "See you at seven."

It was a busy evening for Holloway. His first stop was at the FBI's forensic chemistry laboratory to drop off the capsule he had found in Slayton's apartment. An old friend had agreed to analyze the contents. Next, he visited Slayton's athletic club and personal physician. In spite of Holloway's Defense Investigative Service identification card and a good line, the physician would tell him very little except that Slayton had been depressed before his death, but was otherwise in excellent health. The athletic club staff was more forthcoming and provided the details of Slayton's exercise schedule and deteriorating attitude. It seemed that in his last days, Slayton was only happy when playing tennis. Once he stepped off the court, he was moody and withdrawn. That was a big change from his days before the Iran-Contra investigation became front page news.

Holloway squeezed in a quick dinner at Lenny's and eyeballed a winsome brunette named Veronica, who, based on his past visits, seemed to be permanently attached to one of Lenny's barstools. After some discreet inquiries at the bar, Holloway was assured that Veronica did indeed get down from the barstool. "And I mean get down," said the informant. "Understand what I'm saying?"

Holloway assured the informant that he got the drift, but it was getting late. So, he bid Veronica and Lenny's goodbye and headed for his seven o'clock appointment with Dan Vogle in Alexandria.

Vogle was prompt. He expertly picked the lock on the door of Slayton's apartment, switched computers and went back to his shop to discover the dead man's secrets, if there were any. Holloway's interviews with the neighbors were a waste of time. They could add nothing to what the detective had told him during his earlier visit. He headed back to Lenny's for a nightcap. To his disappointment, Veronica was not there. He took his drink back to the phone booth and telephoned his forensic chemist friend at home. When Holloway heard what was in the capsule, he called Ellis Eaton immediately.

*   *   *

It was near midnight when Holloway arrived at Eaton's Georgetown house. Eaton responded to the doorbell wearing grey slacks and a matching cashmere sweater over a lemon shirt and ascot. He could have just finished a photo session for *Gentleman's Quarterly*. The house gave Holloway the impression of a comfortable museum. It was filled with antiques, Old World, Ming, and Persian. A couple of European masters graced the walls. Holloway glanced at the delicate French chairs in the living room and wondered if they were for sitting or show.

As if he had been reading Holloway's mind, Eaton said, "Come into the study. It's less formal." They walked noiselessly across the Bukaras to a room done in dark wood, creaky leather, and lots of books. It was cozy and less orderly than the rest of the house. A high-intensity lamp and some papers on the leather desktop were the only evidence that the room was used for anything but an after-dinner retreat for the brandy-and-cigars crowd. Eaton was a tidy man and a collector. The house was his showplace. Holloway momentarily amused himself by fantasizing that Eaton's real pad was a pigpen at the Watergate, where he kept a Rubenesque mistress who spent her days washing down Godiva chocolates with Dom Perignon and throwing the candy wrappers on the floor. He smiled, enjoying the image, while his host poured Scotch.

When they were comfortably seated, Eaton asked, "How did your inquiry go? Was all in order at the scene of Mr. Slayton's demise?"

"Not quite." Holloway took a small plastic bag from his pocket and handed it to his host. It contained the blue capsule with the orange stripe. "I found this in the apartment."

Eaton took the bag by a corner and held it at eye level for examination. "Looks like some kind of medication."

"I had a chemist analyze the contents. It contained a liquid, amyl nitrate. You inhale the fumes from it to relieve arterial spasms, angina pectoris, for example."

"Then Slayton did have a heart condition?"

"Slayton had a heart attack, but, according to his doctor, no history of heart problems. He had a complete physical exam after leaving the White House and played tennis several times a week."

"Perhaps the recent strain of dealing with the Iran-Contra publicity took its toll," suggested Eaton.

Holloway disagreed with that diagnosis. "Slayton was on the tennis court the day before be died, according to the staff at his club."

"Then what is the significance of this capsule?"

"The capsule is part of an assassination kit."

"Good God! Are you sure?"

"Yes. Let's say you wanted to kill someone and make it look like a heart attack. If you travel in the right circles, you can get the chemicals to do that. The stuff comes in either gas or powder form. When you release the chemical into the target's face, he inhales it and gets an immediate arterial spasm, which results in a killer heart attack. The target is dead in seconds. The problem is, how do you release the chemical up close and not get a whiff of it yourself? You have two options. The first is to wear a gas mask. A mask is bulky and hard to hide. Also, if it's not properly fitted, you die along with the target. The second option is to inhale the fumes from one of these amyl nitrite antidote capsules just before you release the chemical. The pill keeps you from getting the spasm and is the protection of choice. You might also be interested to know that no commercial medication capsules have exactly those markings and color code. That is definitely the hit man's happy pill."

Eaton looked grave. "This is extremely distressing news." He put down the whiskey glass and held the plastic bag in both hands. "I'll keep this, if you don't mind." Before Holloway could object, Eaton went to his desk and deposited the bag and capsule in a drawer. He stood there for a full minute, lost in thought. When he turned and walked back to Holloway, his manner was crisp. "You must say nothing about this until I get guidance from the White House."

Holloway was uneasy. If Eaton wanted a cover-up, he would have to ask for it. "You don't want the police department informed?"

Eaton understood the trap and had no intention of falling into it. "I've been in touch with the police already. They have determined that Slayton died of natural causes. His body has been released for burial. It would be devastating for his family if this capsule business surfaced just now." He looked over his reading glasses at Holloway. "It might be awkward for you, too. Removing evidence from the scene and so forth. Let's see what the President has to say, shall we? I'll get back to you soon." Eaton walked Holloway to the door. "Thank you for coming out at this hour, Edward. It's been an educational experience."

Holloway could have told him that Dan Vogle was busy dredging the memory of Slayton's computer, but decided to wait. The situation was getting sticky and he might need whatever bargaining chips Vogle turned up.

* * *

Vogle was good at turning up things. The next morning when Holloway arrived at the store, the computer whiz greeted him with a broad grin and a printout. "Look what I found in Slayton's computer!"

The letter read as follows:

The President of the United States
The White House
Washington, D.C.

Dear Mr. President:

I have tried to speak to you on the telephone or arrange a meeting. My attempts have been rebuffed by your staff, and I fear that entrusting my information to anyone other than you would be disastrous for us both. Therefore, I feel duty-bound to make one final attempt to see you through your wife. She has agreed to speak with me this evening because of our long friendship. If you receive this letter, you will know that the First Lady did not support my request to see you and that this letter is my last resort.

It is with regret that I inform you that I and other members of your staff have not served you well, particularly during the last two years. Whether motivated by selfishness, concern for our Nation, or a desire to counter the unproductive relationship between the Congress and the White House, we have not been good soldiers in your cause and the cause of democracy. The Iran-Contra affair has brought all of this to a head for me. Like John Dean of a decade ago, I must tell you that a cancer is growing on the Presidency. It is a malignancy of desperate men whose reputations, fortunes, and very lives are at risk. Beware of The Seven

"Jesus!" exclaimed Holloway. "Where is the rest of it, Dan?"

"That's all there was."

CHAPTER 4

<u>April 23, 1975, Saigon, Republic of Vietnam</u>

It was morning outside the room at the Caravelle Hotel. Inside, the shades were drawn and it was dark, except for a small lamp that spilled a pool of light onto a table. The table seated four men: Sergeant Randy Dillworth, the embassy man, the captain, and a Vietnamese named Trung.

The embassy man was speaking. "Did you locate the safe house where our submarine travelers are hiding?"

"It's right where the good Dr. Nu said it would be," answered the captain. "We scouted the place last night."

"Good. We've got to eliminate the remainder of that raiding party as soon as possible. When do you go in?"

"We don't. It's too risky."

"What do you mean, 'too risky'?" asked the embassy man. "If you don't take out that house, we'll have to fight both the NVA and the South Vietnamese when we go after that cargo."

The captain took a piece of paper from the pocket of his fatigue jacket and unfolded it under the lamp. "The safe house is not far from Tan Son Nhut Airport. This is a diagram of the area. This alley," he pointed to the diagram, "is called Binh Dinh. It comes to a dead end at this field, which is about three hundred meters square and overgrown with high grass. The safe house is here, about a hundred meters into the field from the end of the alley. It's a two-story building, surrounded by a high masonry wall with camouflaged firing ports and broken glass imbedded along the top. During the day, visibility from the house is good in all directions from the second floor. The place is a goddamned fortress."

"Can't you get in close after dark?" asked the embassy man.

"We could blast our way in at night, but that's not the problem." The captain nodded to Dillworth who continued the explanation.

"A gully runs along the north edge of the field that surrounds the house. I found a nicely camouflaged tunnel entrance in the wall of that gully, just big enough for a man to wiggle through. Next month's paycheck says that the tunnel connects to the safe house."

"So what?" asked the embassy man. "It's probably an escape route from the safe house. All you have to do is put a man there to shoot them as they come out."

"A tunnel could mean *lots* of bad guys," observed Dillworth, who had more tunnel experience than he cared to remember. "The entrance is small, but who knows what's underground?" He paused to let the embassy man consider that possibility. "If we're gonna bust into that house, we better damn well know what we're up against. There's only five of us. That includes me, the captain, Trung, and the two guns that we hired." Dillworth did not count the embassy man, who wasn't coming and would probably be in the way if he did.

"Could be anything at the end of that tunnel," added the captain. "A hospital, an ammo dump, or sleeping quarters for a couple of infantry companies." He pushed back from the table. "For all we know, it could be NVA headquarters in Saigon. This submarine business requires high level coordination."

The embassy man looked at them with disdain. "Are you telling me that the NVA has a tunnel complex in the middle of the city? That's ridiculous!"

"Maybe," said the captain, "but take a look at the facts. Real estate is scarce in Saigon, and yet there is this safe house sitting out there on a big vacant lot. How come there aren't any buildings around?" Silence. "I think that if anybody tried to build anything on that lot, it would fall right through the ground into the tunnels."

The embassy man was not convinced, but he was paying attention now. "The people in that house must be dealt with before we go after the cargo. How do you propose we do that?"

"Have you found a pilot to fly the cargo out?"

"Yes."

"Military or civilian?"

"Military. Why?"

"I need a 500-pound bomb. Has he got those kind of connections with the Vietnamese Air Force at Tan Son Nhut?"

The embassy man recoiled. "You want to neutralize the safe house by detonating a 500-pound bomb in the middle of Saigon? You must be insane!"

The captain spoke firmly. "I've given it a lot of thought. This is the only way, unless you want to bring in more people. The more people, the greater the chances that someone will talk . . . and our individual shares of the cargo would be reduced. Even if we could find more people, we wouldn't know how many to hire, because we don't know how many VC and NVA are in or under that safe house. We have to go with the bomb. Anything else is too risky."

Reluctantly, the embassy man asked, "How do you propose to get away with exploding a bomb that size in the city?"

"Does the NVA have any artillery within range of Saigon?"

"Yes. I'm surprised that they haven't started shelling us."

"When the bomb goes off, why shouldn't everyone assume that it was NVA artillery?"

The embassy man considered the proposition. "I don't like it. It's too loud. It's too messy."

"It's perfect," countered the captain. "In a few days, some NVA general will liberate Saigon. The first thing he's gonna do is head for Hangar 11 at Tan Son Nhut to check on that cargo. When he doesn't find it, guess where he's going next?"

"The safe house."

"Right. Now, when he gets there he can find one of two things. He can find a bunch of dead bodies riddled with bullets, in which case there will be one hell of an investigation and people will be looking for us. Or he can find a big hole in the ground, a few body parts, and no real evidence that the safe house was deliberately hit." The captain hunched his shoulders. "Could have been a stray artillery round. Could have been a bomb accidentally dropped from a plane landing at the airbase. Who knows? Case closed and we're home free."

"Your scenario does have certain advantages," admitted the embassy man. He stared at the safe house diagram and worked out his next moves. "I'll contact the pilot immediately to arrange for the bomb. Then, I'll have to get bribe money for the Vietnamese guards at the ammunition dump. That shouldn't be too difficult. They're making plans to burn the embassy contingency funds before we evacuate." He looked up at the captain. "It will take another twenty-four hours to pull this together. Meanwhile, you find transportation for the bomb."

The captain turned to Dillworth. "Randy, we'll need a truck and one of those little Lambretta taxis. Can you handle that?"

"No problem, Cap'n."

"When will you take the safe house?" asked the embassy man.

"Tomorrow night, if you can deliver the bomb."

"And your arrangements to get a man into the control tower?"

"They're on track. Trung will be our inside man. I need a little bait to get him into position. Can you get a passport for this kid by tomorrow?" The captain slid a grainy head-and-shoulders photograph of a Vietnamese teenager across the table.

The embassy man looked at the picture and turned it over to read the identifying information on the back. "I'll work on it." He pocketed the photograph. "Well, I suppose that's it for now. I'll meet you upstairs in the bar at 0900 tomorrow."

* * *

When Trung and the embassy man had gone, Dillworth raised the curtains and daylight spilled into the room.

The captain said, "Hey, Randy, how about losing yourself until tomorrow morning. I may need the room." The captain pulled an overnight bag from beneath his bed and threw in a set of clean underwear and a bottle of cognac.

Dillworth grinned. "What are you up to, Cap'n?"

"I'm going on a search and debauch mission. Gotta find my Sweet Thang. She might want to come here and visit with me for awhile."

"My compliments to the captain. She is one fine hammer. She's also smart enough to be out of the country by now."

"Sergeant, you been hanging around with the enlisted swine too long. You just don't remember the power of officer magic. Ten 'P' says she's waiting for me on Tudo Street." The captain tossed a Vietnamese ten-piaster note on the table.

"You're on," grinned Dillworth. "You are also a sick man. Ever hear the story about the ol' tomcat that ran across the railroad track and got his tail cut off by a passing train?"

"Never," said the captain with a finality that conveyed his lack of interest in hearing it even now. He shoved some toiletries into his bag.

Dillworth would not be discouraged. "Well, the cat missed his tail so much that he went back to look for it. While he was looking, another train came along and cut off his head. Moral of the story: don't lose your head over a piece of tail." Dillworth broke into a howl of laughter.

The captain paused at the door and gave Dillworth a bored look before leaving the room.

Even as he elbowed his way through streets jammed with soldiers and refugees, the captain was barely conscious of them. His mind was focused on Li Minh Bach and the growing heat in his loins. Li was half Vietnamese, half French and a beautiful nineteen, even after a lot of street time. She dressed exclusively in Western clothes: high heels, nylons, and dresses that she had to be poured into. She was well-built and larger than the average Vietnamese. Her hair cascaded from a part in the middle of her head down onto her shoulders and she had cheekbones that a fashion model would kill for. They complemented a straight nose, almond eyes, and a large sensual mouth that laughed easily. Li was intelligent and her English was functional. A year or two at a stateside finishing school and she would be star quality. And in the sack, she was the Magic Lady, the one every man dreams about and few ever find.

He knocked on the door of Li's apartment.

Li opened the door and squealed, "Sweet Thang!!!" She threw her ripe body into the captain's arms.

"Hello, Sweet Thang," he said, his voice a husky whisper.

Li closed her eyes, opened her sensuous mouth, and gave him a long French kiss. Forgetting about the bottle of cognac, he dropped the AWOL bag and put both arms around her, lifting and sliding her crotch over his erection.

"Ah-ha," she said with a devilish smile. "You miss me. I can tell by your dipstick reading. Vung Tau women don't take care of you?"

Li neither wanted nor waited for an answer. She took his hand and led him into a modestly furnished living room. As he entered, he collected his bag with his free hand and kicked the door closed. Li wore a white lace blouse with puffy sleeves that buttoned above the elbows. Her skirt was blue denim and for the life of him he could not understand how she could sit down in the thing and not have the seams pop. She pulled him onto the couch beside her and the skirt disappeared into her navel, revealing a band of tan-yellow flesh above stocking tops held in place by white garter belt straps. Li gave him another long kiss. It started out hungry and turned tender. When he pulled away to reach for his bag, he saw that her eyes were moist. He kissed her on the cheek.

"I brought you something." He took the bottle of cognac out of his bag and sat it on the table.

Li smiled as she tilted the bottle and read the label. "You always bring the good stuff." She let her other hand slide down between his legs and withdrew it quickly as though the move had been accidental. They looked hungrily at each other. The kissing and groping that followed took on an urgency that they both knew well. She gasped as he slid his hand inside her blouse. He withdrew it and began to undo the buttons.

"No," she whispered and her tongue flicked into his ear. "Not here. We go to your place. Where you stay?" Long ago, she had made a rule that they would not make love at her place of business. She felt that it took away from the special quality of their relationship.

"The Caravelle," he answered, glad that he had remembered to kick Dillworth out of the room. "But we can only be together tonight. I have some business people coming in the morning."

Li did not protest. She had been involved in his "business" before.

*　*　*

They were sprawled naked on the bed. Li was lying with her head in the hollow of the captain's shoulder gently stroking his chest and enjoying the twilight between sex and sleep. She had deliberately waited until now to raise the issue. He would be brutally frank in less relaxed circumstances and she would rather hear a lie in the warmth of his arms than bad news in the cold light of day. She moved her lips to his ear and said quietly, "This your last time in Saigon." It was a simple statement of fact. "Soon, you leave, like everybody else."

He said nothing, but turned his face so that his cheek was resting on her forehead.

"You say you take me to States when time come," she reminded him. "NVA be here very soon. Time for me to go is now. You keep your promise?" she asked tentatively. "I go with you?"

Reluctantly, the captain forced his mind to focus until he was wide awake. He thought about the embassy man. "When my 'business' people come, I'll make the arrangements. Do you have a passport photograph with you?" he asked.

"No, but I get one."

"Never mind. I'll take a shot of you with the Polaroid before you leave." He drew her close and gave her a reassuring kiss.

They were quiet for a time. Finally, Li said, "I go see my family tomorrow, say goodbye." She was referring to her mother and sisters, whom the captain had heard of but never seen. Li's father was dead.

"How is your mother?" he asked captain.

"Same. She hate me because I work on street. Hate my street money. Hate me because she need my street money to live. No love, only hate."

The captain felt hot tears plop onto his chest; he drew her closer.

They were awakened by a loud knock on the door. The captain sat up. "Who is it?"

"Randy. We need to talk."

With obvious displeasure he said, "Come on in, Randy."
Li and the captain looked at each other. She smiled and he cursed as they pulled the sheet over their naked bodies.

As soon as Dillworth entered the room, Li squealed, "Randy!" She ran into his arms, taking the sheet with her and leaving the captain naked on the bed. The captain cursed again.

Li and Randy ignored him as they renewed their acquaintance.

"How are you, Li?" asked Dillworth.

"Good! Good!" she repeated with a broad smile. "How you been?" Before he could answer, Li said, "You thinner. Looks good. How long you been in Saigon?"

Over Li's shoulder, Dillworth saw the captain nod and walk to the bathroom.

To Li, Dillworth said, "I'll tell you all about it after I have a talk with your naked friend." They laughed and Dillworth followed the captain into the bathroom and closed the door.

Irritated, the captain asked, "What the hell do you want, Randy?"

"'Bout two minutes ago, I was coming into the hotel to get some breakfast and ran into our friend from the embassy. He wants to see you right away. I told him you had company. He's waiting for you in the bar."

The captain looked at his watch. "He's early. Are Trung and Doyle there yet?"

Randy didn't know.

"I don't want Li to see me and the embassy man together," said the captain. "Get her some breakfast in the dining room, then take her over to her mother's." He turned to step into the shower. "And take a picture of Li with the Polaroid. I'm going to have our friend get her a passport so she can go to the States."

Dillworth hesitated, then said in a low voice, "That's not smart, Cap'n. We need to cut our connections with this place—and anybody who might link us to the hangar."

"I'm not leaving her, Randy. You know what the NVA did when they took Da Nang? They rounded up the women who had been with Americans and pulled out their fingernails."

"Then put her on the next flight to Thailand. She'll be safe there. She doesn't have to go to the States."

"No. If she goes to Thailand, she'll end up in another whorehouse. She's paid her dues. It's her time for a shot at the good life."

"Bullshit! You want her, don't you?" The captain said nothing.

"Look, man, she's just another piece."

"That's not what you said when you introduced us. You said she was a quality lady who got herself caught in a bad situation."

"This is crazy, Cap'n. You don't have to feel guilty because you screwed her for a couple of years."

"That's enough, Sergeant." The captain opened the bathroom door and said, "Li, Randy's going to take you to breakfast and drop you off at your mother's. Meet me here day after tomorrow. I'll have your passport then."

Dillworth forced a smile at Li and walked back into the bedroom. While the captain showered, Li perched on the edge of the bed with the sheet wrapped around her and chatted with Dillworth.

"Shame on you, Randy. You been in Saigon almost a week and you don't come see me?"

"Sorry. I was busy. This is a difficult time."

"Randy, you don't have to stay away because of him." She glanced toward the shower. I know you long before I know Sweet Thang." She smiled gently. "You like my brother." They talked.

A few minutes later, the captain came out of the bathroom fully clothed. He examined the photograph that Dillworth had taken of Li. Then he kissed her and went up to meet the embassy man.

The morning was humid. The embassy man sat in the noisy penthouse bar at the Caravelle Hotel, high above the swirling flood of foot and wheel traffic that coursed through the streets below. Saigon's normally impossible traffic was aggravated by an ever-growing tide of refugees who poured into the city, now just days ahead of the relentless North Vietnamese Army. The bar buzzed as reporters and other media types exchanged notes on the progress of the war and their preparations to leave before Saigon fell. There was also a scattering of lone Western drinkers and Vietnamese, both obviously out of place. Both types sat quietly and waited for, or drank, their deliverance from what was to come with the arrival of the NVA.

The captain entered and went straight to the bar for a bottle of Vietnamese beer. He took a swig and pulled a face. Horrible stuff. He frowned at the label, assuring himself that the liquid was in fact meant for human consumption. After looking around the room to see that his people were in place, he walked over to the embassy man's table and sat down. "You're early," noted the captain in an unfriendly tone.

The embassy man wore a khaki bush jacket and beige slacks. He opted not to deal with his companion's ill humor and went directly to business. "The bomb is laid on. Can you have the truck at Tan Son Nhut by 1400 hours today?"

Unable to pick an argument, the captain replied, "Sure."

"It will have to be marked in some way."

"White engineer tape across the grill. Randy will be driving."

"An Air Force officer named Roper will meet you outside of Gate 1 at Tan Son Nhut. Start early. Refugees have formed a *cordon* un*sanitaire* around the airport. They all want to get out of the country before Ho Chi Minh's legions arrive. It will take you a while to get through them. The guards have to literally beat them off." A pause and the embassy man said, "Well, that's settled."

The captain took a swig of his lukewarm beer with the distinctly formaldehyde taste and comforted himself with the thought that in a few more days, he would be up to his armpits in Budweiser.

"Have you made arrangements for the control tower?" asked the embassy man.

"Yes. Did you bring the bait?"

The embassy man withdrew a U.S. passport from his pocket and passed it to the captain. "Courtesy of our overnight services department. Where's your customer?"

"Down there at the quiet end of the bar." The captain pointed. "The balding one with the wasted look. Patrick X. 'Steamer' Doyle."

The embassy man looked at Doyle with disdain. "One of the resident degenerates, I see. What's his story?"

"He's a maintenance supervisor at Tan Son Nhut Airport. Several years ago, he started a family with a Vietnamese woman. They had two sons, but forgot to get married. So, the kids are legally Vietnamese. Now that the commies are about to take over, Steamer wants to evacuate his family to the States. The problem is that one of his sons is draft age and, as you know, no draft age Vietnamese males are permitted to leave the country. I hear that the Vietnamese Government, what's left of it, has threatened to halt the evacuation of Americans if we fly out any of their draft age men. If that's not bad enough, his wife and mother-in-law won't leave if the oldest son has to stay. I intend to facilitate their departure by conferring instant U.S. citizenship on young master Doyle, the draft dodger." The captain tapped the passport with a finger.

"Excellent," beamed the embassy man.

"One more thing." The captain flipped the Polaroid of Li Minh Bach across the table. "I need a passport for her—by tomorrow."

The embassy man took a quick look at the photograph and a long look at the captain. "Who the hell do you think I am, MacPassport?"

The captain stared at him saying nothing. The embassy man looked at the photograph again. "Don't I know this woman?"

"Possibly. She's worked for us on occasion."

The embassy man eyed him suspiciously. "She's your piece."

"That too, but it doesn't matter. I want her out."

The embassy man was angry now and talking in a savage whisper. "We should be trying to cut every contact with Vietnam to cover ourselves, and you want to jeopardize the whole operation by dragging some street whore out with you? Christ, man, all the blood must have drained out of your brain and into your crotch. What about your wife and kids?"

"You let me worry about my life," the captain said angrily. "If we move that cargo, I can have a goddamned harem if I want to. I'm taking her back. That's final. Get me a passport!"

The embassy man was smoldering, but this was not the time to deal with his anger. He stuffed Li's picture into his pocket and left the bar without a word.

The captain watched his back disappear through the doorway and turned his attention to Steamer Doyle. He looked at Doyle's wasted face and tried to remember anyone he had known in Vietnam who had been touched by the war and not corrupted or destroyed. He could not think of a single person. Doyle was a classic example of what Vietnam did to foreigners who failed to get out in that brief interval between loss of innocence and loss of self-respect. He was a victim of what Randy Dillworth called "The Terrible Toos: too much booze, too many broads, too much money, and too long in Vietnam."

Doyle was raising the latest draft of poison to his lips when the captain slid onto the next stool and said, "Hello, Steamer."

Doyle turned and tried to focus his bleary, suspicious eyes. "Do I know you?"

The captain smiled in an effort to put Doyle at ease. "You know what they say: there are no strangers in the world, just friends who haven't met before."

Doyle looked the captain up and down, snorted, and turned back to his gin.

Ignoring Doyle's rebuff the captain said cheerfully, "I'm looking for an American expatriate with a Vietnamese wife, mother-in-law, and two sons, one of whom needs a U.S. passport."

Not quite sure that he had heard the answer to his prayers, Doyle put down his glass and looked at the captain again. "You picked a weird freakin' time to conduct a survey, friend."

"That's because I have a unique product." The captain took the passport from his pocket and put it on the bar. Doyle covered it with his palm and opened it to find his son's picture inside. "This ain't much good unless you got a way out," he said hopefully.

"Five seats on Air America are reserved for your family. All I have to do is give the word."

"What's it gonna cost? You want gold, like the rest of the vultures?"

The captain feigned a hurt look. "Steamer, I'm surprised that you think I would take advantage of a fellow American at a time like this. I'm just trying to help people who need it. Now, you take my friend over there by the door in the jungle fatigues, he needs a job." Steamer turned to see a tough looking Vietnamese grinning at him over a beer glass.

"That's Mr. Trung," continued the captain. "He repairs windows. He wants to work for you."

Doyle started to laugh. "Mr. Trung is gonna have one helluva lot of work when the NVA gets within artillery range of Saigon." Doyle's laugh turned into a tubercular hack that continued until he squelched it with a swallow of gin.

After Doyle recovered, the captain said, in a low voice, "Mr. Trung is a specialist. He specializes in repairing control tower windows. Anything happens to the windows in the control tower, you send him up there to fix them. Nobody else. If he needs help, he'll let you know."

Doyle squinted through his alcoholic haze. "What makes you think somethin's gonna happen to the control tower windows?"

The captain's face hardened. "You picked a weird freaking time to do a survey on airport window damage. Do you want the passport or not?"

"Yeah," answered Doyle, finally comprehending the terms of their deal. "I get the passport and a way out. Mr. Trung gets the window franchise."

The captain beamed with approval. "That's right, Steamer." He moved very close to Doyle and said, "There are two things that you have to remember. First, I work for some serious people. If you ever mention this conversation to anybody, you won't have any grandchildren." He took Doyle's arm above the elbow and dug his forefinger into the nerve. The grip generated a flash of excruciating pain, but it was gone before the cry could escape Doyle's throat. Tears formed in his eyes.

"Point number two. When you get to the States and your son is safely through customs, you burn the passport or tear it up and flush it down the toilet. If you use it after that, you will call attention to yourself and the people I work for. That would be bad for you and worse for your family. Understand?" The captain made a threatening, but deliberately slow, move toward Doyle's elbow.

"I got the picture," said Doyle, turning so that his elbow was out of harm's way. "When do I fly?"

"As soon as Mr. Trung repairs the control tower windows." The captain reached over and deftly twisted the passport out of Doyle's grasp. "You get this back when the job's done." The captain got up to leave and Doyle started to follow him. "Stay put for a few minutes, Steamer," advised the captain. "Have a cup of coffee. Mr. Trung will come over and tell you how he likes to work."

* * *

It was shortly after lunch when Randy Dillworth, the captain, and Mr. Trung climbed into the cab of the Army two-and-one-half-ton truck and headed for Tan Son Nhut Airport. The two Americans were dressed in their Army fatigue uniforms. Mr. Trung was wearing the stolen uniform of a South Vietnamese air force colonel. The main traffic arteries had become clogged rivers of humanity. The truck barely made it to the airport gate by two o'clock. It arrived with its grill marked with white engineer tape for easy identification. As it inched through the mob of Vietnamese refugees in front of the gate, an American Air Force major in jungle fatigues shouldered his way through the crowd and jumped onto the running board.

"I'm Roper. You Dillworth?" he asked the driver.

"Right."

Roper saw Trung, smiled knowingly and saluted. Trung gave him a grin. "Sir," he addressed Trung, "if you will come with me, it will be easier for us to get in."

Roper and "Colonel" Trung walked ahead and had words with the gate guards, who waved the truck through while fighting off a crowd of Vietnamese refugees desperate for a flight out of Saigon. Randy slid out from behind the wheel, walked to the back of the truck, and climbed over the tailgate into the cargo bed. The captain took the wheel and Roper and Trung joined him in the cab. Roper directed them across the base to an isolated corner on the Vietnamese Air Force side of the installation. As the truck rolled down the tarmac, they passed within a hundred meters of a large hangar inside a barbed wire enclosure. A sandbagged machinegun bunker squatted at either end of the hangar. Two Vietnamese guards leaned against one of the bunkers smoking.

Roper nodded toward the enclosure. "Hangar 11," he said, grinning.

"Looks well protected," observed the captain.

"And they have occasional roving patrols around the building. A major is in charge of the guard detail. He probably has orders to disable the plane if the hangar is attacked. We'll have to go in quickly and kill everybody before they make any mischief."

"What kind of communications do they have?" asked the captain.

"One hotline to VNAF,"—Vietnamese Air Force Headquarters— "and radios: one at each machinegun position and the major in charge has one."

The truck continued down the tarmac until they came to another road leading to a large ammunition bunker. Roper directed them behind the bunker. Off to the right stood a dolly holding the sleek cigar-shaped form of a 500-pound bomb. The captain pulled up next to the dolly. Roper and Trung got out of the truck and spoke to a Vietnamese officer standing nearby. From where the captain was sitting, it appeared that Roper was introducing Trung to the officer in charge. There was a brief three-way conversation during which Roper delivered an envelope to the Vietnamese officer and signaled to the captain that it was okay to load the bomb. All smiles, three

Vietnamese minions popped out of the bunker and helped load the bomb and lash it to the truck bed. Roper took his leave on foot. Dillworth got to ride in the back with the bomb. Trung and the captain tied the canvas down to conceal their cargo. The captain slid under the wheel and drove off of Tan Son Nhut.

One final item was needed to complete the operation—a Lambretta taxi. The Lambretta was a three-wheeled motor scooter-truck hybrid, a motor scooter seat with passenger compartment mounted behind. It was just large enough to carry four people uncomfortably—or a 500-pound bomb.

* * *

It was 1:35 in the morning. A Vietnamese sentry wearing black pajamas and armed with an AK-47 rifle patrolled the yard of the NVA safe house. His job was to give the alarm if he saw unusual activity in the field around the house or the alley Binh Dinh. Since midnight, he had circled the yard looking out through the carefully spaced holes in the wall surrounding the building. As usual, he had seen nothing suspicious. He was bored and careless. His sandals scraped against the tiled yard as he shuffled to the next peephole and looked out. Something odd obstructed his view. It was the muzzle of the silencer on an automatic. The captain fired three bullets in the man's brain. The sentry's body slumped to the ground. The captain cringed when the man's AK-47 rifle clattered onto the tile. He waited for a reaction from the house. There was none. He unhooked the elbow flashlight from his belt, pointed it toward the far side of the field and pressed the switch twice. Then, he dashed across the field to where his four men were waiting. They began pushing the Lambretta quietly toward the safe house. The 500-pound bomb was securely blocked into the passenger compartment of the little taxi. The captain walked behind, playing out the detonating wire. They parked the Lambretta against the safe house wall and the captain attached the wire to the bomb. The front door of the house opened and they froze as the dead sentry's replacement walked into the yard.

The captain whispered, "Let's get the hell out of here!"

They dashed across the field to the spot where the bomb detonator was located. There was commotion at the house as the captain worked feverishly to attach the wire to the detonator. Lights came on in the yard.

The captain yelled, "Fire in the hole!" Everyone dropped to the ground and he twisted the detonator handle, sending an electrical impulse to the bomb.

The bomb blew away most of the wall and safe house. What was left of the building collapsed into a heap of burning rubble. A fireball mushroomed upward from the crater caused by the detonation, rolling under and into itself until it turned into a gray-black cloud. Before the fireball disappeared, there was the *Boo-Boom!* of overlapping explosions somewhere under the earth. Suddenly, the field erupted like a volcano, spewing a burning lava of twisted bodies and equipment into the sky. The captain watched as flaming bodies, arms and legs outstretched, rotated through the air like grotesque pinwheels. The bodies and debris arched up slowly, then plunged back into the inferno where the house had been. Flames leaped high into the darkness as the fire raced through the dry grass. The earth heaved again and there was a low rumble, followed by five minutes of firecracker-like noises. "Ammo dump," observed the captain. He started the truck engine and drove away. Li Minh Bach would be waiting for him at the Caravelle.

* * *

It was minutes before the explosion at the house in the alley Binh Dinh. The loft of Steamer Doyle's airport maintenance building was dark and deserted, except for Mr. Trung and Randy Dillworth. Dillworth opened a window that gave him an excellent view of the Tan Son Nhut control tower. Carefully, he removed the canvas wrapping from his M-14 rifle. The sniperscope was already mounted on the weapon. Dillworth took a long, black silencer from his accessory bag and screwed it onto the muzzle of the rifle. Meanwhile, Trung unwrapped five specially prepared bullets that would break apart on impact, spraying the target with lead. In that manner, they hoped to destroy large sections of window, while having it appear that the control tower had been hit accidentally by debris from the safe house bomb. Dillworth took the magazine from Trung and inserted it into the receiver of the weapon. He squinted through the sniperscope at the control tower. It was thirty seconds to detonation.

Dillworth relaxed, then took a breath and held it. When the bomb went off at the safe house, he emptied his magazine into the control tower.

CHAPTER 5

<u>February 1987, Washington, D.C.</u>
Jack Slayton's unfinished letter to the President lay on the desk. Holloway frowned at it and started pacing his office again. There was something spooky about having the dead man's letter in his possession and the contents didn't make it any easier to have around. Holloway was starting to dislike Slayton—and Ellis Eaton for dragging him into this mess. A few days ago Holloway had been a carefree and prosperous security consultant. Now, he was a two-bit gumshoe, breaking and entering, withholding evidence from the police, up to his armpits in what looked like a murder . . . and closer to the Iran-Contra scandal than he had ever dreamed he would be. "Poor bastards," he had called the White House staff, when the scandal broke, and thanked his lucky stars that he was not involved. Now, he was one of those poor bastards. Holloway looked at the letter again and realized that he had delayed the inevitable as long as he could. The President had to be told. He picked up the phone and called Ellis Eaton's office.

"This is Ed Holloway. Is Dr. Eaton in?"

"No," said the secretary, "but he did leave a message for you, Mr. Holloway."

"Is it sealed?" Holloway asked.

"No, sir."

"Would you read it, please?" Holloway heard paper rattle.

"The message says: 'If you have discovered any new information concerning our research project, hold it until I contact you.' "

Holloway sighed. "When will Dr. Eaton return to the office?"

"I don't know, sir. He's out of the city and won't be back for several days."

"Did he leave a number where he can be contacted?"

"I'm afraid not. However, he does call in periodically for messages."

"When he does, tell him I found some correspondence that the gentleman was preparing for the White House just before his death."

Holloway hung up the phone and started pacing again. He was agitated by Eaton's absence and he would be damned if he was going to sit on Slayton's letter any longer. He had to get it to the White House. There were a couple of ways to do it. He could call his good friend, Sid Mitchell, who was assigned to the President's Secret Service detail and try to arrange something, but that would mean sharing the Slayton secret with another person. Not smart. No. This situation required the direct approach. Reluctantly, Holloway took the telephone book from the credenza behind his desk and looked up the number for the White House. The switchboard put him through to the First Lady's appointments secretary.

A cultured female voice identified its owner and asked, "Can I help you?"

"My name is Edward Holloway of Holloway Security Consultants. Several days ago, the First Lady had a business meeting with one of our clients, a Mr. Dean. During the course of that meeting, she requested certain information that she wanted to pass on to the President. I have that information in a personal letter from our client. He asked us to deliver it to the White House because he had to leave town unexpectedly. I'm calling to request instructions on how the First Lady would like this matter handled." He sensed hesitation and pressed on. "The First Lady met Mr. Dean at the Kennedy Center. If you mention it to her, I'm sure she'll remember."

"Very well, Mr. Holloway. Where can I contact you?"

Holloway gave her his office number and hung up. Ten minutes later, the appointments secretary called back with a three o'clock invitation.

* * *

Holloway arrived at the White House a few minutes before three. While he identified himself to the uniformed gate guard, a man in civilian clothes walked up behind him and said, "Hello, Ed."

Holloway turned and saw the smiling face of his friend Sid Mitchell. Sid's brown hair was thinning on top and going gray at the temples. He had a lean, worried face that had spent too many years searching crowds around the President for potential assassins. His body was starting to get heavy at the beltline.

"How the hell are you, Sid?" They exchanged perfunctory health reports and Holloway said, "I've been meaning to call, but the last few weeks have been busy. Are you my welcoming committee?"

"You got it. I've been transferred to the First Lady's detail. I heard your name mentioned and I volunteered to meet you. Come on." Mitchell turned and started walking toward the White House.

Holloway was surprised to see that they were headed for the residence. He had assumed that he would be going to the West Wing— the business end of the White House. Maybe the First Lady—or the President—didn't want this to be a high-profile meeting. It was just as well. Holloway didn't want to be seen meeting with White House people concerning Iran-Contra any more than they wanted to be seen with him.

Mitchell interrupted Holloway's thoughts. "Dare I ask what you're doing here or will I have to throw myself into the shredder if you tell me?"

"It's nothing heavy, Sid. I'm just delivering a personal message to the First Lady from an old friend."

"Sure," said Mitchell, unconvinced. He led Holloway into the residence and upstairs to the Green Room. Taking Holloway's coat, Mitchell said, "Make yourself comfortable. The First Lady will join you in a few minutes." He departed.

Holloway remembered the Green Room from the tour that he and the other awardees had been given before they got their medals in the Rose Garden. The room took its name from the soft green fabric covering the walls. The ceiling was white and the floor was covered with a Turkish carpet of multicolored design on a green field. The Turkish element struck Holloway as odd in a room he considered primarily early American in character. There was some story behind the carpet, but Holloway had forgotten it. He did remember that the furniture style was called American Federal and that the room contained pieces by Duncan Phyfe. Directly across the room, a fireplace dominated the wall and Benjamin Franklin looked down from a large painting above the mantle. Clusters of chairs and tables stood like sentinels at either side of the fireplace. The wall at the far end of the room had two doors and was decorated with paintings. It was the least interesting part of the room. The centerpiece of the wall to Holloway's rear was a settee covered in cream fabric with green stripes. It was flanked by colonial end tables. A sofa table stood in front of the settee with green upholstered chairs at either end. The gleaming surface of the table contained a silver coffee urn and matching candlesticks. To Holloway's right, green and coral draperies framed two large windows facing the Washington Monument. The ambiance was impressive. A chill passed through his body as he looked out at the Monument and contemplated the responsibilities of the President and the gravity of Slayton's letter. He turned from the window as Sid Mitchell and the First Lady entered the room.

The President's wife wore a red dress and pearls. She smiled, extending her hand. "Good afternoon, Mr. Holloway."

"Good afternoon." Holloway squeezed her hand gently as he looked down at the petite woman. He had never been in her presence before. She was smaller than he had imagined.

"Please," she said, motioning him to one of the upholstered chairs while she took the settee. "You're no stranger to the White House, Mr. Holloway. I'm told that the President gave you an award in the Rose Garden last year."

"Yes, he did." Holloway felt uneasy. He didn't want to be a person. He wanted to be a nonentity who delivered Slayton's letter and got the hell out.

"I understand that you have a letter for me."

Holloway reached into the inside pocket of his coat, took out the envelope containing Jack Slayton's letter and handed it to her.

She removed the letter and read it. At the end of the page, she looked up at him. "Did you read this, Mr. Holloway?"

"Yes."

"Then you know that it's incomplete. Are there other pages?"

"I don't think so. I don't believe he ever finished it. I'd be glad to give you the details . . . if you'd like to have them now." Holloway made a point of looking past her at Sid Mitchell, who stood near the door trying very hard to look like he wasn't there.

The First Lady turned to Mitchell and said, "Would you excuse us for a few minutes?" Sid nodded and left.

"All right, Mr. Holloway, please tell me who wrote this letter and how it came into your hands."

"I can't be positive, but I think Jack Slayton wrote it. Maybe I should start from the beginning." Holloway told her about Ellis Eaton calling him in to look into Slayton's death at the request of the President. He left out the part about finding the amyl nitrate capsule and his suspicion that Slayton had been murdered. "After the police investigation had been completed, I got access to the computer in the apartment where Mr. Slayton died and was able to retrieve that letter."

The First Lady stiffened. "Then the police have this letter too?"

"I doubt that. If they had found it, I don't think they would have closed the case on Slayton so quickly. Also, their normal procedure would have been to get a copy to the White House immediately. If the President doesn't already know about this letter, it's because the police didn't find it."

The First Lady seemed relieved. "How is it that you found this letter and the police did not?"

"Well, the document had actually been erased, but I was able to retrieve it from the computer's memory."

"How is that done?"

"Are you interested in the technical details?"

"In layman's terms, please."

"When you create a document in the computer, you basically reserve a space in memory for that document, Mr. Slayton's letter, for instance. A block is set up which prevents you from writing over the letter while you're working on another document. When you have no further use for the letter, you press the 'erase' button and it disappears from your screen and document index. However, it hasn't really been erased. It remains in the computer's memory. What the erase button does is remove the block so that the memory space where the letter resides is no longer reserved. Therefore, you can create a new letter by writing over the old one. In the case of Slayton's letter, he started to write it. Then, he apparently changed his mind and erased it. By coincidence, the portion of his letter that you have in your hand had not been written over."

There was silence while the First Lady reread the letter.

Holloway took the opportunity to try to get himself off the hook with the White House and with Eaton. He cleared his throat and said, "I'm sure that Dr. Eaton would have wanted to bring this to the attention of the President himself, but he's out of town and I felt that you would want to know about this immediately."

"You were quite correct to bring this to our attention, Mr. Holloway." The First Lady rose from the settee. "I hope you won't mind waiting for a few minutes. I want to show this to the President." Holloway stood and watched her leave.

After a few minutes the door opened and the First Lady entered, followed by the President. He wore a dark suit and regimental tie. He looked the part.

The First Lady hung back while the President flashed his famous smile and pumped Holloway's hand. "Thank you for coming, Ed. Sit down, please." The President and First Lady took the settee. Holloway returned to his chair. "Let me offer our condolences concerning your family. That was a terrible loss."

"Thank you." *Sid Mitchell talks too much.*

"My wife told me how you got the letter. That was a nice piece of work. Any ideas about this 'beware of The Seven' line at the end?"

"No, sir. I thought it might mean something to you."

"I'm afraid not. Well, so far, it looks like you're doing a better job with this than the police. I'd like you to stay on the case and see what else you can dig up. I need to know if Slayton was talking through his hat or if there's any truth to his allegations. If you could find out what or who 'The Seven' are, it would be a big help to me."

"Mr. President, I'll be happy to help in any way I can, but I think the Secret Service is better equipped to handle this than I am."

"I appreciate your frankness, Ed, but here's my situation. This Iran-Contra inquiry is taking its toll on my staff in terms of morale and personnel. All those people are dedicated, loyal Americans, as far as I know. If I start poking around in everybody's background at this point, it'll look like I'm conducting a witch hunt for someone to take the Iran-Contra heat. That would completely demoralize the staff in this time of crisis, when I need them most. I'm just not willing to do that without hard evidence—something harder than an unsigned, unfinished letter, anyway. The Secret Service has a good network. If there is some kind of outside plot against me personally, I'm confident that they will find out about it and take care of it. If someone inside the White House is trying to harm me, I'd be very surprised and the Secret Service probably won't be able to protect me anyway. Does that make sense to you?"

"Yes. I see your point. What can I do?"

"I want you to find out if there is any hard evidence for the Secret Service to go on. Do whatever has to be done. If you turn up something, I'll give it to the Secret Service. If you can't, we'll forget the whole thing. Let's give it a couple of months and see what you have. I'll talk to Ellis when he gets back to Washington. Then the two of you can work out an approach."

All of Holloway's instincts were telling him to run for the hills. Instead, he heard himself saying, "All right, Mr. President." One just did not say "no" to the President. That sounded very loyal—and very stupid. Aside from the stupidity, there was something unsettling about this meeting that Holloway could not put his finger on.

The President stood and shook Holloway's hand. "Thank you, Ed. Keep in touch through Ellis." He moved toward the door.

The First Lady took Holloway's hand. "Thank you, again. Mr. Mitchell will show you out."

Holloway was surprised to hear himself saying, in a low voice that he hoped the President would not hear, "A private word with you, please?"

It was the First Lady's turn to be surprised. She recovered quickly, turned to the President's retreating back and said, "I'll be along in a minute, dear."

The President waved an acknowledgment and left the room.

"What is it, Mr. Holloway?" asked the First Lady.

"Ellis Eaton travels frequently, according to his secretary. If I turn up something and he's out of town, I'd like to be able to get it to you through Sid Mitchell—sealed, of course. It might get awkward if I tried to contact you or the President directly again."

The First Lady considered his request. "I think that would work. I'll tell Mr. Mitchell to relay your messages. Good afternoon, Mr. Holloway."

As the First Lady departed the Green Room, Sid Mitchell entered with Holloway's coat.

Sid winked and said, "Just delivering a message from a sick friend, huh?"

"You'll find out soon enough, Sid."

"What's that supposed to mean?"

Holloway smiled. "I'll contact you in a few days and we'll discuss it." On the way to the gate, Mitchell tried unsuccessfully to pump Holloway for information. Holloway's mind was elsewhere. He was trying to get in touch with a vague, uneasy feeling about the Green Room meeting. It was too . . . easygoing. Neither the President nor the First Lady were concerned enough to suit him. Or, was it more accurate to say that they were not concerned enough about the right things. There was something about the way they referred to Slayton . . . or didn't. That was it! They didn't ask any questions about how Slayton died. It occurred to Holloway that Ellis Eaton had not told the President that Jack Slayton had been murdered.

CHAPTER 6

<u>April 24, 1975, Saigon</u>

The NVA safe house fire raged well into midday and you could take your pick of the rumors as to the cause. Meanwhile, the evacuation of Americans and other nationals was in full swing. Tan Son Nhut had become one of the busiest airports in the world. It was difficult to run such an operation with a crippled control tower, but thanks to Dillworth's marksmanship, the tower windows were a shambles. Doyle got the request for a repairman at first light. Trung deliberately delayed his arrival in the tower until just before the 8 a.m. shift change and was able to take advantage of the confusion to work his mischief. He carried in two repair kits, but brought out only one. The kit that remained in the tower was filled with plastic explosives and carefully concealed.

When Trung returned to Doyle's shop, Dillworth and the embassy man were waiting outside. Dillworth waved Trung over. "How is the window repair business?"

"I think it will be booming any day," he grinned.

The embassy man asked, "Do you still have Doyle's passport?"

"Right here." Trung tapped his shirt pocket.

"Keep it. We need to adjust our arrangements with Mr. Doyle."

Doyle was alone and pouring a shot of brandy into his coffee cup when they entered. Trung and Dillworth looked on while the embassy man did the talking.

"Good morning, Mr. Doyle. My name doesn't matter. I'm your travel agent at Air America. I understand that you'll be flying with us."

Doyle was suspicious of the new face. Ignoring the embassy man and turning to Trung, he asked, "Those windows fixed the way you want 'em?"

"The windows are fine," said the embassy man, trying to establish control. "We appreciate your cooperation."

"Then I'm ready to fly," said Doyle, finally acknowledging the newcomer.

"I need one more favor," said the embassy man.

"What's that?" Doyle asked warily.

"I have some friends who need a place to stay for a couple of days. I'd like to put them in your loft."

Doyle was relieved. "Ha! You can have the whole damn place for all I care. I just want to know when I can fly outta here."

"You can leave when my friends leave."

Doyle's face fell. "Whadda you trying to pull? The other guy said I could leave after the windows got fixed." Doyle turned to Trung. "Where's the other guy, the one I talked to in the bar?"

Trung gave Doyle his inscrutable look.

"Mr. Doyle," said the embassy man, "let's not make this difficult. Either you do as I say or you don't get the passport."

"S'pose I tell the airport police how bad you wanted to get into the control tower?" The coffee cup was giving Doyle backbone.

Calmly, the embassy man said, "In that case, one of us would have to kill you."

Doyle took a swallow from his cup. "When are your friends coming?"

"They'll be along in a day or so. Meanwhile, Mr. Trung will stay here and keep you company. It's nice to do business with a sensible man. Good day, Mr. Doyle."

The embassy man took Dillworth outside for a private chat. "I suppose you're wondering why I wanted you to come out here without telling your captain?"

Dillworth looked at him, but said nothing.

"I know you and the captain have been friends for a long time, but I need some straight answers. Do you trust his judgment?"

"Most of the time."

"Do you believe that Doyle will follow our instructions and destroy his son's passport when he is safely in the States?"

"No."

"Your captain thinks he will."

"I said that I trusted the captain's judgment *most* of the time. This time, he's wrong. No way Doyle's wife is going to let him burn her son's passport."

"What about this woman, Li? He wants to take her to the States to be his mistress. Do you think that's in our best interests?"

"I get your point," said Dillworth. "The bad judgments are starting to stack up."

"You and I are of one mind. What do you suppose we should do about Mr. Doyle and Miss Bach?"

They discussed solutions. When the decisions were made, the embassy man shielded his eyes against the sun and looked up to watch the planes as they circled, landed, and took off with another load of Vietnamese refugees or U.S citizens. On the ground, there was near-panic, as a steady stream of would-be evacuees on trucks, buses, and foot, headed for the so-called "Dodge City" processing station and then, hopefully, to board aircraft for the States. But the queues were long and time was running out. A lot of them were not going to make it. The embassy man made up his mind. "Tell your captain to assemble the group in his room at the Caravelle day after tomorrow for an operations briefing. Let's do it early."

"He'll want to know about Li's passport."

The embassy man gave his pipe stem a thoughtful chew. "Tell him I'll bring it with me."

"But you won't?"

"Of course not."

* * *

April 25th was devoted to preparations. The embassy man met with the pilot and crew chief for the operation and kept in touch with his other contact to be sure that the cargo would not be moved. Dillworth and the captain plowed their way through the madness of Saigon's traffic to collect the last of the equipment and supplies required for the operation and to notify other team members of a meeting the following day at the Caravelle. The fact that the North Vietnamese Army was closing fast on the city added urgency to their labors.

* * *

On the morning of April 26th, in the captain's room at the Caravelle, the embassy man unrolled a large engineer's drawing of Tan Son Nhut and stuck it to the wall with strips of masking tape. He turned to the assembled raiding party with a look of satisfaction and counted them. His audience consisted of seven men. The captain sat at the table beside a rugged looking civilian named Ackerman. He was ex-Special Forces and had a reputation for doing anything that would turn a profit. Major Roper, their Air Force pilot, and Sergeant Yarborough, his airplane crew chief, sat across the table. A tough-looking pair of Nordic types with crewcuts and civilian clothes sat on the edge of the bed. Dillworth stood to the side where he could see everyone. All of them were armed, but Dillworth's gun was most accessible. He carried an M-10 submachinegun suspended from his shoulder by a makeshift sling that was long enough to allow him to rest his hand causally on the pistol grip.

"I see we're all here, except for Trung," observed the embassy man. He's keeping Mr. Doyle company. This is the last time that we will be together before we move on Hangar 11. Let's make sure that we all know what's going to happen and who does what. We will attack the hangar on the 28th of April. According to my sources"—he was referring to Dr. Nu—"the NVA timetable for getting the cargo out of Hangar 11 is as follows. They planned to capture Thanh Song Airfield yesterday with some of its fighter-bomber aircraft intact. This has been accomplished with the help of NVA agents at the airfield. Thanh Song, by the way, is on the coast near the city of Phan Rang, about 170 miles northeast of Saigon. At 1730 hours on the 28th, the NVA will use those captured aircraft to launch an attack on Tan Son Nhut Airport. The aircraft launch was supposed to have been coordinated by radio with a group of NVA commandos in Saigon whose job it was to be in control of Hangar 11 by the time the planes from Than Song hit Tan Son Nhut. The air strike is nothing more than a diversion. Amid the confusion created by the strike, the commandos were to roll the C-130 and its precious cargo out of Hangar 11 and fly off to Phan Rang under the protection of their fighter escort. Fortunately for us, we have disposed of the NVA commandos and will execute the plan exactly as they would have, with one important exception. Instead of heading north to communist-held Phan Rang, we will head for the friendly skies of the South China Sea. Are there any questions so far?"

"What's the cargo?" asked one of the crewcuts.

The embassy man ignored him and addressed the group. "You're being paid fifty thousand dollars apiece not to concern yourselves with that. Are there any other questions?" There weren't.

He continued. "In the event that the commandos were unable to get the plane airborne during the air strike, the NVA have plans to destroy Tan Son Nhut's runways with rocket and mortar fire so that no planes can take off, including the one in Hangar 11. The idea is to keep the cargo at Tan San Nhut until NVA ground forces arrive to claim it. Therefore, we have got to get the plane off the ground as soon as the NVA air strike comes in. Otherwise, we'll be stuck when they rocket the runways."

Dillworth wondered aloud, "Do you think the NVA changed their plans when they couldn't contact the safe house?"

"They can change anything they want as long as we get to Hangar 11 and fly out that cargo before they do. And that is what I mean to do."

Sergeant Yarborough, the crew chief, asked, "What happens if the South Vietnamese or the Americans decide to move the cargo before we get a shot at it? They've got to know that it's just a matter of time before the NVA takes Saigon."

"I have a source who will contact me immediately if a decision is made to move the cargo. If that happens, I will notify you gentlemen immediately and we will preempt the move with our raid.

"If I receive word that the cargo will be moved, getting from this hotel to the airport could be a problem, considering the heavy refugee traffic. Therefore," he said, replacing his glasses, "I have arranged for you to be quartered on Tan Son Nhut air base, to remove the necessity for travel. Our Mr. Doyle has 'volunteered' his loft. The facilities are limited, but the location is close to our objective, Hangar 11."

The idea of moving onto the air base did not sit well with the captain. There was Li to think about. He wanted to be sure that she got out of Saigon. He also did not like the embassy man's reference to "Our Mister Doyle." The captain had been running Doyle. Now, the embassy man was making arrangements with Doyle behind his back. That could be a bad sign. However, from an operational point of view, he couldn't quarrel with the decision to move closer to the hangar.

Saxby, one of the Nordic twins, spoke up. "Why the hell do we have to wait around for the NVA air strike anyway? Why not just go in tonight, knock over the hangar, and fly away?"

"We need the confusion of the air strike to make a clean getaway. There are control aircraft in the air over Tan Son Nhut all the time, monitoring in- and outbound flights. They might call and ask us for identification or information. If we didn't respond properly, they could call for fighters to 'escort' us back to the air base. In that event, all of us would be tried for murder and hijacking."

Saxby gave him an indifferent shrug.

"Very well," said the embassy man. "Let's get down to the specifics of the raid on Hangar 11." The embassy man turned the meeting over to the captain, who described the plan in detail using the air base diagram. It took an hour to assign and explain responsibilities to the members of the raiding party and answer questions.

When the captain had finished, the embassy man stood and cleared his throat. "I believe that the captain advised each of you beforehand that you would be somewhat restricted in your outside contacts after getting the operations briefing. Judging from your backgrounds, all of you are familiar with this practice. As of right now, you are so restricted; no outside contacts will be permitted unless you are in the company of someone else in this group. You do everything in twos. Anyone caught breaking this rule will be dealt with harshly."

"Sounds like you're not used to dealing with people you trust," observed Saxby.

"I don't trust anyone. It cuts down on my disappointments."

Speaking again to the group, the embassy man said, "Sergeant Dillworth has a truck downstairs to transport you to your new quarters at Tan Son Nhut. Major Roper, Sergeant Yarborough, and I have jobs, so we will not be sharing your accommodations in Mr. Doyle's loft. Your quarters have been stocked with food, water, clothes, weapons, and communications equipment. If you need anything additional, tell Trung."

The embassy man paused and looked over the group. They had accepted the conditions of their isolation and were awaiting orders. Good soldiers, all. This was the best time to give them the bad news. "The captain told you that we would be moving out to Tan Son Nhut at 1500 hours today. We've had to change our plans because of a transportation problem. We're going to the air base now." There was an immediate roar of protests from everyone except Dillworth. He looked on impassively and fingered his submachinegun. Saxby was on his feet and talking again. "I've got things to do before we go to Tan Son Nhut. What's this goddamn 'transportation problem'?"

The embassy man replied coldly, "The transportation problem, Mr. Saxby, is that anyone who doesn't go with us right now is going to be transported to Tan Son Nhut in a body bag." Dillworth cocked the M-10 for effect, but kept it pointed at the floor.

Every head turned toward him, except the captain's. He kept his angry eyes focused on the embassy man and his ear tuned to an inner voice. *Randy has found a new partner. Better watch your back.*

The embassy man ignored Saxby and addressed the rest of the group. "All of you have had experience with covert actions. You know that it's simply good security procedure to keep everyone together after the final operations briefing. Right?" There were murmurs of reluctant agreement. The captain said nothing. "All right, let's move down to the truck." Shuffling and bitching, they collected their things and headed downstairs.

The embassy man stayed in the room. He didn't want to be seen with the raiders. The captain hung back too.

"Did you bring Li's passport?"

"No," replied the embassy man. "It will be ready tomorrow."

"Don't jerk me around on this," warned the captain.

"I wouldn't do that. The document will be ready tomorrow. Where and when were you supposed to meet Li to deliver it?"

"Here, between noon and two."

"Unfortunately, it won't be ready until late tomorrow afternoon. I'll give it to Dillworth and have him deliver it about suppertime. Write the lady a note to that effect before you leave."

The captain bristled. "I don't want Dillworth involved. He's your man now. I'll deliver it myself."

"Don't be ridiculous. I had Dillworth go through his little act with the submachinegun to put him on the outside of the group and you on the inside. When he cocked the weapon, they all looked first at him and then at you to see if you were in on the move. You were busy being angry with me for spoiling your date with Li. They saw that. You recruited these men and they see you as one of them. If they get any ideas about taking a peek at our cargo or hijacking it once we get airborne, you will probably be included in on the plot. Dillworth, I, and the airplane crew will not. So, I want you in there talking and listening to them right up until we cash in our cargo. You are our insurance against a mutiny." The embassy man flashed a genuinely warm smile. "I really am good at this, you know." He patted the captain on the shoulder.

"I want to see the passport before Dillworth delivers it," insisted the captain.

"That can be arranged."

The captain scribbled a note to Li and left it on the bed. Then he went downstairs with the embassy man and joined his companions in the truck. The embassy man disappeared into the mass of humanity clogging the sidewalk.

* * *

The next afternoon at three o'clock, Dillworth stood across the street from the U.S. Embassy watching a howling mob of desperate Vietnamese demanding to be evacuated on one of the helicopters taking off minutes apart from the embassy grounds. Marine guards in battle gear held the mob at bay with fixed bayonets to keep the more agile would-be refugees from climbing the compound fence. Dillworth saw the embassy man elbow his way out of the crowd and walk over. "It appears that none of the natives want to be in Saigon for the coming communist utopia."

"The mobs are starting to get ugly," observed Dillworth. "At Tan Son Nhut, they tried to prevent a bus carrying U.S. personnel from entering the base. I also heard that some of our evacuation aircraft have taken ground fire from South Vietnamese soldiers outside of the airport."

"I'm not surprised. They feel betrayed." He handed Dillworth a passport. "This is just to show to your suspicious captain. After you see Li and give her the bad news, I want it back."

"Right. I'll go back to the airport now and show this to him. I meet Li about 1800 hours." The embassy man nodded his approval and Dillworth pocketed the passport. "How's the war going?"

"Straight to hell. The NVA has cut the road to Vung Tau and is massing for an attack on Bien Hoa. Saigon's days are numbered—in single digits."

"Any word from your source on what the South Vietnamese are going to do about the cargo in Hangar 11?"

"There's no talk of moving it. The government is paralyzed. Ex-President Tieu has departed for Taiwan. Vice President Huong is keeping the chair warm until the government can be turned over to General Minh. There is some hope that Minh can negotiate with the NVA. Personally, I don't think he has a chance. The communists are winning. Why should they negotiate? My best guess is that the cargo will remain in place until the political situation is clarified. Of course, by then, it will be too late."

Above the din of the mob, they heard a scream and looked in the direction of the embassy. A woman was hanging from the embassy fence, her arm caught in a tangle of barbed wire strung along the top.

The embassy man turned away. "Is Trung keeping an eye on the hangar for us?"

"Yeah. There's been no change in the guards' routine."

"Good. Well, you'd better get going. And don't get soft-hearted with Li. We're dead if she ever connects us with the hangar."

* * *

Dillworth stood at the Caravelle's bar and surveyed the room, sensing its mood. For the media types who lived in the hotel, the room provided a sanctuary for the final drinks with friends made over years of covering the war. At one end of the bar, a band of longtime residents and hard-core drinkers, from the Doyle mold, considered their options. To go or to stay? That was the question. If they survived at all, they would suffer most under the communists. They were the epitome of Western decadence that the communists loved to expose and vilify. Among the Vietnamese staff, there was apprehension about how the coming regime would affect their lives. The Caravelle was a Western hangout. In many places, the victorious NVA had not been gentle with those who had catered to round eyes.

The bar had also become a prearranged rendezvous point where Americans met the Vietnamese they had promised to get out before the end came. A middle-aged Vietnamese couple sat in one corner. They looked strangely out of place. He was dressed in khaki pants and a white shirt with the tail out. She wore black pajamas. With the exception of an occasional hopeful glance at the door, they sat uncomfortably erect, looking straight ahead, waiting. Dillworth guessed that the parcels at their feet contained the possessions they intended to take into their new lives, somewhere away from Vietnam. The woman held a smaller bundle in her lap. That would be the usual stash of gold and perhaps some American dollars, hoarded over a lifetime as a shield against the uncertainties of Vietnamese economics and politics.

Dillworth was still at the bar when Li entered and joined him. She looked ravishing in a blue blouse and jeans that she had been poured into. Heads turned. He pushed a cognac toward her. She sipped and looked around for the captain. Dillworth had a need to get it over with quickly.

"Li, the captain isn't coming. He left for the States today."

"He leave?" she asked in a disbelieving whisper. "What 'bout me? What 'bout my passport? He promise me. I go United States with him."

"Look, I hate to tell you this but the captain is married. He's got a wife and two young kids. I'm sorry," he said lamely.

Li stared at him in silence. He grew uneasy. Finally she asked, "How long you know 'bout . . . his family?"

"Long time," he said, softly.

Li's nostrils flared and she raised her voice. "Why you don't tell me?" Heads turned in their direction again.

"I don't meddle in other people's love lives unless they affect me personally." *Like now.* "What happens between a man and a woman is nobody else's business." He was having difficulty looking her in the eye.

Her stare never wavered. "Six months 'go, I got pilot who want me to fly Thailand with him. Your captain," she said viciously, "say to me, 'Don't go Sweet Thang. Stay Saigon with me. You, me, we go United States when things get bad.' Das what he say." Suddenly, her eyes widened and she shouted, "Why you don't tell me he marry! Why you don't tell me!"

A reporter who knew Li came up and said, "Can I interrupt the crisis line for a drink?" He brushed between Dillworth and Li and slammed his glass on the bar. Dillworth motioned for Li to move away from the bar, but when he reached for her arm she drew away.

The reporter turned to her and said, "Hey, Li, don't you worry about your lost love. To hell with him. The whole North Vietnamese Army is gonna be in Saigon soon. I hear some of them NVA soldiers been in the bush for five years. Their dicks are gonna be harder than Japanese arithmetic and you are gonna be a fucking millionaire." He threw his head back and let the belly laugh roll out of his foul mouth.

Li glared at the man while he enjoyed his laugh. Then she slapped him as hard as she could. In an instant, the reporter's expression went from amusement to surprise to anger. He lashed at her and she was ready. Only her head moved when his open palm connected with the side of her face. She rolled with the slap and turned her head slowly back to fix him with a glare of contempt.

When he raised his hand to hit her again, Dillworth grabbed the man's arm and said, "You don't really want to do that again, do you?" It wasn't a question.

The reporter looked first at Dillworth, then at Li. His handprint was rising on her cheek and the defiance in Li's eyes was slowly dissolving into wells of tears. Her bottom lip began to quiver and her beautiful face distorted into a mask of pain. She hugged herself, sank into the traditional Vietnamese squat and wailed, "Sweet Tha-a-ang, you son-'bi-i-i-tch! You son-'bi-i-i-tch! Why you leave me here!" Li raised her face to the ceiling and let out a howl of anguish that curdled the blood of everyone in the room. It was the kind of sound that Dillworth had only heard after combat, when the women discovered the death of a mate or child.

The reporter snatched his wrist from Dillworth's grasp and moved away. Li was sobbing and docile when Dillworth led her to a chair in the corner. She sat down and slumped across the table with her head in her arms, sobs racking her body. Dillworth got cognac from the bar and held her in his arms while she drank with trembling hands. When the other customers had turned their attention elsewhere, Dillworth said quietly, "The captain isn't coming and I don't know anyone else who can get you out of Vietnam. I'm sorry.

"I hear a boat convoy is forming up at the docks. They're going to try to make it to some of our warships. If you get that far, the Navy might pick you up and take you to the States, okay?"

Li cried while Dillworth looked on uncomfortably.

Through her sobs, Li said, "I must get out of Saigon. NVA hurt me bad if they find me here. You hear what they do to women in Da Nang who sleep with Americans? Sometime I give you information on Viet Cong. NVA kill me when they come to Saigon. I have to get out of here!" she said desperately.

Dillworth drew a deep breath. "There might be a way. The U.S. Defense Attaché's Office at Tan Son Nhut is responsible for getting Americans and what they call 'high-risk Vietnamese' out of the country. High-risk people are Vietnamese brass, their families, and other supporters of the Saigon government, people who might be subject to NVA revenge when the city falls.

"Every night," Dillworth told her, "the DAO sends buses out to secret pickup points to collect these people and take them to the air base. From there, they're flown to the States by the U.S. Air Force. There's a pickup point not far from here. You'll have to sneak onto the bus and smuggle yourself into Tan Son Nhut. Once you get on base, you'll have to talk someone into putting you on a plane. There are no guarantees, but it's a chance to get out."

"Tell me how," pleaded Li.

He did, never believing for a minute that she would get out. Better for her to live with hope than despair. Dillworth stuffed money into her hand and left.

* * *

At 10:45 p.m., the DAO bus pulled into the alley adjacent to the courtyard with its lights out, as always. The driver cut his motor and coasted to a stop, steering so that the side of the bus was almost flush against the courtyard wall and the bus door perfectly aligned with the archway leading into the courtyard. That would ensure that the bus could only be entered from the courtyard. The passengers waited in the house adjoining the courtyard as a precaution against trouble. The sight of Americans with suitcases waiting outside to be taken to the airport would not sit well with Vietnamese who felt they were being abandoned.

Dressed in traditional black pajamas, Li waited in the shadows not far away. The driver opened the door of the bus and went through the courtyard and into the house. As soon as the door closed behind him, Li slipped across the alley and tossed her small suitcase under the bus and into the courtyard. She followed on her belly. Once into the courtyard, she snatched up her suitcase, entered the bus and went to the last row of seats. There, she began to transform her image. She was less likely to get close scrutiny if she had a Western look. Li got quickly out of her pajamas, slipped into a yellow cotton dress and draped a sweater around her shoulders. She topped the costume off with a plain dark headscarf that hid her prominent cheekbones and lay down out of sight on the back seat. Li's heart pounded as the passengers shuffled through the courtyard and boarded the bus. They filled the front seats first. When the bus was about a third full, Li sat upright in her seat. In the darkness and confusion, nobody noticed. The bus filled and the driver closed the door and drove off.

The trip through the city was tense. Even though a curfew was in force, Li saw roving bands of armed soldiers who could have been deserters or military police enforcing the ban on travel, but the bus was not stopped. Occasionally, there were bursts of gunfire off in the distance. As they approached Gate 1 at Tan Son Nhut, the passengers were silent. The bus squeaked to a halt and a bout of haggling broke out between the gate guards and one of the American passengers, who appeared to be in charge. Finally, the guards waved them through. Once the bus was inside the compound, the passengers breathed audible sighs of relief and started nervous chatter. Li remained silent. The bus accelerated down Republic Avenue and turned right into the street leading to the U.S. Defense Attaché Office Annex, where outprocessing for the States was in progress. The bus stopped near a large building. Li could see hundreds of people in lines or clustered in family groups. The passengers began to unload. The driver stood outside the door, helping women and children down the steps. Li hung back to be the last person off. If there was any difficulty, she wanted running room in as many directions as possible.

When Li stepped off of the bus, the first thing the driver noticed was her shapely figure. He had watched each woman board and that body was not familiar to him. When he looked at Li's face, he was positive that she had not been in the courtyard.

Before the puzzled driver could react, Li thrust something into his hand and said, "I find 'dis on back seat. You keep it."

The driver turned toward the light and saw that he was holding a roll of twenty-dollar bills, neatly bound with rubber bands. He turned back to speak to Li, but she had disappeared into the mob.

* * *

It was 4:30 p.m. on the 28th of April. Most of the raiders were assembled: Dillworth, the captain, Trung, Ackerman, and the intense-looking pair with crewcuts, Saxby and Walker. Everyone was dressed in U.S. Army fatigues, except Trung, who wore the uniform of a Vietnamese Air Force colonel. The embassy man had not yet arrived. Roper, the pilot, and Yarborough, his crew chief, were to be picked up later. Those present were gathered around a sealed packing crate in the supply room of Steamer Doyle's maintenance shop. The crate was the size of a large footlocker. It was too big for one man to get a grip on and too heavy for two men to lift. Metal rings were attached on two sides to accommodate long poles so that the crate could be carried like a sedan chair.

Ackerman tried to push it with his foot. "Damn! This thing must weigh a ton! It'll take a platoon of Vietnamese to lift it."

"That's the idea," said the captain.

"What's inside?"

"Generators." The captain turned to Trung. "Get the poles."

Trung produced two metal rods, each six feet long, and slid them through the rings on either side of the crate.

"Okay, let's get this out to the truck and be careful. We don't have time for a hernia repair," cautioned the captain.

Dillworth, Ackerman, and the two crewcuts lifted the crate and carried it to the truck, complaining all the way about the weight. As they were loading it, the embassy man arrived on a bicycle and followed them back into the maintenance shop. He moved to the center of the circle rubbing his hands together in anticipation. "Well, are we ready to get under way?"

"All set," said the captain. "The security guards in Hangar 11 have two means of communicating with the outside world. One is by radio and the other is a direct telephone line to the Vietnamese Joint General Staff Headquarters down near Gate 1. Ackerman will cut the telephone line and jam their radio frequency just before we hit the hangar. The rest of us leave here in the truck in . . ." he checked his watch, "five minutes. We'll swing by Dodge City to pick up Roper and Yarborough and head for the hangar. Trung, Randy, and I will ride in the front. Everybody else rides in the cargo compartment with the crate. When we get to the hangar, Roper and our crew chief will stay in the truck until we take out the guards. I don't want them hit by any stray bullets. Otherwise, we won't have a way out of here. The rest of us will take out the guards. Ackerman joins us and we wait for the NVA air strike."

"What have we got for firepower?" inquired the embassy man.

The captain reached into a gray aviator's kitbag and withdrew a submachinegun. It was less than a foot in length and looked like an oversized automatic pistol with a black sausage attached to the barrel. The captain shoved a long magazine into the hollow pistol grip and handed the weapon to the embassy man. "That's an M-10 Ingram, equipped with silencer. It shoots seven hundred rounds a minute, if you can reload that fast. The mag holds thirty-two rounds of nine-millimeter Parabellum. Each of us has an M-10, courtesy of friends at Air America. Those Vietnamese guards will never know what hit 'em."

"Ugly-looking little devil," observed the embassy man.

The captain turned to the others. "Okay, people, let's move it!"

The raiders picked up their kitbags and started for the door. Trung hung back. So did Dillworth. The embassy man and the captain lingered in the doorway while the others climbed aboard the truck.

"Trung. Give Doyle his passport," ordered the captain. Trung nodded and walked toward Doyle's office at the front of the building.

The embassy man said, "Dillworth, why don't you see if Doyle has a spare bottle in his office. We can use it to celebrate our success in a couple of hours."

"Right." Dillworth followed in Trung's footsteps.

When Trung entered the office, Doyle was standing at the window holding a cup of brandy-laced coffee. Doyle's Vietnamese wife, his two sons, and mother-in-law squatted in a corner talking quietly. They fell into silent anticipation when Trung entered.

"I saw your men loading up," said Doyle. "You all finished here?"

"All finished." Trung held up the passport.

Doyle sat his coffee on the counter and reached for the document, but never got to touch it. Trung heard a series of popping sounds behind him. Bloody holes appeared in Doyle's chest and throat. He collapsed on the floor. Doyle's wife opened her mouth, but her scream was aborted by a hail of nine-millimeter death. She fell near her husband. The old woman sat stoically while Dillworth fired another burst. The boys died without a whimper, begging Dillworth for their lives with scared, sad eyes.

Trung turned away from the carnage and Dillworth took the passport from him. "Orders from the embassy man. Keep quiet about this. I don't want trouble with the cap'n."

Dillworth moved from body to body insuring that there were no survivors. Then, he went to Doyle's desk and removed a half empty bottle of brandy. "Let's go, Trung—and be cool."

* * *

With the captain at the wheel, they drove east on New Republic Avenue until they neared Gate 1, then turned into a street that took them in the direction of the evacuation center and their rendezvous with the pilot and crew chief. As they approached "Dodge City," crowds of people forced the captain to slow the truck to a snail's pace. The embassy man had been right. In spite of the fact that the DAO had scraped together a small contingent of Marines for crowd control, the situation was, at best, chaotic. About five thousand people, mostly Vietnamese, clustered around the gymnasium where a small, overworked staff of Americans screened applicants for asylum and processed the lucky ones for a flight out of the country. The mob at the gym had spilled over into the adjacent tennis court and bowling alley and onto the edges of a nearby swimming pool.

Li Minh Bach had been standing in line at the gymnasium for seven hours. In her right hand, she clutched a piece of paper that had cost her a gold bar and the night on her back with the man who issued the paper. The man had embossed the paper with a seal certifying that Li was a U.S. Government employee and requesting that she be given asylum in the United States. It was her ticket out, if she could make her way through the long line to the processing center inside.

The captain guided the truck through the crowded street and brought it to a halt near the gymnasium. Roper and Yarborough were waiting. They threw their flight bags into the cargo compartment and scrambled over the tailgate with assistance from the crewcuts. The captain put the truck in gear and honked his horn at the mob obstructing his path.

Li turned in the direction of the sound and saw Dillworth's profile in the front seat. She yelled, "Randy!" But he was fifty yards away and her cry was lost in the roar of the mob around her. Li elbowed her way to a vantage point in front of, but not much closer to, the slow moving truck. She saw Trung and the captain sitting next to Dillworth. She yelled again and waved frantically, but they didn't see her. The truck bulldozed its way through the mob, slowly gaining speed. Li ran after it, yelling. The truck cleared the worst of the mob and accelerated. Losing ground, Li took off her shoes and ran as fast as she could, following the truck as it headed north toward the runway. She soon gave up hope of catching it, but continued to trot along, keeping the truck in sight. It reached the fuel storage tanks, turned left, and dashed across the runway to the north side of the airport. To Li, the truck was a blob on the horizon when it stopped at the east end of Hangar 11.

The hangar was a huge rectangular building surrounded by coiled barbed wire anchored to the concrete parking apron with sandbags. The long side of the building with the large main door faced south, overlooking the runway. The north side faced an open field. The east and west walls of the building formed the short sides of the rectangle and each had a normal entry door in the center. Just outside each door, but inside the barbed wire, a semicircular sandbag bunker had been constructed. Each bunker had a wide machinegun port that covered the approaches to the hangar. The flaw in the placement of these structures was that the soldiers in one bunker could not observe events at the other. It was in front of the east bunker that the captain brought the truck to a halt.

Behind the sandbags, a young Vietnamese guard trained his M-60 machine gun on the truck. Trung, resplendent in his colonel's uniform, got out of the cab and approached the wire. A Vietnamese Air Force major stepped away from the protection of the sandbags and saluted. "Good evening, sir. Are you aware that this hangar has been declared a restricted area by the General Staff?"

Trung returned the salute. "Yes. I'm from the General Staff."

"Sir, my instructions are to verify that before you enter."

"No need for that," Trung said with an impatient wave of his hand. "I don't want to come in. I have additional cargo for the plane. The American ambassador sent a gift for Vice-President Huong." That explained the presence of American soldiers in the truck. Trung waved again and the captain began backing the truck toward a narrow opening in the barbed wire. The bunker guard still had the machinegun trained on the truck and the Vietnamese major seemed to be trying to make up his mind about what to do.

Trung reassured him. "I'll have the Americans take the crate off the truck and leave it outside the wire. Get some of your men out here to take it into the hangar."

The captain and Dillworth dropped the tailgate and wrestled the crate to the ground with help from the two crewcuts. The major was relieved to see that none of the Americans were armed. The crewcuts got back into the cargo compartment. Dillworth and the captain secured the tailgate and returned to the cab. The embassy man, the pilot, and the crew chief sat quietly at the front end of the cargo compartment.

Behind the sandbags, the Vietnamese major opened the hangar door and yelled instructions. A sergeant and two privates appeared and came through the opening in the wire. While the sergeant and major looked on, the two privates attempted to lift the crate. It didn't budge. Both privates complained to the sergeant about the weight. The sergeant gave them a disgusted look and yelled into the hangar. Two more privates came out in their T-shirts. The sergeant barked instructions and the men took hold of the metal lifting rods and put their backs into raising the crate. At that moment, the crewcuts, Saxby and Walker, leveled their submachineguns and killed all four of the privates. The embassy man shot the sergeant in the forehead with his automatic. The machinegunner in the bunker had relaxed. Now, he tried to bring his weapon to bear on the truck again, but Trung produced a silenced automatic and fired four rounds at him. The machinegunner and his weapon fell behind the sandbags with a thud. The major was trying to wrestle his .45 automatic out of a stiff U.S. holster when the embassy man shot him twice through the heart.

Walker and Saxby dashed over the bodies and through the wire, running the length of the building toward the bunker on the west side.

The captain and Dillworth followed them through the wire and entered the east end of the building. They went into the hangar cautiously, pressing themselves against the wall on either side of the door, guns at the ready. The hangar was silent. A Lockheed C-130 Hercules cargo plane stood alone in the center of the hangar, its nose facing the main hangar door. The rear cargo ramp was down. Dillworth and the captain were facing the side of the plane.

From outside the far end of the hangar, they heard the faint popping sound of M-10 submachineguns snuffing out the lives of the guards in the west bunker. Dillworth looked at the captain and held up a finger, indicating that one guard remained. The captain nodded. They began to move away from each other, the captain circling toward the front of the plane, Dillworth toward the open loading ramp in the rear. They froze when the west door flew open, banging loudly against the wall, as Saxby and Walker burst into the far end of the room. Everyone realized that if there was a guard aboard the plane, the door noise had alerted him. Saxby was the first to move toward the aircraft. He was cut down in a hail of gunfire from the cockpit window. The remaining three raiders ran for the aircraft and dove under it for cover, the captain under the wing, Dillworth and Walker under the body near the ramp. The cockpit guard began to yell for help. Walker and Dillworth had a quick conference. Walker went to the front of the aircraft, under the cockpit window and yelled, "Chieu Hoi! Chieu Hoi!," indicating that he wanted to surrender. The guard shouted something in Vietnamese and Walker threw his submachinegun out from under the aircraft so that the guard could see it laying on the hangar floor. Meanwhile, Dillworth quietly removed his boots and crept up the loading ramp into the plane. Walker and the guard continued to yell at each other in Vietnamese and English. The guard was still trying to convince Walker to come out from under the aircraft when Dillworth leaned into the cockpit and shot him in the back.

"Got him!" yelled Dillworth.

Walker darted out from under the plane and ran over to Saxby, who lay motionless on the floor. He checked the wounded man and yelled, "Saxby's hit bad!"

"Leave him!" commanded the captain. "We'll take care of him later. You and Dillworth check the plane. Make sure we got all of the guards. Then, go out to the west bunker and drag those bodies in here. They can be seen from the air."

The captain ran back to the door through which he and Dillworth had entered. Trung and the embassy man were crouched on either side of the entrance, ready to shoot.

"What happened?" asked the embassy man.

"Saxby's down. One of the guards got off some rounds before we took him out. It's safe, now. Get the pilot and crew chief in here. Trung, help me move these bodies inside."

The embassy man alerted Roper and Yarborough. They jumped from the truck and darted into the hangar to begin their preflight checks. Meanwhile, the other raiders finished the grisly task of dragging the dead guards into the hangar. They left the Vietnamese in piles just inside the doors at either end of the hangar. The embassy man drove the truck to the north side of the hangar, where it couldn't be seen from the main air base. Dillworth and Walker cut the barbed wire in front of the main hangar door and pulled it aside so that the plane could exit. Finally, they brought in the crate and plunked it down next to the bodies at the east door. The embassy man paused to look at the crate and the dead guards. To no one in particular, he observed, "After all these centuries, the Trojan Horse still works."

Inside the plane's cargo compartment, crates were stacked chest high and lashed to metal pallets anchored to the deck. The embassy man's heart was pounding as he pried a wooden slat off the nearest crate, fumbled through the sawdust, and found what he was looking for. He examined the object quickly, then covered it with sawdust and hammered the crate shut with his pistol.

"Is it there?" asked a voice behind him.

He turned grinning at Dillworth and the captain. "It's here, just like the good Doctor Nu said it would be." They all grinned.

At that moment a scream echoed through the cavernous hangar. The three men ran down the loading ramp and saw Li. She was standing in the doorway, hands over her mouth, staring down at the dead Vietnamese guards. She looked up and saw the captain and Dillworth. "You lie to me!" she screamed.

The captain shot a suspicious glance at Dillworth and made a move toward Li. The embassy man reacted instantly. He raised his pistol and fired. Li spun under the impact of the bullet and fell face down on the floor, her long, black hair forming a halo around her head.

The captain yelled, "Nooo!" and went for the embassy man, but Dillworth grabbed him from behind with an assist from Trung. Just then, Ackerman came through the east door and shouted, "The air strike is coming in now!"

The embassy man raised his automatic and aimed it at the back of Li's head. As he pulled the trigger, the building was rocked by an exploding bomb from one of the NVA planes. Everyone, including the embassy man, instinctively ducked. The movement threw his aim off a fraction, but his second bullet grazed Li and a red stain began to spread through her hair.

Roper, oblivious to the ruckus over Li, leaned out of the cockpit window with a bullhorn he had brought along to defeat the noise of the attack and yelled, "Let's get this crate off the ground!"

Some of the raiders began to scramble for their designated positions. Yarborough pulled the blocks away from the landing gear wheels. Ackerman and Walker brought Saxby aboard and ran to open the main hangar doors.

Roper's bullhorn came to life again. "Blow that tower, now!" He threw switches and the C-130's engines coughed to life, joining the bedlam of exploding bombs and pounding antiaircraft fire outside. The noise was deafening. As the C-130 rolled slowly toward the hangar exit, Roper could see at least three communist-flown A-37s bombing and strafing the airfield.

Dillworth and Trung had placed themselves between the captain and the embassy man. They pushed the captain toward the hangar door where he had left the detonator for the control tower. The captain was in a blind rage after seeing the embassy man shoot Li. The embassy man was fiendishly persistent. Realizing that he had missed the center of Li's head, he raised his automatic to fire again, taking careful aim. The captain punched Dillworth hard in the stomach and twisted free from Trung. He took a short step toward the embassy man and lashed out with his foot, connecting with the gun. It spun out of the embassy man's grip. The captain drove the embassy man to the floor, both men punching and blocking blows. Trung stepped up and brought the edge of his hand down on the back of the captain's neck, knocking him unconscious. Then he grabbed the captain under the armpits and dragged him up the loading ramp into the plane.

The embassy man sat up swearing and bleeding from the mouth. He looked around for his gun. It was just out of reach. Dillworth stepped between him and the weapon and said, "Forget it. Blow the tower. You two can kill each other after we get out of here." The embassy man gave Dillworth a hateful glare and staggered toward the detonator. Dillworth picked up the gun and walked over to Li's crumpled form. The pool of blood around her head was widening slowly, being fed by a wide gash in her neck where the second bullet had hit. Dillworth felt for a pulse. Then he carried Li to a corner and laid her down gently.

In the cockpit, Roper was on the bullhorn again. "Is somebody going to blow that fucking tower!"

The embassy man picked up the electronic detonator and searched the sky for NVA planes. The A-37s rolled in for another pass at the airfield, running a gauntlet of antiaircraft fire. Bombs separated from the planes. When the first one hit the ground, he pressed the detonator button. A blast erupted from the control tower, mingling with the sound of exploding bombs. Black smoke billowed out from under the roof. Trung was as good at installing plastic explosives as he was at replacing windows. The embassy man ran to the plane's side entry door and Yarborough hauled him aboard. Ackerman and Walker removed the last section of wire barring the exit from the main hangar door and followed the embassy man into the plane. Dillworth was the last to scramble aboard. The C-130 rolled out of Hangar 11 and onto the parking apron, the plane's rear loading ramp closing as it picked up speed.

From his vantage point in the cockpit, Roper could see South Vietnamese flight crews and pilots working frantically to get planes into the air to meet the attacking A-37s. The captain, now conscious, and Trung were also in the cockpit, occupying the copilot and navigator seats. The others were in the cargo compartment. Dillworth had deliberately stayed with the embassy man to calm him down. Ackerman and Walker had broken open a first aid kit and were tending Saxby's wounds. The crew chief, Yarborough, darted from window to window, reporting what he saw to the pilot through his radio headset.

Other cargo aircraft were scrambling to get off the ground and avoid bomb damage. Since there was no control tower to clear aircraft for takeoff, Roper watched the other planes and waited for a break in the runway traffic. When it came, he wheeled the C-130 onto the runway and gave it the throttle. His timing was perfect. There was a collective sigh of relief as the plane cleared the ground and gained altitude. The antiaircraft fire was still intense and on the ground, several VNAF jet fighters were taxiing for takeoff to meet the NVA attack. Roper guided the C-130 into a shallow climb. It looked as though they would make a clean getaway, until a warning came over his earphones. Roper turned to the captain and Trung. "We're not home free. The crew chief says one of those NVA fighters is coming up to look us over. What's gonna happen when he sees round eyes in the cockpit?"

Seconds later, the NVA pilot flew his A-37 into a position slightly above and forward of the C-130's cockpit so that he had a good view of the flight deck. He could see Roper's grim face looking up at him and Trung, sitting in the copilot's seat, holding a pistol against Roper's head. Trung gave the NVA pilot a thumbs-up signal and a toothy grin. The NVA pilot held his A-37 in position while he considered the situation. If this was the plane he had been sent to escort, it would be on his frequency. He spoke into the radio.

"Quang Ngai! Quang Ngai!" The demanding, singsong voice of the NVA pilot filled the C-130 cockpit. "Quang Ngai! Quang Ngai!"

"What is this 'Quang Ngai' crap?" asked the captain.

"I don't know," answered Trung as he waved this pistol and gave the fighter pilot another grin.

"'Quang Ngai' must be a challenge code," guessed Roper. "If we don't come up with the right password, this jet jockey is liable to blast us out of the sky. Anybody know the password?"

"There ain't no damned password!" grumbled the captain, but he realized that there was. Dr. Nu had held back something after all.

The NVA pilot challenged them once more. When he got no response, he rolled his fighter into a tight right-hand turn and fell in on the C-130's tail.

The crew chief's voice came over the intercom to Roper's earphones. "Major, that A-37 is flying right up our loading ramp. He's gonna blast us for sure."

"Quang Ngai! Quang Ngai!" yelled the NVA pilot.

Roper twisted in his seat to get a look at the A-37 and saw salvation out of the corner of his eye. "Trung, I'm gonna turn on the radio so that you can talk to that NVA pilot. Repeat exactly what I say, only say it in Vietnamese."

Trung nodded and Roper flipped the switch and said, "Quang Ngai aircraft, F-5s closing on your tail from seven o'clock low! Break off! We will rendezvous with you over Bien Hoa."

The NVA pilot suspected a bluff, but it was too risky for him not to look. When he did, he saw two F-5s streaking up toward him on afterburners. Quickly, he searched the sky for his wingman and saw him being chased off to the northeast by more VNAF Phantom jets. It was time to relocate. He rolled away from the C-130 and went for altitude with the F-5s in hot pursuit.

In the C-130 cockpit, everyone was relieved. Bien Hoa was to the north. Roper leveled off the C-130 and headed east toward the South China Sea.

CHAPTER 7

Holloway was slumped in a low leather chair in Eaton's Georgetown study, while his host sat at a desk, halfway across the room. "It was a mistake for you to go to the White House with Slayton's letter," said Eaton, trying hard to conceal his anger. "Our understanding was that you would handle the inquiry and I would take care of communications with the President."

Holloway was defensive. "Slayton's letter indicated that the President might be in danger. In my judgment, that called for immediate action."

"I appreciate the implications for the President's safety, but I must insist that you deal with me on this matter. You must not go to the White House again. Your inquiry won't remain discreet for very long if you keep making cameo appearances in the Green Room."

Now, Holloway was angry. "You were out of town. Was I supposed to wait?"

"Of course."

"Did the President complain?" Holloway asked, testily.

Eaton avoided the question and softened his tone. "The Iran-Contra matter has put the President in a delicate position. He neither wants nor needs to know the small details of your inquiry."

"Do you call the fact that Slayton was murdered a 'small detail'?"

"What do you mean?"

"When I talked to the President, he didn't know that somebody had engineered Slayton's heart attack. I told you, but you didn't tell him. I don't consider murder a 'small detail.' "

Unruffled, Eaton asked, "Did you tell him?"

"No."

"Why not?"

"I'm not sure."

"You thought it was my place to tell him, didn't you?"

"Yes," admitted Holloway.

"You were quite right. I haven't told the President for several good reasons. First, our knowledge about how Slayton died was obtained in a somewhat 'unorthodox' manner." He gave Holloway a conspirator's smile. "Explanations at this late date could be embarrassing. Don't you agree?" Eaton didn't wait for Holloway's response. "Anyone having evidence that Slayton was murdered who hasn't come forward by now could be charged with obstructing justice."

Or anyone who removed evidence from the scene of the crime, thought Holloway.

"I don't think either of us wants to put the President in that kind of difficulty," purred Eaton.

"The second reason for not telling him is that there is more to this than simply blurting out every available fact. The President wants to know if there is substance to Slayton's allegations. We need to address that concern first. The circumstances of Slayton's death are of no possible value to the President in that regard and could force him to take actions he would prefer to avoid. Slayton's death may or may not be connected to the allegations. My reading is that we need to know a bit more before we make our report. I find it hard to imagine, but if someone on the White House staff did murder Slayton to keep him quiet, announcing our suspicions at this point would drive the culprit underground or make him even more desperate. Either course could be detrimental to the President."

Holloway said nothing. He was wondering how many years he could get for obstruction of justice.

Eaton leaned forward to indicate his concern, "Edward, I hope you plan to continue this inquiry. The President needs you."

Eaton went to the liquor cabinet. "Drink?"

"Gin and tonic."

Holloway broke the extended silence that followed. "I'd like to interview Slayton's widow. She might know something."

"I thought you might want to do that," said Eaton, as he topped off the drink with a twist of lime. "I mentioned that possibility to the President. He wouldn't hear of it. Miriam Slayton has taken her husband's death very hard and is in seclusion at the family home. Sorry. Perhaps later, when she's recovered. Talk to me first."

Holloway's anger flared. "How the hell am I supposed to conduct an inquiry if I can't talk to the people who might have information?"

Eaton served the drink and returned to his desk. "You're a man of wide experience, one of the best at what you do. You are also my valued adviser in your area of expertise. May I be your trusted adviser in these political matters? I have a suggestion as to how you might proceed."

Holloway knew he was getting Eaton's famous velvet glove treatment, but it felt good and he was out of ideas. "Okay, Ellis. It's your ballpark and your game. How do you want to play it?"

Eaton sat back comfortably and laced his fingers together over his stomach. "The only lead we have now is that this 'Seven' business is somehow linked to the White House staff and the Iran-Contra scandal. I'm an academician by inclination. When we academicians have a problem, the first thing we do is search the literature to see if anything has been written about it. I recommend that approach to you. Why not review the available documents on the Iran-Contra matter. See if you can turn up any reference to 'The Seven' or evidence of a conspiracy targeted at the President. If you find something of that nature, the inquiry might then proceed along the more conventional lines that you have suggested."

Holloway looked at him skeptically. "What documents are you talking about?"

"The Tower Commission has completed the Administration's official investigation of the Iran-Contra affair. They have thousands of documents. I can make those available to you, along with anything else you might require, within reason, of course."

Holloway's hopes were dashed. He could visualize a dump truck full of documents showing up at his house the next day. Swamping a troublesome investigator with enough paper to keep him inactive was a standard bureaucratic ploy. In Washington, it had been elevated to an art form.

Holloway tapped his gin glass impatiently. "Sounds like a job for a platoon of librarians. Besides, what am I going to find that the Tower Commission didn't?"

"It's a job for a man with your instincts, and you will be looking for things the Tower Commission never dreamed of. Personally, I hope you don't find anything, but if something is there, we had damn well better know, and you are the man who can find it."

Holloway was trying to decide if he should just walk away from the whole mess.

Eaton sensed his mood. "This is important work, Ed."

Holloway noticed that Eaton had stopped calling him "Edward."

Eaton continued. "I know this is not exactly your style, but give it a few weeks and let's see what develops."

* * *

In response to Holloway's call, Sid Mitchell was waiting in front of the White House. They talked while Holloway drove to Donna Goodwin's place.

"Sid, I need your help. Did the First Lady tell you why I was in the Green Room last week?"

"Just that you were doing some confidential work for her and the President. She said you might require some assistance from me, passing messages and such. She wants me to 'cooperate fully with Mr. Holloway.' You must be into something heavy."

"I am. This is close hold, Sid. Keep it between us." Mitchell nodded his agreement. "I'm reading some documents for the President. I want you to help because I trust you and you've got the security clearance. You'll be working three hours a night, four or five on the weekends. I'll pay you my standard consulting fee."

"Okay. Anyone else in on this?"

"Dan Vogle and Donna. They're waiting for us at Donna's place."

Mitchell nodded again. He knew both of them as Holloway's business partners, and Donna Goodwin was Mitchell's close friend.

Half an hour later, around Donna's dining room table, Holloway briefed Mitchell, Goodwin, and Vogle on his dealings with Ellis Eaton. To protect himself and his friends, he said nothing about Jack Slayton's murder. He also kept Eaton's identity his own personal secret. When Holloway had finished, he turned to Vogle. "How are we going to handle the computer end of this, Dan?"

"Shouldn't be a problem. We'll get the documents into the computer using a high-speed optical scanner with automatic feed. Meantime, I'll write a program to search for the key words you're looking for. That will take a few days. Then we run the program and the computer will give us a printout of any key word it finds and the document, page, and paragraph where the word is located. You can pull the page up on the monitor or get a hard copy. It's a piece of cake. The hard part is going to be reading all of those pages after the computer identifies the ones we want."

Holloway looked around the table. "That's where the rest of us come in. Donna, you, Sid, and I will do the analysis of whatever the computer kicks out. At least two of us will have to read and initial each lead. That should keep us from missing anything, and the initials will help us keep track of what's been read. Any interpretation that two readers disagree on goes to the third person for evaluation. Now, any ideas on a place to work?"

"Let's do it in the basement," suggested Donna. "The vault is down there and Dan will have room for his computer equipment."

"Good," said Holloway. "We start next Monday."

* * *

During the weeks that followed, they established a routine. Before noon each workday, Holloway arrived with several cartons of documents. Donna logged them and put them into her basement vault. Vogle came later and fed the documents into the computer. Sometimes, the four of them had dinner in Donna's apartment while the computer scanned the thousands of pages for key words that might give them a lead: "The Seven," "Seven," "seven," "seventeen," "seventy," "Slayton," "White House," "White House staff," and so on. After dinner, Dan Vogle repacked the documents for delivery to Eaton the following day. Meanwhile, Holloway, Donna, and Sid went through the printouts of computer-generated leads and read the corresponding documents. The analytical work was slow and tedious. A month later, documents were still arriving with no end in sight, and no solid leads had materialized. Frustration was mounting as fast as the useless stacks of printouts.

It was the first Friday in April and they were in Donna's basement. Piles of loose documents and bound volumes were everywhere. Donna was curled up on the couch, her eyes darting back and forth between a printout beside her and the pages she was holding. Dan Vogle worked at the computer keyboard, programming yet another refinement to the search program. Sid Mitchell stood at the coffee urn, blowing into a cup of steaming brew and wondering what he was doing there. The only sounds in the room were the rustle of pages and Vogle's incessant tapping at the keyboard.

Without warning, Holloway said, "Balls! This a waste of time!"

Donna put down the paper she had been reading and said, in an exaggerated Boston accent, "Whatsa mattah, Big Boy? Doncha like it down heah in the stacks?"

"We're on a wild goose chase, gang," declared Holloway.

"The money's good," Donna reminded them.

"We must have gone through a million pages and we're exactly where we were the first day." Holloway flopped back into his chair.

"Except that I now know more about the Iran-Contra mess than I ever wanted to know and more," added Mitchell.

Donna turned to Vogle. "Dan, can the computer do anything else for us?"

Vogle raised his palms in a helpless gesture. "Sorry. There isn't even a suggestion of anything called 'The Seven.' I think Ed's right. It's just not here. There ain't nothing in this cellar but us four mushrooms and a lot of fertilizer."

"Are you saying that we ought to throw in the towel?"

Vogle stood and arched his tired back. "I'm saying that we're on a cold trail. If there is a 'Seven,' we need to take a different approach to finding it."

"So?" Donna said to no one in particular.

"So," replied Mitchell, "after reading all this stuff, the only question in my mind is, 'Why did all these smart people do all these dumb things?' You've got a group of superachievers in some of the most influential positions in the world breaking laws, destroying their careers, and risking jail just to ransom a handful of hostages and save a banana republic from communism. Very noble, but I just don't buy it. If we could discover the real reason for Iran-Contra, we might have the answers to a lot of questions, including the riddle of 'The Seven.' "

Holloway stared at the wall, wrestling with his internal conflict. He wasn't sure he wanted the answer to Mitchell's question. If he quit right now, he could go to Ellis Eaton in good faith and say that they had searched every available document and had found no evidence that "The Seven" existed. Eaton would pay him a fat fee, tell the President, and everyone would rest easy—unless something bad happened to the President later, something that Holloway might have prevented with a bit more diligence. That had always been his curse. He had to run down every lead, check every detail. Holloway took a deep breath and crossed the line of no return.

"The logic of the thing has been worrying me, too," he confessed. "The key people in this mess have a lot of successful service in the civilian and military bureaucracies, which means they played by the rules. Now, all of a sudden, they become renegades. Why?"

"They had something to gain," suggested Donna.

"What?" Holloway flipped through a stack of biographies that had come with the Tower Commission papers. "Poindexter could look forward to a shot at promotion to four-star admiral. North was a shoo-in for brigadier general. Slayton's star was still rising. These people were going to keep moving up even if the hostages never came home. So what did they have to gain?"

Donna hunched her shoulders and did her thinking aloud. "Some military types value personal loyalty as much as they do the rules. Maybe they owed their loyalties to someone who told them to do the Iran-Contra deal."

"You mean the President?"

As gently as possible, Donna observed, "He seems to be a strong candidate in everyone's mind except yours."

Holloway considered the possibility. He simply did not want to believe that the President was involved, because if he was, this search for "The Seven" could be part of a cover-up. After what Holloway had done for the White House in times past, he refused to believe that the President of the United States would use him like that. Reluctantly, he pulled a yellow legal pad towards him and picked up a pencil. "Okay. Why did they do the Iran-Contra deal? Possibility Number One: the President ordered it." He scribbled a note. "But what if he didn't?"

"In that case," replied Donna, "they would have needed a strong motive, one that would outweigh their loyalties to the President and his policy of not negotiating with terrorists. It would also motivate them to break the law against lethal aid to the Contras."

Holloway took up the thought. "Something more important than their careers and a jail term."

"How about good old-fashioned fanaticism?" asked Vogle.

Holloway shot him a disapproving glance, but wrote it down.

"How about political ambitions and really big money." Holloway finally uttered the words that had haunted the dark corners of his mind since the early days of the scandal.

"Rule out politics," advised Sid Mitchell. "Slayton was not a political animal. Neither is Poindexter. North has the instincts and, maybe, the ambition, but none of them had a political base."

"Try money," Donna suggested. "How much would it take to buy you Holloway . . . if you were in their shoes, I mean?" She gave him a wicked smile.

"Let's see. North is the one who appears to be worse off financially. If Iran-Contra hadn't caused a problem, he was in line for a decent military pension and some lucrative post-retirement employment. Balance those against a jail term, a house full of kids to educate, and the loss of his pension and some post-retirement income." He looked up at Donna. "If I was Ollie North, I wouldn't even discuss a bribe of less than a million-five to do the Iran-Contra deal. That's a lot of money and whoever would be paying this alleged bribe has not even dealt with Poindexter, Slayton, and God knows who else. If all of the key players were in on the payoff, this deal could cost ten million in bribes alone."

"Which one of the principals had that kind of money?" Dan Vogle wondered aloud.

"The Iranians," answered Holloway. "They were in the middle of a war with Iraq and losing. They had American missile launchers and were hungry for new missiles and spare parts. They needed a quick fix and price was no object, but America wouldn't sell to the Iranians for political reasons. So, they got an intermediary to contact somebody on the National Security Council with an offer that the White House couldn't refuse: the Iranians would get the hostages released if the U.S. would sell missiles to Iran. The Iranians also dangled the possibility of political accommodation with moderate elements in their government. After some initial jockeying and foul-ups, Ollie North becomes the worker bee for the deal. As North begins to work out the details, the Iranians sweeten the pot by offering him a million-five to be sure the deal goes through. Maybe other members of the NSC were bribed, maybe not, but from that point on, North was committed to the deal." Holloway paused and looked at them. "How do you like that scenario?"

With detachment, Mitchell observed, "It's got a lot going for it: political intrigue, greed, bribery, and everybody wins—except the Iraqi pilots on the wrong end of those missiles. There's just one thing wrong with your story. I don't believe it happened that way."

Donna had no such reservations. "I like it!"

"That's too bad," said Holloway, "because what comes next goes against your theory that the people involved were smart."

"Assume that the deal went well. Iran got the missiles. North and the others collected their bribes. North takes a chunk of the proceeds from the missile sale and buys arms for his favorite charity, the Contras. Everybody is happy until a Lebanese newspaper exposes the missiles-for-hostages deal and the Iran-Contra connection begins to unravel.

"At that point, North had three problems. The first one was credibility. The arms deal was in violation of the White House policy of not negotiating with terrorists. This was an embarrassment to the President, but no reason to commit hara-kiri. Since North was the bag man, his mission was simply to protect his superiors and make sure that any cover story they chose to tell would hold water. If you were North, what would you have done?"

"Gotten rid of the evidence," said Vogle.

"Right. You'd go to the office immediately and destroy every piece of paper and computer document related to the deal. That didn't happen. Why? Was North lazy or stupid?"

"Maybe there were too many documents to get rid of," suggested Vogle.

Holloway rummaged through a stack of papers and came up with a floor plan. "This is North's office in the Executive Office Building. He had two five-drawer file cabinets. North could have purged them in a couple of nights, with the help of his loyal assistant, Jack Slayton. So how come, twenty days later, we still have North's secretary sneaking out of the White House with Iran-Contra documents in her underwear? Meanwhile, North himself is shovelling documents in the shredder while Justice Department investigators are pounding on his office door. It doesn't make sense."

Donna lowered her head and moaned in frustration. "Let's leave that one for a while. What are North's other problems?"

"You won't like them any better," warned Holloway. "Assume that North accepted a bribe from the Iranians. Unlike violating White House policy, accepting a bribe is a criminal offense. He needs to cover his tracks. How would he do that?"

"By destroying the documents relating to the missiles-for-hostages deal," sighed Donna, "and that takes us right back to the first problem and the first question: 'Why didn't North destroy the documents?'"

"Exactly. Now, for problem three. Even if North didn't take a bribe, he violated the law by funding lethal aid for the Contras with the proceeds from the missile sale to Iran. How would he cover himself?"

Donna spoke the works in unison with Holloway. "By destroying the Iran-Contra documents in his office." She added, "Holloway, I hate you, but I can't argue with your logic."

Holloway dropped the pencil and rubbed his tired eyes. "To explain the presence of the Iran-Contra evidence, we have to believe one of two things about Colonel North. Either he took a bribe and was too stupid to destroy the evidence or he didn't take one and did not feel the need to destroy the evidence because he viewed Iran-Contra as nothing more than a political battle between the President and Congress. North was not stupid. So, that shoots a hole in your 'big payoff' theory."

Donna would not relent. "There had to be a payoff of some kind. My theory still holds. Maybe they wanted the Iran-Contra documents to be found to cover something bigger."

"Like what?" demanded Holloway.

"Murder. Treason. How the devil do I know?"

Holloway gave her a skeptical look. Vogle waited expectantly. Sid Mitchell maintained his detachment.

"Well," said Holloway, "from all we've read, there are a few things we know for sure. Too many smart people in the White House, including Jack Slayton, did a lot of dumb things, with no explanations. We've got Iran-Contra: two classic CIA-type covert operations being run, not by the CIA, but out of the White House by Slayton and North. On one hand, we had a policy of not dealing with terrorists and, on the other, we traded with them for hostages. We had a law withholding arms from the Contras, and the White House continued to provide them arms through secret Swiss bank accounts. The President says he didn't authorize any of this, but North says he did. Investigators found evidence of the Iran-Contra conspiracy, even though the conspirators had two weeks to destroy it." *And there's Jack Slayton, an Iran-Contra conspirator, officially dead of a heart attack, but, in reality, murdered.* "That's just too many contradictions for me to swallow. Something is very wrong here. Our deck is a few cards shy."

Sid Mitchell nodded in agreement and added, "I don't think we're going to understand what Slayton was trying to tell the President in that letter until we know more about Slayton's role in Iran-Contra."

Holloway made a decision. "Let's call it a night. Tomorrow, I'm going to Kansas and have a talk with Jack Slayton's widow."

CHAPTER 8

The next morning, Holloway caught a nonstop flight to Kansas City. This time Ellis Eaton had not objected to the visit because Holloway had simply neglected to tell his employer that he was going. Nor had he announced his arrival by calling ahead. Holloway did not expect the welcome mat to be out for him. The papers had not been particularly kind to Slayton or his wife. He surmised, correctly, that Miriam Slayton had her fill of questions about her dead husband. One more stranger with a new set of questions was probably the last thing she wanted in her life at this moment. Holloway checked into Kansas City's Crown Center Hotel and spent the day doing some local research on the Slaytons. The following day, he hired a van and drove out of the city to the rolling farmland near Mission, Kansas. The Slayton house sat well back from a secondary road and there were no neighbors for miles. Holloway parked the van in the semi-circular driveway and walked up to the luxurious brick rancher. He rang the bell as he took a final glance at the clipping containing Miriam Slayton's picture. The door opened and Holloway found himself staring at the face in his clipping—or so he thought. It was a beautiful, fresh face with green eyes and framed by corn silk-blond hair. The woman standing before Holloway did not fit his image of a grieving widow.

"Mrs. Slayton, my name is Holloway. I'm here concerning your husband's affairs." He was intentionally vague. "Could I have a few minutes of your time?"

The woman's jaw hardened. "I'm Denise French, Mrs. Slayton's cousin. Are you from the media?"

"No. I work for the government. I just flew in from Washington." He gave her his Defense Investigative Service card.

Denise French read the card and looked Holloway over. "I don't know who is least welcome here, media people or government people. Just a minute." She closed the door in his face, and not gently.

After a short wait, Denise French opened the door again. "You have ten minutes. After that, we call the police." She led him to a spacious living room and opened the drapes, revealing a large picture window with a magnificent view. As she was leaving the room, Miriam Slayton entered, wearing a sleeveless cotton dress. She was a drawn and tired version of Mrs. French. In fact, Mrs. French looked more like Miriam Slayton's photograph than Miriam herself. Denise French gave her cousin a comforting pat on the arm as they passed.

"Good morning, Mr. Holloway." The widow extended an ice-cold hand, which Holloway held for an instant. "Please sit down."

"Mrs. Slayton, I'm sorry to intrude—"

She cut him off with a quiet, "What do you want, Mr. Holloway?"

"I'm sorry to disturb you. I wouldn't be here if it wasn't important."

"Things that are important in Washington are rarely important in Kansas. Please tell me why you are here."

"When someone with a high-level security clearance dies, such as your husband, it's routine for us to do a closeout inquiry," Holloway lied. "I have to ask you a few questions. I promise to be brief. After that, I'll tell you why these questions were necessary."

Miriam Slayton gave him a disinterested nod.

"You and your husband were friends of the President and his wife?"

"Yes."

"And still on friendly terms?"

"There were times when I hated Jack's job and I certainly had no love for Washington. It can be a hellish place. The President and his wife are just good people surrounded by . . ." Her voice trailed off and the corners of her mouth turned down, reflecting her bitterness. Her lips quivered a bit and she said, "I bear the First Family no ill will, if that's your question."

There was a momentary silence.

"Your husband was extremely loyal to the President, right up to the day he passed away." Holloway watched her carefully. He didn't know what he was looking for, but caught a brief reaction. Was it more bitterness? Surprise? Something struck a responsive chord in the woman.

Her reply was matter-of-fact. "Of course Jack remained loyal to the President. He knew the rules. When the Iran-Contra story broke, he became a political liability and had to leave. It wasn't the President's fault. That was just reality. It was our treatment by the press that I resented."

"Did your husband have any information of a personal or professional nature about the Iran-Contra business that he was trying to communicate to the President?"

A fountain of crimson raced up Miriam Slayton's neck and splashed into her cheeks. "I beg your pardon?" It was impossible for her to have missed the question. She was stalling. Holloway knew it, and she knew that he knew.

"I asked if your husband had been trying to communicate information to the President during the interval after he left the White House staff and before his death?"

"No. Not that I am aware of."

"Why did he stay in Washington when you came to Kansas?"

"He had business to complete."

"Related to his Iran-Contra problems?"

Her nostrils flared, but her answer was controlled. "Family business. There was a house to sell and so forth."

The lady had repaired the cracks in her facade. Holloway realized that he was not going to get anywhere unless he provided some bait.

"Mrs. Slayton, I need your help in a matter vital to the President. In order to convince you how important this is, I must confide in you. May I have your word that you will not repeat what I am about to say?"

Miriam's eyes locked on Holloway. "A matter of national security, is it?" She got up, walked to the picture window and stood there, her back to Holloway and her arms folded defensively beneath her breasts. The warm sun streamed through the window, highlighting the peach fuzz on her exposed limbs. She wasn't wearing a slip. Holloway could see the outlines of her long, shapely legs through the dress. His libido began to stir.

Without turning from the window she said, "I'm not sure I want to know any more secrets. Secrets restrict one's freedom." She returned to her chair. "I want to be free. I made the sacrifices for God and country, just as Jack did. Now, I want to be free." There was something wild, yet sad, in her eyes. She waited for Holloway to make the next move.

"Your husband met with the First Lady the night he died. He told her that he was the President's John Dean. Does that mean anything to you?"

Miriam hesitated, then said, "No. I have no idea why my husband would make a statement like that."

Her words were too deliberate, too cool for Holloway to believe. John Dean was not a name to be taken lightly. He was the man who blew the whistle on the Watergate scandal. Miriam should have shown some surprise, some concern, something.

"Mrs. Slayton, I need to know about this John Dean business. So, I'm going to tell you something that will be painful for you. I think your husband had something important to tell the President about the Iran-Contra deal and someone killed him to keep him quiet."

The woman's eyes went wide with terror and her hand shot up to cover her mouth. She shook her head from side to side, denying Holloway's words. Suddenly, the tears came in silent torrents. Holloway offered her his handkerchief and she accepted without comment.

"I'm sorry I had to tell you like this. There's no easy way to say these things." He stood up, but knew better than to try to console her.

"Would you like to be alone?"

Through her tears, she said, "Yes, please." She didn't look up.

"If you feel like talking later, I'll be in Kansas City for a couple of days. I'm staying at the Crown Center." He let himself out under Mrs. French's hostile glare. Holloway would have given his eyeteeth for a tap on Miriam Slayton's phone. Instead, he settled for visual surveillance. He drove to a deserted stretch of road half a mile away, made a U-turn, and parked on the shoulder. He had a clear view of the house and watched until well after dark. At ten o'clock, the lights went off in the dining room and came on upstairs in what Holloway guessed was Miriam Slayton's bedroom. Those lights went out after midnight and Holloway drove back to Kansas City.

* * *

The call reached him the next afternoon in his hotel room.

"Mr. Holloway, this is Miriam Slayton. Are you enjoying the sights in Kansas City?"

"To tell the truth, I haven't been out of this room since I returned from your house. How are you feeling today?"

"Well enough to treat you to one of our famous steaks, if you're not busy for dinner. I haven't been to Kansas City for quite a while. I feel the need for bright lights and people. Would you like to join me?"

"My pleasure."

"We have reservations for seven o'clock at Harry Starker's on the Plaza. Anyone in the hotel can direct you. I'll meet you there."

The food and drink were good at Starker's, but it was a tad busy for Holloway's tastes. He preferred the slower pace of Lenny's in D.C. After some small talk, Miriam took Holloway's card out of her purse and read aloud, "Defense Investigative Service." She cocked her head to one side and studied him. "You don't look like 'Defense Investigative Service.' My husband worked with those people several years ago. They were unimaginative souls in double-knit polyester sports coats with everything color-coordinated, except their white socks. You, on the other hand, have a rather roguish look." Holloway laughed. Miriam smiled, exposing two rows of almost perfect teeth framed by blazing red lipstick. She was beautiful.

Miriam caught Holloway eyeing the cut of her red dress. "I suppose you expected me to be all sadness and widow's weeds?"

"You can't mourn forever." She could have come in flour sack and ashes for all Holloway cared. He just wanted to know about the John Dean business, but the dress was easy on the eyes.

"I've mourned Jack ever since he went to Washington. Sixteen-hour workdays . . . and the weekends just did not exist. He's been dead for two months and the only thing I feel is . . . abandoned. At this moment, I don't care how he died or who was responsible. I may change my mind tomorrow or next month, but right now, I simply don't care. When Jack died, a chapter closed in my life. I will not drag leftover baggage into the new pages. Not even if it belongs to the President of the United States."

Then what the hell are we doing here? he wondered.

Miriam must have read his mind. "Don't worry, Holloway. I'll tell you what I know about Jack's last days in Washington. But I warn you, you may walk away with more questions than answers. In the meantime, relax and enjoy your dinner."

The steak was excellent and the gin-and-tonic loosened Holloway up a bit. He and Miriam chatted through dinner, staying with the safe topics initially: the plight of the Kansas City Chiefs, the sights Holloway wasn't going to see before he left town, and exotic places they had been. Finally, the subjects became more personal.

"I had two children in two years," said Miriam. "My dad said I should have been a farmer's wife." She smiled sadly, remembering her father. "But I was a soldier's wife. Jack was a captain in Army intelligence when our last child was born. He was always off on some hush-hush mission to Vietnam or God-knows-where. I had to raise the kids by myself most of the time." She paused. "Were you in the military, Holloway?"

"Yes, but I don't like to talk about it."

Miriam gave him an appraising look. "You were a spook too, weren't you?" There was amusement in her voice. Holloway didn't answer. "I should have known. I'm always attracted to the silent warriors."

This was the first Holloway had heard that she was attracted to him. The news was flattering. It also made him uneasy.

Miriam realized what she had said and changed the subject. "There's a band in your hotel bar. The last set starts in fifteen minutes. We can make it if we leave now."

The Signboard Bar was more to Holloway's liking. The music was mellow and the crowd was thin enough to make dancing not only possible but enjoyable. Miriam was quiet and graceful on the dance floor. Holloway sensed that she was working up the strength to talk about Washington. He was wrong. Halfway through the set, the crowd had thinned to a hard core, leaving Miriam and Holloway an unpopulated corner.

Holloway was saying, "This place isn't bad."

"I'm surprised you didn't discover it before tonight. What did you do with all your free time here?"

"I studied."

"What?"

"You," he was tempted to say. Instead he said, "People."

She smiled slightly. "What a fascinating pastime. Did you learn anything?"

"That I'm not always right about them." He laughed.

"Did you study me?" Her smile broadened.

"Yes."

"And what did your studies reveal?"

He felt heat in his cheeks. "Nothing bad."

"Evidently you were not very thorough." They shared a nervous laugh. "I do agree," Miriam continued, "that it's a good idea to know the people one is dealing with. So, are you the Holloway of Holloway Security Consultants or the Defense Investigative Service Holloway?"

Surprised by Miriam's knowledge, he managed to say, "Both. I do some contract work for DIS."

"Sounds boring."

"It usually is, down among all those double-knit sports jackets and such." He smiled "I like 'boring.' I've had my lifetime ration of excitement." Holloway wanted it to be so, even though he had not quite reached that point. "Besides, the pay is good and you meet a better class of people." He raised his glass to her and drank. "How did you find out about Holloway Security Consultants?"

"I called Washington and had you checked out. I still have a few friends there."

"You waited until your friends gave me a clean bill of health before inviting me to dinner, right?"

Miriam suppressed a smile. "I might have invited you to dinner whether you checked out or not." She raised her glass to him, drained it, and ordered another.

"My husband taught me a lot of things, Holloway. One of them was not to drive home after four Scotches. May I spend the night in your room?" Miriam's eyes were downcast, watching her finger circle the rim of her glass.

As tenderly as he could, Holloway said, "I take that as a compliment, Miriam, but I don't think it's the right thing to do." This was the first time that he had called her Miriam.

She raised her eyes to meet his. "Are you married?"

"No. It's just not ethical to get involved with you here and now."

"An honest spook." There was feigned amazement in her voice. "Who would have believed it?" She tossed her head and said, "I don't need your code to protect me. I can take care of myself."

"Sometimes *I* need the code to protect *me*."

She took him by the hand. "Let's dance." The music was slow and Miriam's body was hot against his. Her perfume sent his head spinning and her lips brushed his neck. "Take me to your room, Holloway. This is the first nice evening I've had since the Iran-Contra mess started. Don't spoil it for me. Tomorrow, I'll give you secrets. Tonight, I need to give myself."

* * *

It was late morning in Holloway's hotel room. Coffee was all that remained of breakfast. Miriam sat by the window, wrapped in a hotel bathrobe, looking over the rim of her cup at the Kansas City skyline. Holloway pulled up a chair and joined her. They sat in silence until Miriam was ready to tell her story.

"If you want to understand what Iran-Contra did to my husband, you have to know something about his personality. Everyone said that both of us were organized. I'm organized like a juggler. Throw in another ball and I'll make room for it. Jack was organized like a mechanic. When he set out to do something, all the tools were laid out. He knew all of the parts and exactly which screws to turn. Things rarely went wrong for him. When they did, he made a smooth adjustment. If something was beyond his control, he didn't worry about it. He would play tennis and sleep like a baby. Above all, he never panicked and had an even temper. Once the Iran-Contra story broke, he was in a continuous state of agitation or gloom."

Miriam took a sip of coffee and let her memory rerun the last difficult months of her marriage. "Actually, the problem started about a year before the Iran-Contra story came out. We were at home in

Washington. It was Friday, the thirteenth of March 1985. I remember because we had been to a birthday party. Jack was tired. On the way home, he said he was going to sleep late, which was rare. Unfortunately, a call came for him at three in the morning. Jack said something like, 'Do you know what time it is over here?' He listened to the caller without saying another word, then put his clothes on and went out.

"I heard him come in a little later, but he didn't come to bed. I went down to see what was wrong. Jack was in the basement and in such a state that he didn't hear me coming. I'm no prude, but he was using curse words that I had never heard before. I thought someone was with him, but he was alone, and drinking. That was also unusual for him. He was raving. He said something like, "That dumb son-of-a-bitch! If he lives through this, I'll cut his balls off and mail them to the Ayatollah myself!' He kept repeating, 'I told him to get out! I told them to pull him out!' And there was murder in his eyes. He wouldn't talk to me about it. So, I left him and went up to bed. Afterwards, he still refused to discuss what had triggered his reaction, but he was never the same after that night."

"How was he different?" Holloway asked.

Miriam looked at him for the first time since she began her story. "Worried and jumpy, or withdrawn.

"Other strange things started to happen. Jack had to travel a lot and couldn't always tell me where he was going or when he would return. We had an agreement that he wouldn't lie to me about it. If he couldn't tell me anything, he would say he was off to Calcutta. Jack kept his agreement not to lie about his trips right up until about two weeks after he got the upsetting phone call. He came in one day, packed a bag, and told me he was on his way to Calcutta. That was Thursday or Friday and I think Jack returned on Sunday night. I didn't give the trip another thought.

"A couple of days later, I ran into Sheila Hamilton, a friend of mine who works at the World Bank. She said that she was in Switzerland for an economic conference and ran into Jack, but he pretended not to notice her. I wasn't surprised. Sheila couldn't keep a secret if you tattooed it in the middle of her back and locked her in an empty room. Anyway, I decided to have a little fun with Jack and asked him if he had seen the newspaper coverage of his trip to

Switzerland. I thought he was going to have a heart attack. He stayed upset even after I told him that I was just pulling his leg. We had a nasty argument and he denied that he was ever in Switzerland. But later I checked his suits before taking them to the cleaners and found a Swiss hotel bill."

"What was the name of the hotel?"

"La Richmond, or something like that."

Holloway made a note. "Where was your husband when Sheila Hamilton saw him?"

"Some bank, but I've forgotten the name."

"Was your husband with anyone?"

"Yes. Another man. Sheila didn't know him."

"Can you remember anything else about the trip?"

"That's it. Sorry." She smiled for the first time that morning. Holloway looked at his watch.

"When does your flight leave for Washington?"

"In three hours."

Their eyes met and held. She looked away. "You had better get started or you'll miss it."

Holloway showered, dressed, and packed while Miriam watched in silence. When he was ready to leave, she was still in her bathrobe. "I think I'll keep the room for another night. It was good to get away from the house. If you're ever in Kansas City again, Holloway, call me." She stood by the window clutching a cup of cold coffee, waiting for an invitation to Washington that didn't come. As he collected his bags, she asked, "May I call you, if I come to Washington? I only have your business number."

Holloway took out a card and wrote his home number and address on the back. She came to him, took the card, and kissed him gently on the lips.

"You take care, Holloway."

*   *   *

The estate was tucked away off of a northern Virginia back road an hour south of Washington. It was large enough to have a separate guest cottage, but small enough not to be considered an ostentatious show of wealth. Of course, there was hardly a person in the capital who did not know that the owner, Jules Vaterman, was rich. But who would want a poor Assistant Secretary of the Treasury. Vaterman, a balding, portly man with a six-foot frame, was in the bathroom completing his nightly toilet when the phone rang. He waddled over and answered his private line.

"Yes?" he growled into the receiver.

"Schaeffer," said the caller. "I've had another call from Kansas."

Vaterman's brow wrinkled with concern. "Same problem?"

"No. A different one. I'm told that Miriam Slayton had a visitor from Washington. He asked questions about her deceased husband."

"That's to be expected. The Iran-Contra investigation is in full swing. People from the Justice Department and Congress are all over the place."

"Her visitor said he was from Defense. I checked him out. He does contract work for Defense once in a while, but he's not working for them on this."

"Well, who *is* he working for?"

"I don't know," replied the admiral.

"Who is this person?"

"Fellow named Ed Holloway. Former Company man. Distinguished record," said the admiral with grudging respect.

"Better find out about him quickly."

"I'm on it. What about Miriam Slayton? Have you made a decision?"

"I need to know what she knows," said Vaterman with some urgency. "I'm going to delay the final decision a while longer. We don't want to act in haste and repent at leisure. We've already had enough of that."

CHAPTER 9

<u>March 1987, Washington, D.C.</u>

Holloway was tired when be returned to Washington. He told Donna that he would take a couple of days off for some rest. The truth was that he had become obsessed with the Slayton case and wanted to screen the Iran-Contra documents again using Miriam Slayton's leads. Holloway sat down at the computer in Donna's basement and called up Dan Vogle's search program. He typed in the new key words: "bank," "Bank," "Geneva," "La Richmond," "Switzerland," followed by "CROSSINDEX WITH SLAYTON." Holloway stayed at the computer for two days, reading documents that the search program had identified for him and finding nothing significant. On the evening of his second day back from Kansas, he decided to turn in early. He had promised Donna that he would come to work the following day, after she had reminded him that they had clients other than the White House.

Holloway had just slid between the sheets when the doorbell rang. When he opened the door, Miriam Slayton was standing there, suitcase in hand, about to cry.

"Miriam, what's wrong?"

She dropped the bag and threw herself into Holloway's arms. Her body began to shake uncontrollably and she broke into a hysterical crying fit. Holloway got her and the suitcase into the apartment. Standing just inside the door, he held her until the spasm passed. "What is it, Miriam?"

She looked up at him and tried to say something, but began to cry again. Through her sobs, Holloway could make out the words, "They killed her!" a phrase Miriam kept repeating.

"Killed who?"

"Denise," she sobbed, "they killed my cousin, Denise. They killed her while I was in Kansas City with you." Miriam launched into another fit of crying. Holloway held her until it passed. Then, he poured a stiff Scotch and waited for Miriam to take a couple of swallows before trying to question her again.

"Tell me what happened."

"Denise was murdered." She looked at Holloway, eyes brimming with tears. "They tortured her, Holloway. They did awful things to her. They were after me!" she screamed. "They thought Denise was me!" She sobbed for several minutes.

When Miriam had regained her composure, Holloway asked, "Did the police catch the killer?"

Miriam shook her head.

"Do they know who did it or why?"

"I told you. They thought she was me! Don't you understand!" She dug her nails into his arm. "They're after me, Holloway! I need a place to hide. Can I stay here with you? Just for a few days?"

"Of course. But tell me who's trying to kill you?"

The question seemed to confuse Miriam. Her mouth worked, but nothing came out. She looked around the apartment, trying to get her bearings. "I need time to think, Holloway. I just got off the plane. I'm tired. Can we talk about it in the morning? I can't deal with it now. Denise was my best friend."

"I understand." He led her to his bedroom.

Miriam slept fitfully and so did Holloway. He dreamed of little blue and orange capsules like the one he had found in the apartment where Jack Slayton was murdered. He woke up sometime in the night and put his automatic under the pillow. His movement awakened Miriam. She wanted to talk.

"After you left Kansas City, I spent another day there. I did some shopping and went to a movie. The following afternoon, I drove back to Mission. When I arrived, the police were everywhere. Denise had . . ." She choked back a sob. "She was dead. Stabbed. They did terrible things to her." Miriam shuddered. "I had to go to the morgue to identify her body. It was horrible." She was quiet again. "They questioned me. I told them that I was at the hotel with a gentleman friend. I didn't give your name, but I'm sure they checked with the hotel." Holloway shrugged, indicating that it didn't matter.

"They asked me not to leave the state, but I was scared and I couldn't go back to the house. I got on a plane as soon as they let me go. I bought the suitcase and some clothes on the way to the airport. I'm afraid, Holloway."

"That's normal. Do the police have any suspects?"

"No."

"How did they find Denise?"

"A friend came by to visit and found her."

"Last night, you said that someone killed Denise because they thought she was you. What was that all about?"

"God, Holloway. I don't know what I said last night. I was out of my mind with fear. After what you told me about how Jack died, I was scared to death."

"You kept saying, 'They are trying to kill me.' Who are 'they'?"

"I don't know. Whoever killed Jack and Denise. Look, I don't want any part of this. I don't even want to talk about it anymore. I want to forget it for now." Miriam rolled her naked body over on top of Holloway. "Help me forget for a little while. Make love to me. Please." She kissed his neck. "Please." She kissed his lips, flicking her tongue into his mouth. "Please." Miriam kissed his stomach. "Please." She nibbled the inside of his thigh.

Miriam was lying on her back on the side of the bed nearest the door. Holloway was sprawled face down beside her with his hand under the pillow. Both were in a deep sleep. The first indication Holloway had that someone else was in the apartment came when he heard the latch click and the knob turn on his bedroom door. He flipped himself over in the direction of the door, cocking the automatic as be turned. When he came to rest across Miriam's body his heart was pounding and he was looking into Donna's gray eyes over the sights of his gun.

Donna's eyes registered shock. Then she smiled at the ridiculous sight of Holloway laying naked across the bed holding a gun. Miriam, awakened by Holloway's movements, was struggling with sleep to comprehend what was happening.

"Coming out of our shell, are we?" Donna asked Holloway.

Awake now, Miriam clawed for the covers and gave Donna a Who-the-hell-are-you? glare. Holloway breathed a sigh of relief and lowered his gun. By way of explanation to Miriam, he nodded in Donna's direction and said, "My mother."

"His landlady," said Donna, correcting him. "Excuse me. I didn't mean to intrude." Slowly, she appraised Holloway's nakedness. "Toodle-loo, you," she said, closing the door behind her.

"A friend?" asked Miriam.

"Not anymore." Holloway pulled on his pants and followed Donna into the living room.

She was waiting for him with a finger on her chin and a coy smile. "Well, well, well. Was that the famous Lady Veronica of Lenny's?"

"That's Miriam Slayton." Donna's eyebrows went up with surprise. "She had a death in the family. She was hysterical when she got here last night."

Donna flashed a cold smile. "Nothing like a nice warm screw to calm one's nerves, hey?"

"Give it a rest, Donna. She thinks somebody tried to kill her." Holloway related the story of his visit to Kansas and Miriam Slayton's arrival the previous evening.

There was an uncomfortable silence when he finished. "What the hell are you doing here, anyway?" asked Holloway.

"In case you didn't notice, it's eleven o'clock. You were supposed to come to work today. You didn't call in and your phone is off the hook. I thought perhaps you had killed yourself with an overdose of presidential loyalty." She added, "And you still may, if you're not careful." Donna nodded toward Holloway's bedroom. "You need to let go of this Slayton thing. I have a bad feeling about it."

"If someone is really trying to kill Miriam Slayton, then maybe we're on to something. We might be able to find out who The Seven are and why Jack Slayton was killed."

Donna was surprised. "I thought Slayton died of natural causes."

"Somebody blew bye-bye dust up his nose. The heart attack was chemically induced."

"How do you know that?"

"Trust me. I know. Anyway, the trail is getting warm. We might be getting closer to discovering what Slayton wanted to tell the President."

"Is that what you really want?"

"Of course. That's what we're getting paid for. Don't you want to know what happened?"

"Slayton knew. He's dead. A heart attack. How convenient. Someone is trying to kill his wife. Maybe she knows, too. No, thanks. I don't want to know because I don't want to be dead. And if you want to stay alive, tell our client that we can't identify The Seven, get rid of those Iran-Contra documents, and run for the nearest exit if anybody mentions Jack Slayton's name. You don't know what you are getting into. I think that the Tower Commission Report and that other stuff we've been feeding into the computer is only the tip of the iceberg. I'm not interested in looking below the waterline.

"This is very big, Holloway. Jack Slayton was involved in an international conspiracy. He dealt with several foreign intelligence services, not to mention various shady arms brokers of undetermined allegiance. That's the fast lane, partner, and you're not with the Company anymore. You're just a civilian. You got no backup but me, Dan Vogle, and Sid. I don't know about the rest of them, but I gave up sleeping with a gun under my pillow fifteen years ago and I don't intend to start that again. You keep picking at this thing and you're going to open a door that you can't close. Something bad is liable to come out and eat your lunch."

"You want me to just drop it?" Holloway asked.

"Yes."

"I can't walk away from the President, Donna. Could you?"

"Is this the same president who claimed that he never got Ollie North's memos about the Iran-Contra deal?"

Donna was getting a look from Holloway that told her she was out of bounds, but she held her ground and gave him a final cut. "Don't become a victim of your loyalty. And if you do, try not to take any innocents out with you this time." Donna took his apartment key from her ring and tossed it on the hall table as she left.

Miriam was waiting when he returned to the bedroom. "I'm sorry that I inconvenienced you by coming here. It was just the safest place I could think of."

"It's not a problem."

"Thanks. Now that I'm here, what do I do next?"

"Help me find out what's going on. Have you ever heard of something called 'The Seven'?"

"No. What is it?"

"I wish I knew," Holloway said.

Miriam did not pursue the subject. Her mind was elsewhere. "Holloway, maybe Jack had a problem in Switzerland that triggered all of this. I told you that he started acting strange after he got the overseas call and went to Switzerland. Maybe you could find something there."

Holloway had been considering that very thing. "You had a friend here who saw Jack in Geneva," Holloway reminded her, "Sylvia-something."

"Sheila. Sheila Hamilton. She works at the World Bank."

"That's the one. Why don't you call and ask her to talk to me."

"She'll want to have lunch and gossip. I'll tell her that I'm in Kansas and that you are settling Jack's affairs for me."

"Ask if I can stop by today at three."

* * *

Sheila Hamilton's office was the most orderly nine square feet of space Holloway had ever seen. Everything appeared to be in the place it was designed to occupy. The desk was a temple of fastidiousness, its printouts and spreadsheets organized into neat piles on either side of a powerful calculator, which held the place of honor in the center. On the credenza behind the desk, a single rose in a slim vase stood vigil over family photographs and proclaimed the dominance of femininity. Above the credenza, a diploma in an oversized frame announced to the world that Sheila Hamilton held a doctorate in economics. What disorder there was had been packaged and confined to a wood-and-cork bulletin board on a nearby easel. From there, it could be whisked into the closet, removing the last evidence that chaos might exist in this otherwise pathologically ordered environment.

The woman herself was small, attractive, and as neat as her office. Only her hair suggested an element of personal disorder. It was swept up into a saucy pile on top of her head and held in place by a black comb with sparkling stones. Auburn ringlets cascaded down onto her face and neck. Below the ringlets, all was precision. Her features were sharp. She wore a ruffled white blouse with a cameo at the neck, black pleated skirt, and polished black boots. Sheila Hamilton came toward Holloway in quick, short steps and thrust out her hand in a manner suggesting that someone had forgotten to shake it in times past.

"Come in, Mr. Holloway. Miriam said you would drop by about this time." She looked at the clock and Holloway knew that his punctuality was being verified.

When they were seated, Sheila asked, "Are you a friend of Miriam's?"

"A business acquaintance, which is why I'm here. Before Mrs. Slayton's husband died, he was negotiating the purchase of a vacation apartment in Switzerland. He apparently put down a substantial sum of money. Since his death, Mrs. Slayton has been unable to find a record of the transaction. She asked me to try and locate the seller to find out if the purchase is still on track or get her money back. Since you saw Mr. Slayton in Geneva, we thought you might be able to help."

"And how might I do that?"

"Mrs. Slayton thinks that the man you saw her husband with in Geneva was the person who was selling the apartment. If I could locate him, we might be able to settle the matter."

"Very well. What would you like to know?"

"Could you tell me about your meeting with Mr. Slayton?"

"It wasn't actually a meeting. I was in an elevator, on my way to a reception in the WorldCorp Building. I didn't see Jack Slayton get aboard. It was a rather large elevator and I was the short person at the back of the crowd." Holloway thought he heard a touch of resentment. "When we reached the top floor where the reception was being held, my group headed for the reception hall to the right. Jack and his companion went to the left into a private wing. It was cordoned off with one of those velvet ropes. As I left the elevator, I saw Jack reach down and unhook the rope. That was when I recognized him. I called to him. He seemed to hesitate, but never looked in my direction. He continued down the corridor. I went after him, but his companion blocked my way. He told me, very politely, that entry into that wing was restricted. I insisted. He took me firmly by the arm, told me that he was with security and threatened to have me thrown out if I continued to make a nuisance of myself. At that point, it occurred to me that Jack might have been there on National Security Council business and didn't want to be recognized. I gave up and went to the reception. That was the extent of the encounter. I didn't see Jack Slayton again until several months later, here in Washington. He didn't mention the incident and neither did I."

"The man with Mr. Slayton, did you get his name?"

"No."

"Could you describe him?"

"Oh, yes. I remember him well. He was about six-four. Brown hair. Blue eyes. Thin face. He had a lean, leathery look, like a cowboy. He even wore cowboy boots, of good quality, too. His suit was dark blue and well-tailored. There was a little identification tag clipped to the breast pocket of his suit. It contained the WorldCorp logo and the word 'security.' "

"Could you tell what his nationality was?"

"He had a slight drawl, southwestern United States, I think."

With unintended skepticism, Holloway said, "You have an exceptional memory, Ms. Hamilton."

Sheila Hamilton bristled. "Photographic, Mr. Holloway." She looked at her watch, not having much time for people who doubted her powers of memory or anything else.

He took the cue, thanked her, and left.

* * *

Holloway drove home as fast as he could. Donna had not returned from work and he was thankful for that. He was not up to another argument with her. He let himself into her basement, got the computer out of the vault and typed "WorldCorp" into the search program. The program ran the new key word against the Iran-Contra documents and came up with nothing. Holloway locked the computer away and went to a nearby shopping center for two orders of his favorite Chinese takeout: Hunan chicken. When he got home, Miriam was delighted with his choice. They ate leisurely at the kitchen table and discussed Holloway's meeting with Sheila Hamilton.

Holloway slid his notes across the table to Miriam. "Here's Sheila's description of the man your husband was with in Geneva. Do you know anybody who looks like that?"

Miriam studied the description and shook her head slowly. "I don't think so." Holloway retrieved the notes and put them into his pocket. "What's the next step?" asked Miriam. "Will you go to Geneva and try to find him?"

Holloway put a piece of chicken in his mouth with the chopsticks while he thought about it. "I suppose so. There aren't any other choices."

"When will you go? Soon?" Miriam seemed eager to get him on the road.

"Might as well get on with it. I'll leave day after tomorrow. Damn! That means more time away from the office. Donna is going to be mad." Thoughts of Donna sent Holloway into a dark mood.

Miriam noted the change. "Is Donna your lover?"

"No. Look, you aren't interrupting a relationship by being here. I haven't had time for a social life lately."

Miriam gave him a lopsided smile. "I could tell that in Kansas City."

"I'm sorry. Was I rough?" asked Holloway.

"No. Just . . . hungry."

They shared a nervous laugh, but Holloway drifted back into his cloudy mood.

"If you and Donna aren't lovers, why are you so glum?"

Holloway was slow to answer. "It was something she said to me this morning. She poked an old wound. Friends do that sometimes."

"Was it what she said about 'taking innocents with you'?"

Holloway's head snapped up when he realized that Miriam had overheard his conversation with Donna.

"I didn't mean to listen," she explained. "I thought Donna had gone. I came to the bedroom door to see if you wanted to join me in the shower. I couldn't help overhearing what she said."

Holloway wondered what else she had overheard.

"What did Donna mean by that comment about 'innocents'?"

Holloway had discussed that subject with Donna only. He was

not sure he wanted to share it with anyone else. Miriam reached across the table and took his hand into both of hers, but said nothing. That helped him make up his mind.

"Donna was talking about my family. They were the 'innocents.' I had a wife and a son here in Washington and a mother and father in Iowa. I was out of the country a lot of the time. On the long tours my wife and son went with me, but even then I couldn't spend much time with them.

"My son couldn't deal with my absences, neither could my wife, for that matter. Both of them developed psychological problems and had therapy on a regular basis. The doctor told me that if I didn't find time for my family, it would fall apart. I was working in Afghanistan at the time. The Company transferred me back to a desk job in Washington. I was having my first Christmas with my family in two years. It was Christmas Eve and we were trimming the tree when I got a call from the Company. A Russian defector had made it to our embassy in Pakistan. He had what appeared to be high-grade intelligence related to one of my projects. My boss wanted me to interrogate him. Unfortunately, the defector had been shot and our people in Pakistan weren't sure he was going to live. They didn't want to risk moving him. The Company asked me to fly to Karachi immediately. I should have refused, but I didn't.

"That was the last straw for my wife. Her parents were dead. So, she packed up my son and flew to Iowa to stay with my parents. My dad and mom were in their seventies, but they drove to the airport on Christmas Day to get my wife and son. On the way back to the farm, some drunk in a pickup truck ran into Dad's car and killed all of them.

"I decided to leave the Company. Donna and her husband were my best friends and ex-Company people, too. They helped me through the rough spots. Later, they took me into their consulting business as a partner. Donna's husband died about a year ago. Then, it was my turn to help her. We're family now, and this time Donna is the innocent. She doesn't want to get hurt because I'm involved in your problem or your husband's."

Miriam laid a gentle hand on his arm. "I'm sorry about your family and I understand Donna's feelings." After some silent time had passed, Miriam asked, "How did you make out with the Russian defector?"

"When I got to Karachi, he was dead."

* * *

The following morning, Holloway was on his way to work before Miriam got out of bed. He visited two clients to consult with them about their computer security systems and was in the office by noon. There, he put in a good five hours under Donna's watchful, but uncharacteristically quiet, supervision. The silence continued when he described his visit with Sheila Hamilton and informed Donna that he was going to Switzerland to locate the man Hamilton had seen with Jack Slayton. Only when he was leaving for his apartment did Donna warn him to "Be careful."

When Holloway got home, Miriam was putting the finishing touches on a spaghetti dinner. They ate a leisurely meal on the living room couch, while Holloway watched the evening news and Miriam read the paper. Both media were full of the Iran-Contra scandal and the news sent each of them into the private worlds of their thoughts. There wasn't much conversation.

Miriam was browsing through the financial section of the paper when, suddenly, she went rigid. Her lips moved as she read the article. When she finished, she dropped the newspaper like it was a hot poker. "Oh, no!" she cried, covering her mouth with her hands.

Holloway looked at her and saw that same fear in her eyes that he had seen the night she arrived. "What is it, Miriam?"

She could not speak. A visible tremor passed through her whole body and she began to cry hysterically. Holloway scooped up the newspaper, and while Miriam clung to him and sobbed, he read about the death of Sheila Hamilton.

When Miriam caught her breath, she babbled, "They killed her! They killed her!"

"Don't be ridiculous, Miriam. The paper says it was an accident." But Holloway didn't believe that anymore than Miriam did.

For an hour, Holloway pumped Scotch into Miriam and tried to convince her that the accident report was true. When she was sufficiently sedated, he said, "I know you don't want me to go right now, but I have to see a man on business tonight. I'll call downstairs and ask Donna to come up and stay with you for a while."

"No!" she protested.

"I have to see him tonight, Miriam. I'm leaving town tomorrow."
As an afterthought he cautioned, "Don't tell Donna why you're upset.
She'll just get mad at me again."

Donna did come to sit with Miriam, but she was angry anyway.
Her displeasure was triggered when Holloway told her where his gun
was and to keep the door locked until he returned. Before Holloway
left the apartment, he called Sid Mitchell to arrange a meeting at
Lenny's an hour later.

Holloway drove to the Crystal City Marriott and found a table in
the lobby bar-and-disco. He finished one drink and had the waitress
bring another. Leaving his fresh drink on the table, Holloway made
a show of asking directions to the men's room, the location of which
he already knew. Once outside of the bar, Holloway walked quickly
past the men's room to the far end of the lobby. He turned right into
the pedestrian tunnel under Jeff Davis Highway, which lead to the
Crystal City Shopping Center. Holloway sprinted the length of the
tunnel, through the Center, to the Metro station escalator. Clutching
his monthly turnstile pass, he bounded down the escalator steps, two
at a time, and arrived at the platform just in time to catch the uptown
train.

Thirty minutes later, Holloway walked into Lenny's. Veronica
was occupying her usual perch at the bar where she could see everyone
and hold court. She was alone for a change, but Holloway had other
things on his mind. He joined Sid Mitchell, who was having dinner at
a table. "Thanks for coming, Sid. I need help."

"I thought you had stopped ruining my weeknights when you
took all of that Iran-Contra stuff back to wherever you got it. And
don't thank me. You're buying this dinner." Sid smiled at his plate.
"I'm having filet mignon and this superb bottle of . . ." Mitchell
picked up the wine bottle and sneered at the label " . . . of wine-
flavored vinegar. An excellent year too, if the bouquet doesn't deceive
me," sniffed Mitchell. "However, Ralph, the sommelier, has assured
me that it was aged overnight in a Styrofoam keg in the basement of
this very building. Lenny will serve no wine before its time." He
shook his head. "Jesus, Holloway, what do you see in this place?"

"People don't come to Lenny's for the wine cellar, Sid. They
come here for delicious food, generous drinks, and luscious women."

Mitchell swept the room with a doubtful glance and said, "Maybe."
He forked a piece of the filet into his mouth. "Anyway, why did you
drag me out to this fleshpot? You sounded hot and bothered on the
phone. Did you find out anything on your visit to Kansas?"

Holloway gave Mitchell the details of his visit with Miriam Slayton
and her subsequent appearance at his apartment. "When Miriam
showed up claiming someone was trying to kill her, I thought it was
pure fantasy. I assumed that the death of her cousin, Denise, was a
coincidence. Now, I'm not so sure."

Mitchell gave Holloway a wry smile. "Miriam, is it? Just one
visit to Kansas and you two are on a first-name basis, with the lady
shacking at your place. Donna tells me that she looks even better
than her pictures. You old dog. And I remember when you couldn't
get laid at Du Pont Circle on Saturday night with a fistful of fifties."

"You and Donna can go to hell."

Mitchell chuckled. "I'll take that under advisement. So, why
aren't you sure that the cousin's death was a coincidence?"

"Miriam told me about a friend of hers named Sheila Hamilton,
who saw Jack Slayton in a suspicious meeting with a guy in Geneva,
Switzerland. Since this was the first decent lead we've had on Slayton,
I thought I'd check it out. Yesterday, I went to see Hamilton. She
didn't know the mystery man in Geneva, but she did give me his
description. Last night, Hamilton was electrocuted when her hair
dryer fell into the tub while she was taking a bath."

Mitchell stopped chewing. "So, what?"

"So, what kind of woman would dry her hair while sitting in a
tub?"

"A careless one."

"Right." said Holloway. "But Sheila Hamilton was not careless.
I was in her office yesterday. It looked like a museum. She looked
like a museum piece. The woman was a neatness freak, Sid. That
kind of person does not sit in a tub and dry her hair. I'll bet she had
a nice little vanity with a big mirror where she could sit and blow-dry
herself to perfection."

"Holloway, that's so thin that I can see through it."

"Well try this. Did you ever see a woman dry her hair in the
bathtub? No. That's because you can't dry your hair while it's
getting a steam bath from the water you're sitting in."

Mitchell chewed thoughtfully on the filet. "It's still thin . . . but I'm starting to hear you. For the sake of argument, let's assume that somebody did whack her. How does that relate to you?"

Holloway smiled and rubbed his hands. "When we were sitting in Donna's basement reading printouts and getting nowhere, nobody died. Then, I go to Kansas and start asking questions about Jack Slayton and Denise French is murdered. Next, I ask Sheila Hamilton about Slayton and twelve hours later she's dead. Is that coincidence, or what?"

Mitchell sipped his wine. "Thin coincidence. But suppose you are on to something and somebody is trying to cover it up. Why are they killing people *after* you talk to them? It makes more sense to whack the women before they give you information or . . . just kill you." Mitchell gave Holloway a worried look.

"Maybe he's not trying to cover up anything. Maybe he's trying to find out something, just like me."

"And you're leading him to the sources?"

"You're getting warm, Sid."

"Somebody is tailing you," concluded Mitchell. Instinctively, his eyes searched the room for someone who didn't fit into Lenny's unique ambiance.

Holloway said, "Don't worry. If I did have a tail, I shook him in Crystal City."

"Any idea who it might be?" asked Sid, really interested now.

Holloway shook his head.

Mitchell gave the matter some thought while he sopped up the last of the Bearnaise with a piece of bread. "Aside from the fact that Denise French was a mistake, why would somebody torture and kill those women just to get information? Why didn't he make up a story, just like you did, get what he wanted, and walk away?"

"Beats me. Either I've got a psycho following me around or whoever it is doesn't want it known that he's interested in Jack Slayton."

Mitchell raised his fork. "I vote for number two."

"Me too." Holloway rubbed his chin. "Sid, I need you to help me flush the tail."

"What do you want me to do?"

"I'm going to Geneva tomorrow to see if I can identify the guy who was with Slayton at WorldCorp. I want you to cover my back."

"Wait a minute. I can't go bouncing around the world whenever you feel like it. I'm not a consultant. I've got a real job."

"You also have a lot of vacation time coming that you're going to lose if you don't take some time off soon." He flashed a satisfied smile. "Donna also tells me about your business. Besides, the First Lady wants you to cooperate with me and I need some cooperation."

Mitchell sighed, "What's the schedule?"

"Today is Thursday. We fly out of Dulles tomorrow, after work. We change planes in Frankfurt on Saturday morning and arrive in Geneva before noon. Sunday is free. Monday, I go to see Slayton's friend at WorldCorp. If I'm being followed, you should be able to tell by Monday night. Maybe we can get some pictures of my tail and have a talk with him. We fly home on Tuesday. You can go back to work on Wednesday.

"Who's paying?"

"I'll give you expenses and a hundred dollars a day."

"Come on, Holloway. A hundred a day in Switzerland ain't even walking around money. One-fifty."

"No dice. You draw full pay on vacation. The hundred is pure gravy."

"I'll take it," Mitchell said grudgingly. "As tight as you are with a dollar, you must be planning to get rich at this consultant scam."

"I need one other thing from you, Sid. I can't find out very much about WorldCorp. Doesn't the Treasury Department have an office in Geneva that keeps track of Americans involved in foreign businesses?"

"Yeah. It's a branch of the Hidden Assets Division. They find big money that Americans conveniently forget to claim on their income tax forms. Do you think Slayton was salting away some ill-gotten gains?"

"Could be," mused Holloway. "You Secret Service types are part of Treasury. Do you know anyone in the Geneva office who we can tap for information, unofficially?"

"No, but I'll do a quick check tomorrow."

"Good. And keep quiet about where we're going and why. For the record, this is just a vacation trip. We're booked into the same planes and hotels, but let's keep away from each other until we find out whether or not I'm being followed." Holloway slid the plane tickets and hotel reservations across the table to Mitchell.

"Damned sure of yourself, weren't you?" asked Mitchell.

"I was sure about you. You're easy, Sid. You'll go anywhere for a hundred a day and expenses." Holloway laughed and got up to leave.

Mitchell stopped him with a final caution. "Could be that Slayton was in Geneva to deal Iran-Contra money or even political slush funds. If that's the case, and you ask the wrong questions, you may get your head handed to you."

"That's another reason why I want you along to watch my back."

*   *   *

The last rays of the sun bathed Baltimore's Inner Harbor in a warm red glow, providing a breathtaking view from Admiral Schaeffer's apartment. Schaeffer turned to his guest, Assistant Secretary of the Treasury Vaterman. "Look at that, Jules. Isn't it beautiful?"

"Magnificent!"

They watched in silence for a time. Finally, Schaeffer got down to the purpose of their meeting. "How are things going on your end, Jules?"

Vaterman replied, "As you know, the idea of an aid package for communist Vietnam never did have much support in Washington. Now, that idea is dead in the water. Neither State nor the White House staff will have anything to do with it. Nobody in his right mind is going to ask the President to trade aid for MIA corpses while the arms-for-hostages deal with Iran is threatening to bring down his Administration. I'm sure this is not coming as a surprise to you."

"Damit, Jules! This is different from the Iran-Contra case. The objective is to provide a final resting place for men who died in the service of their country during a war. We're talking about providing closure for MIA families who haven't known for years whether their loved ones are dead or alive. Did you remind those striped trousers at State of that?"

"Everyone is concerned about the MIAs," Vaterman said soothingly, "but nobody is going to ask for aid right now. The prevailing attitude is that a hostage is a hostage. It doesn't matter whether he's a live hostage in Beirut or a dead MIA in Hanoi. An aid package for the Vietnamese that smacks of ransom is political poison to the Administration and on Capitol Hill."

The admiral cursed.

Vaterman puffed thoughtfully on his cigar. "You're going to have to find some other way to handle the Vietnamese. Of course, as soon as that information is conveyed to Hanoi, your friend Colonel Can may redouble his research efforts. Have you given any thought to buying him off? Could he be persuaded to defect and seek asylum in the comfort of a nice Swiss bank account?"

"I've thought about that. It won't work. He's an ideological purist. A bribe would be proof that he's on the right track. We can't afford to confirm Vietnamese suspicions."

"Then you may have to arrange an accident for your friend."

"He's not my friend, Jules! Don't try to stick me with Can. We all agreed to let him run on a loose leash for a while."

"You are quite right. Well, State won't be talking to the Vietnamese for a while. That will give you some time to come up with something, but make it good. We'll have a serious damage control problem here if the Vietnamese start to talk."

"Speaking of damage," said Schaeffer, "did you know that Miriam Slayton has disappeared?"

"What?"

"She went into hiding after someone killed her cousin, Denise French. It happened at Miriam's home in Kansas. It was probably a case of mistaken identity. French was a ringer for Miriam. Evidently you made your decision, but whoever you sent bungled the job."

"What are you talking about? I didn't send anyone after Miriam Slayton."

The admiral frowned at Vaterman. "If you didn't do it, who did?"

Vaterman looked alarmed. "I think there are some other players in our game. We had better find out who the devil they are. What about this Holloway fellow who visited Miriam Slayton? You said he was an ex-Company man. Has he gone into business for himself? Is he working for someone else? What's his story?"

"I haven't been able to find a link between him and the Slaytons, but we had better start keeping a close eye on Mr. Holloway." Schaeffer took a small notebook from his desk and picked up the phone. "I have his address. I'll put someone on him first thing in the morning."

CHAPTER 10

Holloway and Mitchell arrived in the city on Saturday before noon. Since they planned not to be seen together in public, Mitchell lingered at the airport over lunch, while Holloway went immediately to the hotel. Holloway had booked them into Le Richemond. It was one street away from Lake Geneva and first class. However, he had not selected the place for its amenities. Le Richemond's attraction was that it was the only hotel in Geneva with a name like the one Miriam Slayton remembered from the matchbook cover that her husband brought back from his not-so-secret trip. Holloway wanted to see how Jack Slayton lived when be visited Geneva. As he walked through the plush lobby to the reception desk, Holloway realized that Mr. Slayton had lived well indeed.

With jet lag beckoning him to bed, Holloway had to find some way to stay awake until evening so that his body would adjust to local time. The concierge advised him that he had time to shower and catch a city bus tour, which he did.

Sid Mitchell arrived at Le Richemond at one-thirty and found a message waiting for him. Holloway had left his room number. Mitchell asked for accommodations on the same floor and set about locating their Geneva contact.

When Holloway returned to his room several hours later, he discovered that a note had been shoved under his door. It contained an address in Geneva's international district and the words, "Eighth floor, Sunday, noon." Sid Mitchell had signed the note with the initials,

"H.A.D." for the U.S. Treasury Department's "Hidden Assets Division." Holloway lingered over dinner in the hotel dining room and went to bed exhausted.

He got up early and took a brisk walk along a section of the lakeshore near his hotel. The sun was brilliant and the weather was clear and cool. The walk gave him a hearty appetite. At breakfast in the hotel dining room, he studied a city map and the faces of his fellow diners. One of them might show up later as his tail.

At ten-thirty, Holloway left the hotel at a leisurely pace. He took the Quai du Mont Blanc north along the lakeshore, pausing to look at the dilapidated Palais Wilson. Built as a monument to President Wilson for his peace efforts, the crumbling palace with its broken windows seemed less a tribute to the man than a mocking commentary on peace itself. Holloway raised his camera to get a picture of the palace, his eyes sweeping the crowd behind him. There were too many people for him to pick out a tail.

A short distance beyond the Palais Wilson, the street became Avenue de France and turned west, away from the lake. Within a couple of blocks the pedestrian traffic had thinned considerably. By the time Holloway crossed the bridge over the railroad yard, less than ten people were visible behind him. If he did have a tail, Mitchell should have no trouble picking him out, but where was Mitchell? He strolled past Sismondi College and turned right into the Place des Nations, a bus stop and parking area in front of a gate to the United Nations grounds. Holloway joined a knot of tourists. He gawked, snapped a picture, and abruptly retraced his steps back to the main street, eyeing the tourists moving toward him. None looked familiar.

The street name had changed to Route de Ferney. Holloway turned right. The hill in front of him was steep and pedestrian traffic was down to a trickle. It would be obvious if he looked back now, and he didn't want to scare off the tail. Holloway took Mitchell's note out, verified the address, and focused on his destination.

The Hidden Assets Division had a history dating back to the aftermath of World War II. Although it had a different name then, the Division had been one of the U.S. Government's most important tools for tracking Nazi loot to Swiss bank accounts and business arrangements sheltered by Swiss neutrality. Now, with Nazi treasures redistributed or forgotten, the Hidden Assets Division concentrated on Mafia skim, drug money, and the proceeds of white-collar crime.

Holloway turned left at the appropriate avenue and arrived at his destination at five minutes to twelve. The building appeared to be at least twenty stories high. Holloway entered the deserted lobby and gave his name to the security guard who directed him to a bank of elevators. Hidden Assets Division was not listed on the building directory. Evidently, the Treasury Department also saw an advantage in not having its assets exposed. Holloway took the elevator to the eighth floor.

When the door opened, Sid Mitchell stepped into the car blocking Holloway's exit. A camera with a long telescopic lens hung from his neck. He winked and pushed the button for the twelfth floor. "My compliments on your selection of hotels. I may have to revise my opinion about your stinginess. Putting us up at a nice hotel was the least you could do after sticking me with the dinner tab at Lenny's."

"And a good morning to you, too, Mr. Mitchell," said Holloway, brushing aside the complaint. "Now that the pleasantries are over, who are you taking me to see?"

"Jessica Talbot. She's an accountant, lawyer, and investigator for the Hidden Assets Division, U.S. Department of the Treasury. Ms. Talbot has been working in Geneva for three years. She comes highly recommended by a friend of mine in Washington."

"What did you tell her about me?" asked Holloway.

"That you needed background on the Geneva business community and are the personal representative of someone high up in the Administration. That's why she agreed to see us on Sunday."

They left the elevator on the twelfth floor and Mitchell led the way down the corridor to a suite marked only with the word "PRIVATE." He pressed the buzzer and a woman opened the door. She was of medium height and sturdy build. Straight red hair, pulled back behind the ears, framed her round face. She wore no makeup that Holloway could see and had a fresh, honest look about her. The ends of the white silk scarf around her neck were tucked beneath the collar of a well-tailored red suit. White-and-red shoes and earrings completed the outfit. There was something about her that made Holloway yearn for Miriam Slayton.

She said, "Good morning, gentlemen."

Mitchell introduced Holloway.

The woman smiled, revealing the snow-white teeth that Holloway knew she would have. "I'm Jessica Talbot. Welcome to Geneva."

She lead them through a cavernous suite that housed a typing pool surrounded by private offices. Jessica Talbot had a corner office with windows on two sides overlooking Lake Geneva.

When they were seated around the conference table in Talbot's office, she asked, "How may I be of service to you, Mr. Holloway?"

"I'm conducting a sensitive personnel inquiry concerning an appointee to the White House staff. You understand that what we say here must be kept in confidence?"

"Certainly."

"I've been told that the subject of my inquiry made a secret trip to Geneva. An informant gave me the name of the company he visited and a description of the mystery man he was seen with. I know it's a long shot, but I was hoping you might have information about the company that would help me identify the mystery man."

"That's possible. We keep track of some Americans who visit Geneva, if they are suspected of criminal activities or associate with known criminals. Can you tell me the name of the individual under investigation?"

"Sorry. I can't divulge that."

"Very well. What is the name of the company your man visited?"

"WorldCorp."

Jessica Talbot smiled slightly and nodded her head. "Yes, Mr. Holloway. I can tell you about WorldCorp. In fact, I am probably the U.S. Government's expert on the topic. I've been investigating them off and on for three years."

"Excellent," beamed Holloway. "Are you familiar with their security staff?"

"Yes."

Holloway put his elbows on the table and leaned toward Talbot. "About a year ago, the person I am investigating met with a man who fits this description: six-four, lean, brown hair, blue eyes, wears good suits and cowboy boots. Does that ring a bell?"

Jessica Talbot's ironic smile broadened. "It certainly does. The man you have described is Randolph Travis Dillworth. He's chief of security at WorldCorp—or was, until a month ago."

"What happened to him?" asked Holloway.

"He disappeared."

"Do you know why or where he went?"

"No. A source inside of the company told me that Dillworth's disappearance was a surprise. He just walked out of a meeting one day and didn't come back. There was something of a panic among the board members. I suppose that's normal when the security chief disappears, but it was smoothed over quickly. A few days later, they brought in an equally shady character named Ackerman as Dillworth's replacement."

"Is Dillworth 'shady'?"

"He is, in my book. Do you know anything about WorldCorp?"

"No. That's why I'm here."

"In that case, let me update you on some recent Swiss financial history, WorldCorp, and Mr. Randy Dillworth.

"Mr. Holloway, in the early and mid-seventies, the Swiss banking community was undergoing a shake-up. It was brought on by changing world economic conditions and years of abusive Swiss banking practices, not to mention calculated neglect by the Swiss Government. By looking the other way, the government had allowed many financial institutions, public and private, to build economic houses of cards with the cash of their investors and depositors. In the early seventies, those houses started to collapse. The reasons were as varied as the institutions themselves: speculation in foreign exchange, the oil crisis, the bottom fell out of the real estate market in several countries, and so on. Even the largest Swiss banks were not immune to the crash. They lost millions of francs, but survived. Many smaller financial institutions did not. They either disappeared altogether or were bought up by one of the Big Three: Union Bank of Switzerland, Credit Suisse, or the Swiss National Bank, and became branch offices of the mother institutions. There was another group of small, shaky, private banks that were bought up by other private bankers. This is where Dillworth entered the picture.

"Early in 1976, according to the file, Dillworth appeared in Geneva as an 'adviser' to a group of Swiss lawyers and bankers who bought a small private bank and several other businesses, at bargain prices, I might add. There was nothing unusual about the purchases. However, the odd thing about Dillworth's group was that all of the men involved were experienced in Swiss banking circles except Dillworth himself. As far as I have been able to determine, Dillworth's only banking experience was as a teller at a Texas savings and loan company in the early 1960s. That was after he dropped out of college and before he joined the Army."

"So, the question is, what was his real position with the group?"

"Exactly," agreed Talbot.

"You have a theory, of course," said Holloway.

"Yes, I do. I think Dillworth was the point man for some wealthy Americans who were setting up a tax dodge."

"How does that work?"

"Americans, and any other nationalities, for that matter, who want to hide their assets, come to this country and buy a six-pack of Swiss lawyers or bankers to act as their front men. The Swiss become a figurehead board of directors. With the principals back in the States calling the shots, the front men buy the businesses and handle relations with the Swiss Government and business community. To all appearances, the business is Swiss-owned and entitled to protection under very liberal Swiss tax laws. Our Internal Revenue Service can't touch a cent of the profits."

Holloway was surprised. "Is it that simple?"

"Pretty much, except that the principals have three big problems. First, they have to smuggle their money out of the States. Second, they have to make sure that the front men don't rob them blind or make business decisions on their own. I believe this is where Dillworth came into the picture. His job was to keep an eye on the Swiss front men for the American owners. Once WorldCorp was established, he installed himself as chief of security. That was an excellent cover because it gave him access to any information or area of company operations and it allowed him to be secretive about his own actions." Jessica Talbot sat back with an air of satisfaction at having explained her theory to someone from Washington.

"You mentioned a third problem," Holloway reminded her.

"Oh, yes. The third problem is that the real owners have to keep us here at the Hidden Assets Division from finding out who they are and the fact that they are using a Swiss front to avoid taxation under U.S. laws."

"Did you find any proof of income tax evasion by WorldCorp?" asked Holloway.

"Not according to the Treasury Department," replied Talbot, her voice tinged with bitterness. "We've sent the file to Washington twice requesting permission to initiate a formal investigation in cooperation with the Swiss authorities. The request was blocked each time."

"What do you mean 'blocked'?"

Jessica Talbot hesitated. "Perhaps 'blocked' was too strong a word. The WorldCorp case is an emotional issue for me. It's been my only failure in this job. I've gone as far I can legally go with WorldCorp. Swiss cooperation is essential for any further progress. When the file was reviewed in Washington, Assistant Treasury Secretary Vaterman ruled that we had no basis for requesting Swiss intervention. The Swiss won't get involved unless one of their laws has been broken. Income tax evasion is not against the law in this country unless, of course, one is Swiss. In other words, if you smuggle money out of the United States to avoid taxation and use it to run a business in Switzerland, the Swiss don't give a damn as long as you pay your Swiss taxes." The bitterness had returned.

"Well, if you can't go after WorldCorp, what about Dillworth's personal finances? Anything there?"

"Nothing that will stand up in court. Dillworth is very good. He draws a salary of eighty thousand a year and pays his taxes."

"Then, what makes you think he's crooked?" asked Holloway.

"His lifestyle. Dillworth lives well beyond his means. He lives in a mansion, drives a Bentley, and spends like a man with his hand in someone else's pocket. There's more, if you want to hear it."

"Please," said Holloway.

"Dillworth's family life is interesting, from a financial perspective. He divorced his first wife before he came to Geneva in '76. She was the heavy. Cheated on him while he was in Vietnam, but the divorce was friendly. He got custody of a daughter who is now attending the Sorbonne. His former wife is employed by a travel agency in Dallas, owned by WorldCorp. Dillworth does not appear to keep in touch with her."

Holloway and Sid Mitchell exchanged glances.

Jessica Talbot continued. "A year after Dillworth came to Geneva, he married a French woman. She was beautiful, but as poor as a church mouse. They had a daughter in 1978 and were divorced in 1980. After getting an uncontested divorce from Dillworth, she moved to a villa on the French Riviera and, with no visible means of support, raised her daughter. The daughter is now in a posh boarding school here in Switzerland. The cover story for all of this is that the wife inherited money from a relative while she was married to Dillworth. Last year, I used two weeks of my vacation time trying to track down the source of her inherited wealth. The trail went cold at a private bank in Liechtenstein. That country is notorious as a center for devious financial arrangements."

Holloway asked, "Does Dillworth keep in touch with his French wife?"

Talbot smiled. "In the most intimate sense of the word. He visits her three or four times a year. They have been observed at beaches on the Riviera holding hands and other body parts. However, the second Mrs. Dillworth never comes to Geneva and, in his work world, Dillworth plays the role of the eligible bachelor. He dates a variety of beautiful women."

"You've certainly done your homework," he observed.

"Not well enough for Jules Vaterman at Treasury and not well enough for the Swiss."

Jessica Talbot looked at her watch and noted that she was losing her Sunday, the only day she did not spend in the office. She wondered at what level Holloway was plugged into the Washington power circuit. She would have excused herself, but it didn't pay to be rude to visiting firemen. They turned up as allies or enemies at the most unexpected times in one's career.

Sid Mitchell brought her speculations to a halt. "What about Ackerman, Dillworth's replacement at WorldCorp?"

"Ah, the new mystery man," said Talbot with a touch of disgust. "I haven't had much time to check him out. I was able to get his social security number and queried the Defense Department about his military service. Defense won't release any paper on him. His records are classified. Treasury got telephonic notification that he served honorably in the Army from 1970 to 1973 and took a discharge in Vietnam. He was a communications specialist in a studies and observation unit." Talbot pulled a derisive smile.

"Something odd about that information?" asked Holloway.

"I would characterize it as an unusual coincidence. That was the same response that the Pentagon gave me two years ago when I asked about Randy Dillworth's military service."

Talbot pushed her chair back and added, "That's all I have on Dillworth and WorldCorp, gentlemen. It took three years of hard work to accumulate and it's worthless. I might as well throw the file in the trash can."

Holloway's eyes lit up. "Before you do, mind if I take a look?"

Talbot gave Holloway a nonchalant, "Of course not," but thought, *There goes the rest of my Sunday*.

Her assessment was correct. It was four o'clock when Holloway and Mitchell closed the WorldCorp file and departed. Sid Mitchell led the way to the elevator and rang for a car. "Did you read the list of companies owned by WorldCorp?" he asked, referring to a document in Talbot's file.

Holloway replied with a solemn, "Yeah."

"What did you make of it?"

"The same thing you did. They've got employment agencies, arms manufacturing, light aircraft, boats, travel agencies, a food processing plant, a uniform company, and a bank: just what you need to raise, finance, transport, and provision a small army."

"WorldCorp has 'Iran-Contra' written all over it."

"You don't know the half of it, Sid. Talbot said Dillworth and Ackerman did their Army service with a 'studies and observation group.' That was the Studies and Observation Group, Military Assistance Command, Vietnam; 'MAC-V-SOG,' for short. SOG was the cover name for a unit that took over some of the CIA's clandestine missions in Vietnam in the mid-sixties and early seventies. A lot of people in the SOG bounced back and forth between the regular military forces and the CIA. I wonder how much more CIA talent WorldCorp has in its Geneva operation."

"Is that why Talbot can't get to first base with her investigation?"

"I wouldn't be surprised."

"Ed, I think this is a good time to point out that we have stumbled into a shit pit and if we're not real careful, we could drown in it. It's dangerous for you to visit WorldCorp tomorrow. You'll be a marked man if you walk in there and start asking questions about Slayton and Dillworth. If I was in your shoes, I'd go home and write the Senate Intelligence Oversight Committee a nice, anonymous letter. Then, I'd sit back and read about it in the *Washington Post*."

"I thought about that as we were going through the file, but I can't just walk away. The President asked me to find out what Slayton was up to. What do I tell him?"

"Nothing, if you're dead."

The elevator doors parted. Mitchell and Holloway stepped into the empty car. Mitchell pushed the eighth floor button. "Have you forgotten what happened to Sheila Hamilton and Denise French?"

The two men said nothing more as the elevator glided to a stop at eight and Mitchell stepped out, camera in hand. Holloway pressed a button to keep the doors open. "I appreciate your concern, Sid, but I've got to level with you on a couple of things. The President asked me to do this and I've got to do my best for him. You understand that or you wouldn't be in the Secret Service. The other thing is that I'm doing this for selfish reasons. I want to stop whoever is trying to kill Miriam. She's the first woman I have cared about since my wife died."

Mitchell nodded. "I understand, Ed. Just be non-threatening when you go to WorldCorp. Okay? And be careful. I think I spotted a guy on your tail as you walked toward the building. He peeled off when you hit the open spaces." Sid hefted the camera and winked. "I'll get you some pictures for your trophy wall."

"Oh, I almost forgot." Mitchell handed Holloway a ticket. "Tomorrow, you and I are going to take a castle cruise on the lake. Our boat leaves the Grand Casino at ten-fifteen. I'll give you a rundown on your tail then. Try to lose him before you get to the boat."

Holloway released the button and the elevator door closed.

Sid Mitchell was scanning the nearby streets and park through his telescopic camera lens when Holloway emerged from the entrance eight floors below and headed southwest toward Lake Geneva. Mitchell was unable to pick out the tail until Holloway was well along the avenue. The man had fallen in behind Holloway and it was too late to get a profile shot of him. Mitchell cursed, snapped off three pictures of the man's back and rang for the elevator. On the way down to the lobby, something familiar about the tail nagged at him: the wide-legged, splayfooted walk, with hips going before the body. Where had he seen that walk? His memory answered. He had seen it thousands of times, along hundreds of city streets and dusty provincial roads, along hundreds of dikes and rice paddies—in Vietnam!

Holloway continued to play the tourist, giving Mitchell the time he needed to spot the tail. He walked leisurely, taking in the sights. On the lakeshore at the intersection of Avenue de France and Quai Woodrow Wilson, he paused to take a picture of Geneva's characteristic attraction, the fountain, Jet d'Eau. Located in Lake Geneva near the breakwater, its pressured plume of water soared five hundred feet into the air. Holloway stood admiring it for several minutes. The sun was setting and a stiff breeze was blowing in from the Lake. He used the wind as an excuse to turn up his coat collar and convert his leisurely stroll into a swift stride. The real game was to make the tail speed up his own pace so that Mitchell could pick him out of the crowd.

Holloway strode along the Quai du Mont-Blanc, past the Grand Casino, stopping occasionally—and suddenly—to catch shots of the Duke Charles Monument or the sun setting on the lake. At the end of the Quai, Holloway turned left onto the Pont du Mont-Blanc, which lead across the River Rhone to the old city. The bridge was several hundred feet long and it would be impossible for a tail to follow Holloway across without being seen by Sid Mitchell. Holloway smiled and realized that he was enjoying himself, just as he always had. There was no game like The Great Game.

Holloway turned right off the bridge and plunged into the old city. He made his way through a series of twists and turns until he came to Saint Peter's Cathedral. Continuing south, Holloway approached the Reformation Monument with its huge reliefs of John Calvin, Farell, Beze, and Knox. He took a photograph of the monument and a close-up of Calvin, the man who gave the world the Protestant work ethic. Beyond the park and down some cobblestone streets he came upon a cluster of restaurants and had dinner in one of them. As Holloway ate in the sumptuous surroundings, he realized that they were not for him. He enjoyed patrol rations and steaming coffee in the outdoors on cold mornings. He enjoyed . . . pain, as his wife used to say, on their camping trips. Holloway took a cab back to his hotel. That night he dreamed of his wife and Miriam Slayton.

The telephone awakened Holloway at five-thirty the next morning. Sid Mitchell's voice said, "There's a package for you at the front desk. Don't go to WorldCorp without it."

Room service brought it up immediately. Inside was a Velcro ankle holster and a .22 caliber automatic. The unsigned note that accompanied it advised Holloway to, "Ditch this if you get into a bind. It's untraceable." Holloway burned the note and flushed the ashes down the toilet. Then he got ready to visit WorldCorp's headquarters.

*   *   *

The receptionist was as good as she looked. She sized up Holloway as he pushed through the glass doors of WorldCorp's executive offices. She decided, correctly, to address him in English, rather than one of the other three languages in which she was fluent. "Good morning." The greeting came with a radiant smile. "Can I help you?"

"I'm here to see Mr. Dillworth. He's in security."

The smile remained, but her eyes went cold at the mention of Dillworth's name.

"Mr. Ackerman is our new chief of security. Would you like to see him?"

"My business is with Mr. Dillworth. Is he still employed here?" Holloway observed that his insistence on Dillworth made her uncomfortable.

"Mr. Dillworth is not at this facility," was her vague response.

"I've come all the way from the United States to see him. Do you have an address and phone number where he can be reached?"

"I'll see what I can do." The smile had been replaced by a mask of efficiency. "Please have a seat." She directed Holloway to a bank of comfortable chairs near the carpeted wall and didn't pick up the phone until he was out of earshot. Holloway tried to read her lips but the conversation was over before he realized that she was not speaking English.

The receptionist led Holloway out of the executive offices and down the corridor. They turned a corner and entered the first door on the left. It was unmarked. Donna's caution came back to him in a flash: "You keep picking at this thing and you're going to open a door that you can't close. Something bad is liable to come out and eat your lunch."

Holloway's guide led him past the secretary in the outer office directly into what was obviously the sanctum of someone important. The man behind the desk was blond. He had blue eyes, perfect male cheekbones, and a perfect tan. In fact, everything about him was perfect, except his thick, purple lower lip. Holloway sized him up as a person capable of great cruelty.

The man rose and gave Holloway's hand a perfunctory squeeze. "Mr. Holloway, is it?" He didn't wait for an answer. "I'm Ackerman. Security." He motioned Holloway to a chair. "What can I do for you?"

"I'm here to see Mr. Dillworth. I understand he no longer works for the company." Holloway put some inflection into "company," alluding to the CIA, and watched carefully for Ackerman's reaction. He was disappointed.

Ackerman flashed an amused smile. "Who told you that?"

Holloway bluffed. "I went to the wrong office, downstairs."

"You have been misinformed," said Ackerman, dismissing the issue. "Are you here to see Mr. Dillworth about a security matter?"

"No. It's a personal matter."

"Then, I'm afraid you're out of luck. Mr. Dillworth is conducting a detailed vulnerability assessment of our holdings in the Middle East. The war has made it increasingly difficult to do business there. People have a tendency to blow up things." He tried a smile that only made him look sinister. "In any event, we don't expect Mr. Dillworth back for a couple of months. He moves about quite a bit, sometimes in difficult circumstances. As a result, he has no regular schedule of contacts with this office. If you want to leave a message, I'll see that it's delivered at the first opportunity." He feigned disinterest, then added, "Of course, if the matter is critical, you might want to discuss it with me. Mr. Dillworth did leave me power of attorney to take care of some of his affairs while he's away." He let the bait hang there and waited for Holloway take it.

"Well," Holloway hesitated, "I suppose anything beats a two-month wait. I wanted to talk to Dillworth about a business deal that he was involved in with Jack Slayton." Holloway was sure that he saw a flicker of concern in Ackerman's face at the mention of Slayton.

Ackerman recovered nicely. "You don't mean Jack Slayton of the Iran-Contra scandal?"

"That's the one."

Ackerman frowned. "Did their business have anything to do with WorldCorp?" It was a natural question for a security officer to ask, but Ackerman was no ordinary security man. He was a SOG alumnus.

"I don't think so." Ackerman relaxed. "Dillworth was brokering the purchase of a vacation apartment here in Switzerland for the Slayton family. After Jack Slayton died, his widow found records indicating that her husband had given Dillworth twenty thousand dollars to open negotiations for the apartment. Mrs. Slayton is no longer interested in the apartment. She retained me to get her money back."

"I see. How long ago did this transaction take place?"

"Mrs. Slayton said that her husband visited Geneva about eighteen months ago."

"She waited a long time to start asking questions," Ackerman noted.

"Mrs. Slayton was not aware that a purchase was in the works until after her husband died."

Ackerman nodded his understanding. "Well, I am afraid I don't have the authority to deal with this issue. At least not without some research. What are Mrs. Slayton's intentions if Dillworth is unavailable?"

"She intends to take the matter to court. Twenty thousand dollars is a lot of money to a widow."

"I understand. Do you think Mrs. Slayton would give us, uh, give Mr. Dillworth, a couple of weeks, before she puts this in legal channels?"

"I think that could be arranged, but only if you can guarantee me an interview with Dillworth. She's tried to contact him several times, without success. She's starting to get the feeling that Dillworth has stolen her money."

"That's not an unreasonable assumption, under the circumstances. However, I can assure you that Mr. Dillworth is no thief. I will make every effort to contact him this week. Where can you be reached?"

Holloway didn't intend to make it easy for them to find him. He took out a pad and wrote down Dan Vogle's post office box address.

Ackerman read it and asked, "No telephone, Mr. Holloway?"

"Mrs. Slayton prefers that all communications between herself and Mr. Dillworth be handled in writing."

"A wise precaution." Ackerman stood up, signaling the end of the interview. "I'm sorry you came all this way for nothing, Mr. Holloway. Are you staying in Geneva long?"

"I'm leaving tomorrow?"

"Have a safe trip home." Ackerman tried another smile and, again, it went sinister on him. This time, he seemed not to care.

* * *

Holloway stepped into the bright April sunlight. It was nine-thirty. He walked across the street to a hotel and killed fifteen minutes in the lobby shops. At nine-forty-five, he left the hotel quickly and got into a taxi at the curbside stand. He gave the driver fifty franks and directions to get him to the Grand Casino boat dock on Quai du Mont Blanc at exactly three minutes to ten. The cabbie delivered Holloway on schedule. Everything was going according to plan. The ticket window had just closed and the last passengers were going aboard the castle cruise boat. Holloway made a dash and was the last person up the gangplank. If there was a tail, he had missed the boat.

Sid Mitchell stood at the rail reading a travel guide to Switzerland. He took no notice of Holloway's arrival until they were well under way. Then, both men made their way to the lake side of the boat, away from any prying eyes that might have been left on shore. Since it was Monday, the crowd was thin and they had no trouble finding a private spot for their talk.

Mitchell sidled up to Holloway. "Nice piece of work. You gave all of them the slip."

Holloway was surprised. "All?"

"All. You had more tails than fleas on a junkyard dog. I confirmed the first one as you were leaving Jessica Talbot's building yesterday. Guess what? He's Oriental—Vietnamese, from the look of him. Small and very, very good. When you walked across the bridge to the old city, he got a cab and rode over. He was waiting when you got to the other side. You walked right past him."

"What about the others?" inquired Holloway.

"I only saw two. There could have been more. They were a team. The Oriental spotted them on the bridge. They both followed you across on foot. Dumb."

"The Oriental wasn't with them?"

"No. When he spotted them, he just dropped back and followed them while they followed you."

"What did the others look like?"

"Caucasian males in their thirties, maybe. Nothing outstanding about them. I couldn't tell if they were American, European, or what. One was a little guy, oval face, neat dresser. The other looked like a Marine with long hair, if you can imagine that. I figured the Oriental would have the most interesting story. So, I followed him."

"And?"

"He's staying at our hotel, in the room directly above yours. Name's Long. Carries a French passport. He arrived the same day we did. Odd coincidence, wouldn't you say?"

"Damned odd," mused Holloway.

Mitchell speculated, "My guess is that he's bugged your room. That's how he knows when you go out. If he's fast, he can be waiting in the lobby when you leave the hotel. Cute."

"Any ideas about the team?"

"They could be anybody, even Treasury agents. Hell, I wouldn't put it past Jessica Talbot to have you followed if she thought that would help her bag WorldCorp and Dillworth. That lady has a fixation."

"Sid, this is starting to look like someone has been following me since we left the States. That means they were watching my house."

"That's the way I figured it, too. I called Donna and gave her a heads-up. She called you a lot of nasty names." Sid was serious. "I asked her not to tell Miriam what was going on. I figured you wouldn't want her to worry. If someone was watching the house and wanted to harm her, he would have taken his shot by now."

"Thanks, Sid. Did you get pictures of the people who were tailing me?"

Mitchell turned down the ends of his mouth in a gesture of disgust with himself. "I got 'em all except a clear shot of the Oriental. The guy is an eel. He even had a reversible trench coat that he turned over a couple of times. I would have lost him if it hadn't been for that walk of his." Changing the subject, Mitchell asked, "How did things go at WorldCorp?" Holloway told him.

"Where do you think Dillworth really is?"

Holloway shrugged. "I don't know, but I'd bet money that he's not in the Middle East." He hit the railing with his fist. "We've got more damn questions now than when we came over here. WorldCorp is the key. If it's not, why are all those hoods following me? There's got to be a way to find out what Dillworth, Ackerman, and company are up to!"

Mitchell withdrew from the conversation and listened to the tour guide announce over the public address system that they were passing Chateau Rothschild on the left. He initiated a walk around the deck so they could see it, but Holloway was not interested in the scenery. Trying to get his friend's mind off of WorldCorp, Mitchell said, "Donna thinks you should give this up and come home. I agree."

Holloway waved his hand. "I don't want to hear that record again, Sid. I know the tune."

They walked the deck in silence as the boat glided by the Maison de Saussure and the Port of Versoix.

Mitchell let some time pass and decided to try again. "Suppose you do find that WorldCorp is a CIA front that has been supplying the Contras and Jack Slayton was up to his eyeballs in it. Have you given any thought to the political impact of that news on the government or the country?"

That brought Holloway up short. Until now he had focused on Jack Slayton's allegations about plotting by the White House staff. He had not considered the larger issues and, if the truth were told at this moment, he didn't really give a damn about them. That was how people got into trouble. They started trying to figure out what the President wanted to hear instead of just giving him the facts. "The President's got to deal with the facts and the political consequences, Sid. That's what he gets paid for. My job is just to make sure he has the facts before he starts dealing."

"That's a naive view and you damn well know it. You can't separate the President from politics and, right now, the political battle of the century is shaping up between the President and Congress over who makes foreign policy and how. So far, the political damage has been confined to the National Security Council: a couple of loose cannons down there making policy out of a broom closet. The CIA, for once, has clean hands and a pure heart and Ollie North is taking the Iran-Contra heat by himself. Everything is under control. Enter, Ed Holloway, dragging a dead cat named WorldCorp. All of a sudden it isn't loose cannons. It's a government conspiracy with the CIA leading the pack. The White House has lost control of the Administration. Do you think the President wants that kind of news? And I'm not saying hide it from him. I'm just saying that you don't have to be the one to deliver the dead cat. Deep Throat did a lot of good during the Watergate scandal and nobody found out who he was."

"Are you saying that the President might not want to know the whole truth?"

"Maybe he *already* knows about WorldCorp. Maybe it's not a CIA front. It could be a conduit for political slush funds. It could be anything and it might be nothing. But if it's something, you and your news might not be welcome." Mitchell looked at the far shore and tried to contain his frustration. "You can't separate the President from politics, Ed. He's a political being and WorldCorp looks like bad political news."

Holloway looked at his friend as if seeing him for the first time. "You think the President is involved in the Iran-Contra scandal, don't you?"

Mitchell was angry now. "I try not to think about the President at all. I was a rookie on the White House Secret Service detail during the Watergate scandal. Since then, I don't rule out anything—even after it's ruled out. My job is to protect the chief of state. I don't have to believe what he says or agree with his politics. It's like you and the truth. If the truth is a dead cat, that's not your problem. You're just the messenger. The difference between you and me, Holloway, is that I know the President wants protection, not dead cats."

The two men looked out at the shoreline in silence. Finally, Mitchell said, "I want to say one more thing, then the subject is closed. If you do find that the CIA is behind WorldCorp, you are in danger, my friend, and that's all I care about. These political shenanigans have gone on since the birth of the country and it's the little people who always suffer. The fat cats always walk away."

In his heart, Holloway agreed with a lot of what Mitchell had said, but he was in the mood for action, not political philosophy. "Let me have the camera, Sid. I'll get a picture of the Oriental myself and maybe have a little talk with him. It's time to find out who the other players are."

When the boat returned to the Quai du Mont-Blanc, Holloway did not see anyone who fit the descriptions of the men who had been tailing him. He took a cab at the Hilton and had the driver drop him in the old city. It took him two hours of walking to find the cafe with the perfect location. He made a note of address and returned to his hotel to wait until dark. Aware that his room was probably bugged, Holloway had told Sid Mitchell to call him there and, for the benefit of the microphone, they arranged a meeting. Mitchell would not, of course, show up. This party would be just for Holloway and the listener upstairs, Mr. Long, or whatever his name was.

To the amazement of the chefs, Holloway left through the hotel kitchen. He travelled to the old city, switching cabs twice as insurance. Arriving at the cafe an hour ahead of his scheduled meeting, he took a table giving him a view of the door and waited. Half an hour later, the Oriental entered, without noticing Holloway, and took a table so that he, too, could observe the door. He ordered a beer. Several minutes later, Sid Mitchell came in, bought a pack of cigarettes from the vending machine, and departed. That was the prearranged signal that the Oriental was Holloway's tail.

Holloway finished his drink and walked over to the Oriental's table. The man appeared to be absorbed in the evening paper. He looked up in surprise when Holloway snapped his picture. Then another. The man was cool. His only reaction was to blink at the flashbulbs.

Holloway looked him over; the straight black hair, the cast of the forehead and jaw, the form of the nose and lips. Definitely Vietnamese, Holloway decided. At first glance, the man had that ageless quality that Westerners often see in Orientals. Holloway noted the finely etched lines around the eyes and mouth and the hint of gray at the temples. *You're not ageless. You're about forty-five, I'd guess.* There was something else about him: a look of determination, of a will to endure and prevail. Holloway had seen that look before, in the faces of captured Viet Cong. The man folded his paper and put it aside. Holloway noted short, manicured nails, but an inconsistent hint of callous along the edge of his right hand. *A little hard work or self-defense training in your background. Maybe both. You don't belong here among the decadent comforts of Geneva any more than I do. Our preferred arena is the Other Great Game, where the stakes are high, winner takes all, and losers go home in body bags.*

Holloway said, "You bugged my room. Let's talk. Maybe we can help each other. Or, you might like to trade some information for the pictures." Hollow swung his camera by the strap.

"Not here Mr. Holloway," said the man, in English. "Outside. I believe there is an alley just down the street to the right." The man smiled. He had scouted the area, just as Holloway had earlier.

"Fine." Holloway left the cafe as his tail called for the check.

When the Vietnamese came out of the cafe, Holloway was down the street, near the mouth of the alley. The Vietnamese walked up to Holloway and motioned for him to lead the way. Holloway had only taken a few steps into the alley when he heard the switchblade snap into place. He whirled fast, arms crossed at the wrist to form a block against the knife arm. It was thrusting up toward his kidney. The block worked. Holloway grabbed the knife arm and pulled the Vietnamese toward him, driving his knee into the man's stomach. As the Vietnamese doubled over in agony, Holloway spun him around and pulled his trench coat down over his elbows, pinning the man's arms to his sides.

In a quick motion, which caught Holloway off guard, the man leaned forward, then propelled his head back, smashing it into Holloway's nose. Blood spurted over Holloway's face. Before he could recover, the Vietnamese took a step forward and brought the heel of this other foot up into Holloway's groin. Holloway screamed. The pain was blinding. His knees turned to jelly and tears filled his eyes. Holloway made a feeble attempt to maintain his grip on the overcoat, but the Vietnamese twisted free, side stepped to the left, and swung his leg back in a wide arch. Holloway saw the blow coming, but was in too much pain to move. The man's heel caught Holloway in the chest and the wind went out of him with an "Oooff." Holloway fell backwards against trashcans, knocking over several with a loud crash.

The Vietnamese came at Holloway screaming and straining to free his arms. Holloway heard cloth tear and felt a button bounce off his face. He executed a diving roll to the right to avoid another kick. The Vietnamese scampered after him, freeing himself from his overcoat as he went. Holloway came out of the roll on one knee, in front of a row of garbage cans.

At that moment, a door opened behind the Vietnamese and a man wearing a stained white apron stepped into the alley shouting something at them in angry French. The Vietnamese was momentarily surprised and Holloway took advantage of the distraction to charge him. Holloway pinned the man's arms to his sides and drove him back until they fell to the ground with Holloway on top. The French-speaker took in the scene quickly and darted back into the building, slamming the door.

Holloway and the Vietnamese struggled for control of the knife. Holloway began smashing the man's knife hand against a metal storm drain cover. The Vietnamese released the knife and it fell through one of the drain cover slits and into the sewer. Winded and still hurting from the kicks, Holloway relaxed momentarily when the knife disappeared. That was just long enough for the Vietnamese to deliver several quick, painful blows to Holloway's kidney with his free hand. Holloway shifted his weight in an attempt to avoid the blows. When he did, the Vietnamese shifted his own weight in the opposite direction and was able to slide out from beneath Holloway. Holloway was still holding the man's knife hand in a vise-like grip. The Vietnamese kicked hard at Holloway's elbow, making his fingers pop open like a sprung lock. The Vietnamese rolled away fast, came up on his feet, and delivered another kick to the midsection that doubled Holloway over in pain. Then, the man stepped back and pulled open the left side of his suit coat. Holloway could see the brown leather shoulder holster strap against the white shirt as the Vietnamese reached for his gun. Holloway knew that he would be dead in a matter of seconds. His knees were already drawn up to his chest in response to the last kick, putting his ankle holster within easy reach. Holloway's hand darted down to the holster and he fired as soon as the gun was free, stitching a pattern of nasty little holes up the man's body. The first shot hit the Vietnamese in the thigh, the second in the stomach, the third chest high and the fourth in the forehead. The man fired wild shots as he staggered backward and fell to the ground.

Holloway heard a police siren close by, but knew that he was hurting too badly to get away before the patrol car arrived. He doubted if he could stand up and he knew he couldn't run. He took out his wallet, removed most of the cash and a packet of traveller's checks and stuffed them into his ankle holster. Then he propped himself up against the alley wall and lapsed into unconsciousness.

* * *

The interrogation room in the police station near the cathedral was clean and would have even been comfortable, if Holloway had not been in pain. The doctor finished his examination and pronounced Holloway free of broken bones. Holloway's profession of amazement that such a diagnosis could be made without benefit of x-rays met with stony silence. The doctor departed, leaving him in the hands of two Swiss policemen in civilian clothes. The older man was squat, balding, and wore a black leather overcoat over his gray suit. The younger man was thin and blond. He was attired in a hip-length black leather jacket over a white turtleneck and black slacks. Holloway concluded that black leather was all the rage with Swiss detectives. The policemen started to question him before he had finished dressing from the examination.

"What is your name?" asked the younger man in very precise English. He was holding Holloway's passport.

"Edward Holloway."

"You are American," proclaimed the policeman, as if he had just discovered gold at Sutter's Mill.

"That's right."

"What is your business in Switzerland, Mr. Holloway?"

"I'm a tourist." Holloway buttoned his shirt.

"Why did you shoot that man in the alley?"

"He tried to rob me."

"Did you know him?"

"No." Holloway looked for his overcoat and suit coat, but didn't see them. "Can I have my coats? It's chilly in here."

"Your coats are being examined for evidence," said the blond. "Please sit down at the table."

There was only one chair and it had been placed so that the overhead light would shine into Holloway's eyes.

The interrogator snapped Holloway's passport closed and slipped it into his pocket. "Where did you get the gun that you used to shoot the man who was trying to rob you?"

"I took it away from the robber."

The answer appeared to surprise the young policeman. He was at a loss for a follow-up question. The older detective took over the interrogation. "And how did you take the robber's gun without getting shot?" His accent was heavily Germanic.

"I've had some martial arts training. I can handle myself." Holloway had a flashback to the alley where he was almost kicked to death. He wanted to laugh out loud at his own words.

"Why would a tourist require martial arts training?"

"I'm a private investigator. I run into difficult people at times."

"And you take your gun and shoot them, like you did tonight."

"I told you, it wasn't my gun."

The detective tossed the Velcro holster on the table. "This also is not yours, then?"

Holloway picked up the holster and examined it. "Oh, yes, this looks like my holster."

"Why were you carrying a holster with no gun, Mr. Holloway?"

"I use it to hide my money from pickpockets when I travel. In fact, I had several hundred dollars in it tonight. I assume that you have my money. Are you examining *it* for evidence, too?"

"We have your money." The older detective walked around behind Holloway's chair. "Carrying your money in a pistol holster is a bit unusual, is it not?" Holloway shrugged and the interrogator nodded for the younger man to take over the questioning again.

"How long have you known the man you shot, Mr. Holloway?"

"I told you that I didn't know him. He was a total stranger."

"You have never seen or met him before?"

"No."

"How is that possible? Both of you travelled across the Atlantic Ocean on the same aircraft. Both of you flew from Frankfurt to Geneva on the same aircraft. You were both registered at the same hotel. How is it possible that the two of you have been together in the same places for three days and have never met?"

"Call it luck. Call it coincidence. Call it whatever you like."

The policeman behind Holloway bent forward so that his mouth was level with Holloway's ear. "We call it lying." He strutted to a position in front of Holloway, hands clasped behind him. "Your story consists entirely of lies and not very good ones. Are we to believe that the man who tried to rob you had two guns and one holster, while you had one holster and no gun?"

Holloway's temper flared. "I don't give a damn what you believe. I'm the one who was attacked and I'm through answering questions until I talk to someone from the American Consulate."

At that moment, a buzzer sounded. The older detective went to the door and was met by two uniformed policemen and a distinguished looking man in a cashmere coat with a dark fur collar. They spoke French in low voices. The cashmere coat was getting a lot of deference. Holloway's interrogator seemed to be protesting. The cashmere coat cut off the protest with a loud "*Non!*" and proceeded to give directions. Then, he departed. The two uniformed men waited outside of the room and the interrogator came back to Holloway.

"It seems that you will get your wish. Someone from your consulate is here to speak with you. While you are waiting, I suggest you develop a more believable story. In the meantime, please do not try to leave the room. There are guards outside. Since you are a murderer, they will not hesitate to shoot you. Good evening, Mr. Holloway." The interrogators departed, leaving him alone.

They had taken Holloway's watch so he had no idea how much time passed while he waited. He guessed thirty minutes. During that time, the room seemed to get comfortably warm, then hot. Finally, a guard opened the door and ushered in a man in a dark blue suit. He was short, with the oval, uninteresting face and self-effacing manner of a diplomatic minion. The man put on his best phony smile and strode toward Holloway.

"How do you do, Mr. Holloway? I'm Charles Pinchot from the U.S. Consulate." The guard brought a chair for Pinchot and withdrew, closing the door behind him. Holloway started to speak, but Pinchot cut him off. "I think it's best if we don't talk here. The walls have ears." Pinchot rolled his eyes at the ceiling. "My colleague is upstairs arranging for your release. We would like to move you to a more, ah, satisfactory location where you can tell your story to

American officials. Would you like to see a newspaper?" Pinchot shoved a copy of the *International Herald Tribune* at Holloway and delved into a novel. It was all rather undiplomatic.

Pinchot had come prepared for the wait, but not for the heat. Gradually, both men became uncomfortably hot as they waited for Pinchot's colleague to complete negotiations with the Swiss. Pinchot was sweating profusely and it seemed somehow out of character for him. "A bit warm in here," he announced. Holloway glanced at him and continued to read. A few minutes later, Pinchot jumped out of his chair. "God, I can't stand this heat!" He walked to the door and spoke to the guard in French. The guard responded and Pinchot translated for Holloway. "There's a problem with the heating system. I'm going for a soft drink." Pinchot left and returned shortly with two cups of cola. He handed one to Holloway. "I found a machine upstairs."

"What's the hold-up?" asked Holloway.

"I'm afraid this isn't unusual. The Swiss are neutral. They bend over backwards to inconvenience all nations equally." Pinchot raised the cola in a toasting gesture. "In the meantime, we'd better replace our liquids, or we'll be prunes by the time you're out of here." The two men drained their cups.

* * *

Holloway awakened in response to several assaults on his senses. The first was an incessant throb behind his eyes. A couple of months ago, he would have attributed it to his nightly alcoholic escape from the pain of losing his family, but he had not drunk anything headache-producing recently, except Mr. Pinchot's cola. The second assault was the strong smell of bourbon. He could even taste it. Holloway forced himself to a fully conscious state. When he reluctantly opened eyes, he saw that he was lying on a cot in a cell. His clothes were dirtier than he remembered and he was wearing his suit coat. It was stained and smelled like it had been soaked in whiskey.

A man was sitting in a chair next to the cot shaking Holloway by the shoulder and it wasn't Pinchot. The closer Holloway got to full consciousness the more violently the man shook him. The shaking made Holloway aware that his entire body was a pulsating blob of pain. It was then that he remembered the Oriental using him for a soccer ball in the alley.

"Mr. Holloway! Mr. Holloway!" The voice was strong and insistent. Holloway mumbled something and the shoulder-shaking increased to what he guessed was a point-five on the Richter scale. "What did you say, Mr. Holloway?"

Holloway licked his lips. The bourbon residue almost made him gag. Then, slowly and distinctly, so that there would be no misunderstanding, Holloway said, "If you shake me one more time, I'm going to get up from here and break every finger on your hand."

The shaking stopped and the man leaned closer so that Holloway got a good look at him. Gray slacks and a blue blazer came into Holloway's field of vision. Regimental tie against a blue shirt. The face was in its thirties with a square jaw, intelligent blue eyes, and a hard look around the mouth. It was crowned with short brown hair and connected to a lean body. The face radiated confidence. It belonged to a man who was not fazed by visiting murdering drunks in foreign jails, and that kind of cool made Holloway uneasy.

"Sit up, Mr. Holloway?" The voice coming from the face was American and strong. It was used to giving orders.

Holloway didn't move. "Who the hell are you?"

"Tom Braxton. I'm from the United States Consulate. I'm special assistant to the consul."

"Are you here to spring me?"

"Yes."

Holloway sensed that a lot of time had passed since he and Pinchot had replenished their fluids from the cola cup. He glanced at his wrist, but the watch was still missing. "What time is it?"

"Nine a.m.," announced Braxton.

"You and Pinchot took your damn good time. And why did that little bastard slip me a mickey?"

"I beg your pardon?" Braxton looked puzzled.

Holloway uncoiled himself from the fetal position and, with great pain, swung his legs over the edge of the cot and sat up.

"I said, 'You and Pinchot took your damn good time.' I've been here for twelve hours."

"I'm afraid I don't understand, Mr. Holloway. The duty officer told me about your predicament at seven this morning. I came down here immediately, and I don't know anyone named Pinchot."

"What the hell do you mean, you don't know Pinchot. He's with the State Department. He came in here about ten last night. He said my release was being arranged. Then, the little bastard drugged me!"

Tom Braxton suppressed a smile. "The guard told me that you had nightmares. Maybe you dreamed up this Pinchot. I know all of our people in Geneva who deal with the Swiss on tourist matters. We don't have anyone named Pinchot."

Somewhere behind the throb in Holloway's head, a voice told him to forget Pinchot for the time being and concentrate on getting out of jail. "Yeah," agreed Holloway, "maybe it was a dream. So, when do I get out of here?"

"You're free to go now, if you like."

Holloway was surprised, but said nothing.

Braxton added, "The Swiss did impose one condition."

"What's that?"

"You must leave the country immediately. You have been declared *persona non grata*, no longer welcome in Switzerland. The Swiss are releasing you into my custody with the understanding that I put you on the first flight back to the States. My job is to escort you back to your hotel, collect your belongings, and take you to the airport. I hope you don't object to those conditions."

"Why should I object?" asked Holloway. "No charges?"

"The Swiss don't usually press charges against tourists for public drunkenness. Ordinarily, they would have put you in a cab and sent you back to your hotel. Brawling in the street is another matter. Fortunately for you, they were unable to catch the man you were fighting." Holloway could have asked why the police couldn't catch a dead man with four bullets in him, but why complicate the situation?

Braxton continued. "The Swiss are deporting you because you resisted arrest. The report says you slugged a policeman. They won't tolerate that kind of disrespect for authority."

"That's fair," said Holloway trying not to sound cynical. It was painful for him to walk. So, he let Braxton and a guard help him hobble down the hall to the elevator. On the first floor, they went to separate windows of a bulletproof glass enclosure and conducted their business. Braxton signed papers accepting responsibility for Holloway. Holloway signed a receipt for his property.

Braxton walked over and picked up the holster. "A very unusual place to keep cash." He had read the interrogation report.

"I'm eccentric," said Holloway, as he shoved his money into the holster and strapped it to his leg. He picked up his camera and remembered that he had taken pictures of the Oriental. He glanced at the frame indicator. It should have read "21," but it read "0." Holloway opened the camera. It was empty. He banged on the glass to attract the policeman's attention. "I had film in this camera when I came in here last night. Where is it?"

The policeman removed Holloway's property receipt from an accordion file and read it carefully. He spoke English with a heavy German accent. "Kam-e-ra vas empty." He gave Holloway his most professional blank stare.

Holloway wasn't having any of it. "Look, I know damn well there was film in this camera and I want it!"

The policeman drew himself up close to the glass so that Holloway could see all six-feet-five-inches of his bulky frame. Slowly, he repeated, "Kam-e-ra vas empty. *Kein film!*" He jammed the receipt back into the file and turned away.

Holloway wanted to continue the discussion, but Braxton took his arm firmly and drew him away from the window. "I don't think it would be a good idea to argue with these people right now, do you?"

Braxton led Holloway, still grumbling about his film, to a Mercedes in front of the police station. A dark-suited chauffeur with linebacker shoulders opened the rear door for them while he gave Holloway a disdainful look. Holloway wanted to think during the drive to his hotel, but Braxton wanted to talk.

"I'm sorry your stay in Switzerland was not as pleasant as it might have been. Did you conclude all of your business before you got involved with the police?"

"I didn't have any business to conclude. I was here on a pleasure trip."

"Ah," sighed Braxton. "Well, Switzerland is a wonderful place to get away from the stress of business . . . usually."

"Yeah," said Holloway, absently. He was still thinking about the camera and wondering what had really happened to the man he shot in the alley. "Say, Braxton, I'm a little fuzzy on what happened last night. Can you fill me in?"

"Sure. The police report said you and another man were drunk and fighting behind the restaurant. A citizen called the police. They came and found you drunk and unconscious. When they tried to revive you, you became abusive and assaulted them. They had to use force to subdue you, knocking you unconscious again." A smile played at Braxton's lips. "They brought you into the station, let you sleep it off overnight, and notified us this morning. I came over and got you out. That's all there is to tell." Braxton's smile broadened. "I'm afraid it wasn't your night to win battles."

"That guy in the alley was trying to mug me. Before I passed out, I seem to remember that he had a gun."

Braxton frowned. "No gun was mentioned in the police report."

"A knife, maybe?"

"Sorry. No knife either. No weapons at all."

* * *

Holloway sat on the edge of the bed in his hotel room peeling himself out of his dirty clothes, while his two escorts packed his bags. They left his shaving kit in the bathroom, along with underwear and a change of clothes. In the process of packing, the escorts conducted a thorough search of the room. The State Department had put their deportee in capable and very determined hands. As for Holloway, he had become accustomed to the pain and was concentrating on other concerns. His pictures were gone. The body had disappeared. The only evidence that the Oriental ever existed was a knife in a sewer. Before he could search for the knife, he would have to get rid of his escorts. That might not be easy.

When Braxton had helped him into the car at the police station, Holloway had satisfied himself that the man was not armed, at least from the waist up. However, his muscles were like ropes. The chauffeur, on the other hand, appeared to be packing a holster on his left side and he kept a safe distance between himself and Holloway. It was clear that brute force was not the answer. He was in no shape for a fight. Another plan began to take shape in his mind.

Holloway stood in the bedroom stripped to the buff and under the watchful eye of the chauffeur while Braxton examined Holloway's shaving kit. Satisfied that it contained nothing that could be used as weapon, he tossed the kit on the bathroom sink and gave the room a cursory inspection from the doorway. Holloway prayed that he would not look behind the door, and he didn't. Braxton nodded to Holloway that the bathroom was his. "You've got fifteen minutes to shower, shave, and get dressed. Oh, and take care of your personal needs in there, Mr. Holloway. There will be no more rest stops for any reason until you're airborne." As Holloway limped past him, Braxton eyed his bruised body and shook his head. "You really took a beating."

"You shoudda seen the other guy."

Braxton was not amused. "Leave the door open, Mr. Holloway." He took off his coat and plopped into a chair that gave him a good view of the bathroom sink. He did not have an unobstructed view of the toilet to the left of the doorway or the shower to the right of it. Braxton took the morning newspaper from his coat pocket and alternated between scanning the headlines and watching Holloway's back. The chauffeur positioned himself against the wall, between the bathroom and the door leading into the hall. From that vantage point he could see only the toilet, but he was blocking the only exit from the suite.

Holloway shaved quickly, being careful not to disturb his tender nose. Then, he turned the shower on and stepped into the tub. As he did, Braxton looked up from his paper and adjusted his chair so that he could observe Holloway in the shower by looking into the bathroom mirror. When he was satisfied, he went back to his newspaper.

As soon as Braxton looked down at the paper, Holloway turned up the spray volume and pulled the shower curtain part way around the tub. Then, he reached behind the door, lifted the receiver from the phone on the bathroom wall, and punched four digits. In a low voice he said, "Room service, this is Holloway. I'd like three American breakfasts—"

The shower curtain whipped back and Braxton was standing there red-faced and angry. "What the hell are you doing?" Without waiting for an answer he snatched the receiver from Holloway and listened, his hand over the mouthpiece.

"What's the problem," asked Holloway. "I was ordering breakfast. I haven't eaten since yesterday."

Braxton stepped out into the bedroom, snapped his fingers at the chauffeur and pointed towards the door. The chauffeur leaped away from the wall, gun in hand and pointed at the entrance.

Holloway was still talking about being hungry. The voice of room service was jabbering, "Monsieur Holloway? Monsieur Holloway? Are you there?"

Braxton pointed a finger at Holloway. "You, shut up!" He removed his hand from the mouthpiece and put a smile in his voice. "I'm Mr. Holloway's guest. Could you read back his order? I'm allergic to some foods."

The voice from room service replied, "Of course, monsieur." He read the order.

"Could you also read back the message Mr. Holloway gave you. He was sending it for me and I want to be sure it's correct." Braxton gave Holloway a triumphant look.

"There was no message, other than the order, monsieur. Do you wish a message delivered? I will be happy to inform the concierge."

Braxton's triumph faded. "Never mind. I'll take care of it myself. Thank you." Braxton depressed the phone cradle to break the connection. Then, be unscrewed the mouthpiece, ripped out the contents, and slammed the receiver into its cradle. For several seconds, Braxton eyed Holloway with a controlled fury. He reached into the shower, deliberately wetting his shirt, and turned the water off. "From now on, you do exactly what I tell you, nothing more, nothing less. You get out of line again and you'll fly back to Washington in Intensive Care Class." Eyes riveted on Holloway, he stepped backwards into the bedroom and snapped his fingers for the chauffeur to relax.

The remainder of the dressing and packing ritual went swiftly and in hostile silence. Holloway was about to put on his coat when someone knocked. Braxton walked to the door and said, "Yes?" "Your breakfast, monsieur," came the reply from the hall.

"Leave it and shove your bill under the door. I'll sign for it."

"Very well, monsieur," and the bill appeared.

Braxton gave it to Holloway, who signed it with a pen from the nightstand. Braxton read what Holloway had written and shoved the bill under the door.

"Thank you, monsieur," said the hall voice.

Since there was no peephole, Braxton pressed his ear to the door to monitor the room service waiter's departure. He heard nothing. The hall carpet was too plush to give up a footfall. Braxton stepped away from the door and pointed a finger at Holloway, "You've got five minutes to eat." He turned to the chauffeur. "Bring in that cart."

The chauffeur opened the door quickly and glanced both ways. He saw nothing except the breakfast cart standing to the right of the door, long side toward him. As he stepped into the hallway and reached for the cart, a man in a ski mask uncoiled from behind the cart and pointed a revolver at him. "Turn around. Get into the room," commanded the masked man.

The chauffeur turned back toward the door. As he did, the masked man stepped from behind the cart and lunged forward, driving his shoulder into the chauffeur's back. This action propelled the chauffeur into the room and sent him sprawling onto the floor.

The masked man leaped over the chauffeur's body and landed with his gun pointed at Braxton. "Hands up! Don't make trouble and you'll walk away from this."

Holloway dashed behind the masked man and closed the door. On the way back, he disarmed the chauffeur. The masked man had put Braxton on the floor and was searching him. He found State Department credentials, but no weapon. "What do you want to do with these two?"

"I need to keep them out of circulation for a while," Holloway replied. "Tie them up and leave them."

When the two escorts were bound and gagged, Holloway went into the bathroom and slipped a shower cap into his pocket. He came back and stooped down next to Braxton.

"No offense, but I just don't trust you. Last night, one of your embassy friends came to the jail and drugged me. After that, things and people started to disappear. I don't want to join them. If you're on the level about wanting me out of Switzerland, you'll be happy to know that I'm on my way, right now. I'll take your credentials and your friend's gun and leave them somewhere safe. In an hour, I'll call room service and have them untie you. You wait for my second call. If both of you are still here, I'll tell you where your stuff is. If only one of you is here or you don't answer . . . Well, I'll make sure that the credentials and gun are used to embarrass you. Got it?"

Braxton nodded his head.

"Good. I don't think I'll be coming back to Switzerland. This country is rough on the tourist trade."

Stepping into the hall with his masked companion, Holloway closed the door and hung the "Do not disturb" sign in place. Sid Mitchell ripped off the ski mask and shoved it into his pocket. Without a word, they walked down the hall to Mitchell's room. When they were inside, Mitchell asked, "What the hell's going on, Ed? Last night I saw the Oriental come out of that alley in a basket. Then, you come out in cuffs. Now, we're tying up State Department guys!"

"It's a long story and I don't have time to tell it right now. I'll fill you in when we get back to Washington. Are you packed?"

"Yeah. We're supposed to be on the plane in an hour."

"Okay. I'll reserve my room for another day. That will keep the maid away from our friends. You check out and take my bags. Catch the plane as scheduled. Just before you take off, call the hotel and tell them to untie those two hoods in my room. Their credentials and gun are in the toilet tank." Holloway and Mitchell enjoyed a quick laugh. "By the way, that ski mask was a nice touch. Where did you get it on such short notice?"

"I had a kid from room service get it for me outside the hotel. Gave him a hundred to get it quick and another hundred to keep his mouth shut. It'll be on my expenses report. What are you going to do about getting out? Those two in your room might not be from the State Department or interested in your good health. Someone could be watching the airports for you."

"I thought about that. I'll take the train to Germany and fly out of Munich. But first I need to pick up a souvenir."

* * *

Holloway took a cab to the nearest department store where he purchased and changed into jeans, rubber boots, a heavy wool shirt and a yellow slicker jacket and pants. He also bought a crowbar, flashlight, and rubber gloves. His final purchase was a backpack, into which he shoved his other clothing and the equipment. The transformation complete, Holloway took a cab to within a block of the alley where he and the Oriental had fought. He paid the cab driver and walked the rest of the way.

When he arrived in the alley, Holloway looked like a typical street crew worker. He set his pack against the alley wall, took out the crowbar and pried up the storm drain cover. Then, he pulled on the rubber gloves and climbed down the metal ladder into the sewer.

When his foot touched bottom, he was standing in six inches of very cold water. He eased his gloved hands below the surface and carefully ran them along the bottom of the pipe in ever-widening circles around his feet. He was about to give up on that tactic when his finger slid over a smooth object. Carefully, Holloway picked up the item and held it in the shaft of light from the street above. It was a small, shiny, and almost triangular piece of metal, the tip of a knife blade. Holloway's heart started to pound. He dropped the piece of metal in the hotel shower cap and stuffed it into his pocket. Then, he flicked on his flashlight and played it along the pipe. *Bingo!* There, a few inches above the waterline, was the knife handle with the remainder of the broken blade attached. He turned off his light and put the rest of the knife in the shower cap.

* * *

In Washington, the phone rang at Admiral Schaeffer's quarters at Fort NcNair.

"This is your friend," said Ackerman from his office in Geneva.

"I recognize your voice. Your cold is better," replied Schaeffer, responding with the code words indicating that it was safe to talk.

"I had a visitor yesterday. His name was Holloway."

"I'm aware of that. I had some people looking after him. They lost him after he left you. What did he want?"

"He wanted to talk to Dillworth. He also asked about a recently deceased mutual acquaintance," said Ackerman, in a cryptic reference to Jack Slayton. "I stalled him, temporarily."

"Were you aware that Mr. Holloway got into trouble last night?"

"No," replied Ackerman.

"He solved part of our Vietnamese problem. It was messy. Your local station chief had to provide assistance. Holloway doesn't know who helped him, of course. He's out of harm's way now—on his way back to the States at this very minute. I don't think you'll be seeing Mr. Holloway again. He needs to reduce his travel schedule. If he continues at his current pace, he'll endanger his health."

CHAPTER 11

<u>April 1987, Washington, D.C.</u>

Holloway reasoned that if anyone from Geneva was still interested in him, they would attempt to reestablish surveillance at the Washington airports or at his home. He was determined to avoid both for the time being. He travelled from Geneva to Munich by train and flew from there to New York the following morning. That afternoon, a shuttle flight brought him into Baltimore, where he rented a car for the trip to Washington. Before taking to the road, he called Harvey Burgin of the FBI's Counterintelligence Division and made an appointment.

After two hours of plowing through the evening commuter traffic, Holloway arrived at Burgin's office on Pennsylvania Avenue. Burgin was in his fifties and built like a teddy bear, with complementary apple-cheeks and a gentle, self-effacing manner. He was working in shirtsleeves at his desk when Holloway came in. The briefcase and coat on a chair by the door indicated that he had been ready to leave for some time. Burgin got up and lumbered toward Holloway with a gentle smile and his big paw of a hand extended. They had known each other since the early 1980s, when Holloway was the CIA liaison man to the FBI. "How have you been, Mr. Holloway?"

Burgin distanced himself from everyone at the Bureau by calling them "Mister" or "Miss." There was a remote sadness about the man that he seemed determined to preserve.

After they exchanged greetings, Holloway took out the plastic shower cap containing the switchblade. "Harv, I need a favor. Can you have the lab lift the prints off this knife and run a make?"

"Is this a counterintelligence matter?"

"I don't know. An Oriental—probably Vietnamese—was following me. When I took his picture, he tried to stab me. There was a scuffle. I got the knife. He and the picture disappeared. I'd like to know who he was."

Burgin took the knife and plastic. "I'll see what I can do. Where can I contact you?"

"Okay if I just drop in about eleven tomorrow? I'll call first."

"Fine."

*   *   *

Exhausted from the trip, Holloway took an overpriced hotel room within walking distance of FBI headquarters and went to bed without dinner. A hunger headache woke him at nine the next morning. Holloway consumed the biggest breakfast on the room service menu, showered, and made his call.

Burgin answered the phone with a troubled voice that conveyed bad news. "There was no problem lifting the prints, but we ran into some trouble during the identification process. I'll tell you about it when you get here."

Holloway covered the few blocks to the Hoover Building in less than ten minutes and was out of breath when he walked into Burgin's office.

Burgin was apologetic. "We found a match for the prints on your knife, but when we tried to pull up a name, the computer blocked our access and alarms went off. Deputy Division Chief Kruger called me in and wanted to know what was going on. I told him the truth, of course. He ordered me to bring you to his office when you arrived."

"Damn!" said Holloway. "Okay, Harv. Thanks for trying. Sorry I got you into a mess. Is Kruger going to identify the prints?"

"I don't think so."

Younger than Burgin, Kruger had an imposing physical presence enhanced by white hair and piercing blue eyes. He didn't offer either visitor a seat. Holloway stood in front of Kruger's desk, while Burgin tried to find a neutral zone on the sidelines halfway between his boss and his friend.

"What are you working on, Holloway?" demanded Kruger.

"I might trade that information for the name that belongs to the prints on that knife."

"Trade," laughed Kruger. "I don't have to trade with you. You're not entitled to any Bureau information. You tell me what you're working on and I might tell you something that will keep you out of trouble."

"I'm working on the name of the guy who tried to stab me."

"You don't understand, do you? The prints don't exist, the man doesn't exist. In fact, this conversation is a figment of your imagination."

"I suppose the knife I brought in here doesn't exist either?"

"What knife?" asked Kruger innocently.

Holloway looked at Burgin, who looked at the floor.

Holloway exploded. "Don't give me that crap, Kruger. I'm getting tired of people telling me that I almost got whacked by the little man who wasn't there. I want to know who that guy was and what he was!"

Kruger was unmoved by Holloway's emotion. "You press this and the only thing that will happen is that Harvey, here, is going to get into trouble for trying to help you."

"If you aren't going to help me, why the hell did you ask me in here?"

"To tell you, officially, that this division and all of its personnel are off limits to you. Don't make any more unannounced appearances. If you have business to conduct, I'm your point of contact. I'm doing this to preserve the integrity of the division. I don't want anyone here to get in trouble for doing unauthorized work for you. Harvey, escort Mr. Holloway to the sidewalk."

Burgin apologized all the way down to the street, but that didn't make up for the fact that Holloway had hit a dead end. It was time to get some advice.

*   *   *

When Sid Mitchell arrived at Lenny's, the lunch crowd was already wall-to-wall. Holloway had captured a booth and was devouring one of the tuna fish sandwiches on his plate.

Mitchell slid into the booth across the table from Holloway and snapped a napkin open. "You sounded depressed on the phone. I'm happy to see that you didn't commit suicide with something from Lenny's wine cellar. Who would pay for lunch?"

Holloway ignored Mitchell's attempt at humor. "The FBI knows the guy who tried to knife me in Geneva, but they're not talking." Holloway described his meeting with Kruger. "I'm out of ideas, Sid. What do you think?"

Mitchell took half a sandwich from Holloway's plate. "My advice hasn't changed. Get the hell out." He flagged down a waitress and ordered a diet cola.

"I hate to throw in the towel," Holloway admitted.

"Remember what I told you about dead cats." He put down his sandwich. "You look like hell. Why don't you go home and sleep in your own bed. Donna's been calling me every day asking if I've heard from you. And what about Miriam Slayton? She hasn't been outside since you left. You think she's going to hide in your apartment for the rest of her life while you chase some dead Vietnamese? If you've got a thing for the lady, why don't you start living a normal life with her?" Mitchell's beeper interrupted the conversation. He excused himself and went to the phone. He returned a few minutes later, shaking his head. "How do you manage to get calls on my beeper?"

"What?"

"Donna called. She's got an urgent message for you. She wouldn't give it to me. Call her at the office."

*   *   *

Donna was furious when Holloway called. "Where the devil have you been? I've been worried sick about you."

"I thought you didn't want to be involved. I was preserving your innocence." The statement carried equal parts of truth and sarcasm. Kruger had soured his mood. "Sid said you have a message for me."

Donna decided not to trade barbs with him. "You had a call from a man who wouldn't identify himself. He said that you lost something on Pennsylvania Avenue this morning and that he will return it if you meet him at the Vietnam War Memorial between two and three this afternoon."

Holloway looked at his watch. It was a ten minutes after two.

"Thanks, Donna. I love you and your messages!"

"Save the mush for Madame Slayton," said Donna. Then, with obvious concern, she said, "Holloway, come home. I miss you—and your woman is driving me crazy. I get interrogated about you every night."

* * *

Harvey Burgin was sitting on a bench near the Vietnam War Memorial. He was leaning forward resting his forearms on his thighs and staring across the grass at nothing in particular. Holloway came up and sat beside him. The two men didn't speak for a while. Finally, Burgin said, "Nguyen Van Can. That's his name. He's a lieutenant colonel in the Vietnamese intelligence service."

"The current regime?"

"The current *communist* regime," Harvey said bitterly.

"I'm pretty sure he was following me around Washington. What interest would Vietnamese intelligence have in an ex-CIA employee?"

"I don't know," answered Burgin, still staring at nothing.

"The Bureau is supposed to know," Holloway reminded him gently. "Didn't Kruger have somebody on him?"

"No. Communist Vietnam is not a credible intelligence threat. Besides, we were told to stay clear."

"Where did the order originate?"

"The White House."

Holloway's pulse quickened.

Reluctantly, Burgin focused on the story he had come to tell. "Colonel Can first came to the attention of the Bureau last year. Kruger got a call from the White House telling us that Can was coming to the States as a United Nations 'observer.' He was to be allowed free rein as long as he didn't break any laws. No surveillance permitted."

"Why the special treatment?"

"I don't know. We were just told to keep hands off."

"But you didn't. Otherwise, you wouldn't have Can's fingerprints."

"Foreign intelligence operatives in the United States are, by law, the responsibility of the Bureau. Kruger takes that responsibility seriously." Having stated the legal justification for violating a White House directive, Burgin relaxed. "Kruger got Can's prints as he processed through customs. We conducted a brief surveillance. He didn't visit any sensitive people or places. Kruger became convinced that Can was harmless and the Bureau followed White House guidance of no physical or electronic surveillance. We continued to monitor Can's movements through his credit card usage, airline reservations, and other passive techniques."

"What was he up to?"

"Some kind of research. He visited the Securities and Exchange Commission, all of the stock exchanges, and lots of banks and libraries. He spent time in the Library of Congress reading about the American departure from Vietnam, refugee resettlement, and everything he could find on the role of the CIA in Vietnam."

"Was that the extent of his travels?"

"No. He went to Europe several times."

"Did the Bureau hand him off to the CIA when he travelled abroad? asked Holloway.

"Yes. The White House forgot to tell the CIA to keep clear."

"Who's the CIA case officer?"

"Hugh Stiles."

"What was in the overseas take on Can?"

"The CIA got information on where he went and who he saw."

"Were there copies of the CIA reports in Can's Bureau file?"

"No," replied Burgin. "We got extracts. Can talked to a lot of bankers and lawyers in Switzerland and Liechtenstein."

"What about?"

"Swiss banking history in the 1970s. He posed as a student conducting research for a dissertation in international economics."

Holloway tried to see a pattern or motive in what Burgin had related, but he could find neither. "Any idea what he was really up to, Harv?"

"There are no assessments in the file. The Bureau doesn't know what Can is doing or why."

"Who, in the White House, requested that Can be allowed to roam around without surveillance?"

"Jack Slayton, of Iran-Contra fame."

Now we're getting someplace!, thought Holloway.

Burgin got up wearily. "Could we walk a bit? These benches are hard on my back."

They strolled along the grass, circling toward the front of the Memorial. The crowd was thinning.

"Why is the Bureau keeping Can's file under wraps?"

Burgin gave the question some thought. "There's nothing of intelligence value in the file. I suppose Kruger doesn't want anything to get out that would link the Bureau to Iran-Contra personalities. Bad for the FBI image."

They walked to the front of the Vietnam War Memorial and along the boardwalk in front of the black granite slabs containing the names of the war dead. Burgin stopped in front of a slab near the center of the wall. He turned to Holloway and gave him a plastic bag containing Can's switchblade. "Did Can actually cut you, Mr. Holloway?"

"No."

"Well, you might be interested to know *someone* was cut with that switchblade."

"Oh?"

"The lab found traces of human blood in the handle recess, AB-positive. That's a rare type," said Burgin in a distracted tone. He stared up at the names carved into the slab.

"Harv, I appreciate this. Kruger will have your ass on a high rack when he finds out."

Burgin leaned forward and ran his forefinger over a name cut into the stone. When he turned to look at Holloway, his eyes were blazing with contempt. "Kruger can go to hell." He turned back to the wall. "I lost a son in Vietnam. When I sent my boy into that meat grinder, I never thought I'd see the Bureau cover up for a Vietnamese, communist spy." Burgin's eyes locked on Holloway. "I hope you get the son-of-a-bitch."

Holloway saw the anguish in Burgin's face and had to tell him. "Just between us, Harv, I already did. He's dead."

Burgin's mouth twisted into a tight smile that had nothing to do with happiness. It held for a few seconds, until his lower lip began to quiver and tears welled up in his eyes.

* * *

It was three in the afternoon when Holloway and Burgin parted. The rush hour exodus from the city would be in high gear in half an hour. Holloway knew that he had to talk to Hugh Stiles at the CIA that day. Tomorrow would be too late. By that time, Kruger would know that Burgin had exposed Can. Kruger would certainly try to cut off Holloway's access to CIA information, if out of nothing more than spite. He looked like a man who did not lose gracefully. Holloway drove to L'Enfant Plaza, where he found a phone and called the CIA. The operator put him through to Hugh Stiles' section.

"Three-four-oh-two," answered a male voice, giving only the extension number, in accordance with CIA procedure.

"I'm calling Hugh Stiles. I was given this number by a mutual acquaintance on Pennsylvania Avenue." Stiles would not know whether Holloway was referring to the FBI or the White House. Therefore, he would be less likely to call Kruger for verification. "I have some information about an Oriental gentleman who visits Switzerland and Liechtenstein a lot and likes to pose as a student of economics."

"Who is this?"

"Are you Stiles?"

"Yes."

"My name is Ed Holloway. I used to work there. Pull my personnel jacket so that we don't have to do a mating dance before we talk. I can be out there before four-thirty. And let's keep this between the two of us."

"I'll be waiting. No need to hurry. I'm the watch officer tonight."

Holloway got to Langley just ahead of the worst of the rush hour. The receptionist notified Stiles and he came down to the lobby to meet Holloway. Stiles had a pipe clenched between his teeth and wore a three-piece suit, button-down shirt, and regimental tie. *The intelligence guru in full regalia*, thought Holloway derisively. Up close, Stiles was balding and looked to be in his late thirties. He had a ruddy complexion and wide, inquisitive eyes set above a narrow nose.

Stiles was carrying two folders in his left hand. One was Holloway's personnel file and the other, Holloway guessed, was the dossier on Lieutenant Colonel Nguyen Van Can. Stiles greeted Holloway warmly. "Welcome. The legend lives. I didn't realize who you were when we talked on the phone." Stiles led the way to an interview room and they sat down at a polished table. "I've heard a lot about you," admitted Stiles. "It's a real honor to meet you."

There was a gushiness about the man that put Holloway off, but this was no time to be picky. The red carpet was out.

Stiles opened Holloway's file and read aloud. "Silver Star for bravery with the Army in Vietnam. A tour with the Phoenix Program. Laos. Afghanistan. Awarded the Intelligence Medal for Merit twice and an Intelligence Star. Liaison to the FBI and NSA." Stiles looked at Holloway with a mixture of admiration and envy. "You did it all! How did you cram so much into one career?"

"Some say that the Company moved me around because I couldn't get along with people."

"I heard that you'd have been one of the youngest major station chiefs in Company history if you hadn't quit. Why'd you leave?"

"Family," said Holloway, shifting uncomfortably in his chair, "but that's another story. I came here to talk about Vietnamese." He reached over and tapped the file lying in front of Stiles. It was not one of the official file folders that the CIA used for dossiers.

Stiles cleared his throat. "Officially, this file does not exist. Somebody over at the FBI talks too much."

"Or the White House," said Holloway, trying to throw him off the scent.

"If anybody at the White House knew that I had a file on Can, I'd be out of a job. They didn't want him tailed, as you probably know." Stiles cocked his head to one side. "What's your interest in him?"

"He tried to stick a knife in my back."

"What!"

"I want to know what he was doing and why he was interested in me. I've got information to trade."

"Such as . . .?"

"Colonel Can dropped out of sight recently. I know what happened to him. I'll share that information with you, if you share yours with me."

Stiles' expression turned grave. "I know that Can disappeared. A friend of mine was supposed to be keeping an eye on him when he vanished. Tell me when it happened and I'll know that you know what you're talking about. Then we can deal."

"Can disappeared a couple of days ago in Geneva, Switzerland." Stiles bit hard into his pipe stem. "You go first," said Holloway.

Stiles took the pipe out of his mouth and tapped the burned tobacco into an ashtray. "About a year ago, the Bureau inquired as to what we had on Colonel Can. We had nothing. Later, the Bureau, specifically Kruger in CI, told me that Can would be coming to the States and that the White House had imposed a surveillance ban while he was here. Since there was no prohibition against keeping an eye on Can if he went abroad, Kruger asked me to handle the job quietly through Company channels. He didn't want to make it an official request from the Bureau. I agreed. Can visited Europe several times. I would get a call from the Bureau whenever he booked overseas flights or from the Customs Service whenever he left the country without reservations. In most cases, I had someone on him when he arrived at his overseas destination."

"Who did he contact?"

Stiles took a paper from Can's dossier and passed it to Holloway. "That's the contact list—cities, organizations, and people that Can visited."

The names "Geneva," "Randolph Dillworth," and "WorldCorp" leaped off the paper. Holloway forced himself to say, "I don't see anything familiar here." He handed the paper back to his host.

Stiles gave him a suspicious look, but said nothing.

"What do the asterisks mean?" Holloway asked.

"They indicate contacts whom Can followed, even as we were following him. He made it a practice to shadow many of his contacts either before or after he visited them in their offices."

Holloway asked, "Did you get any audio or video surveillance."

"No."

"Anything on the people he visited?"

"No. Most of them were bankers or insurance people. We had no intelligence interest in them."

"What's the bottom line, Stiles? What was Can up to?"

"I don't know."

"Take a guess."

"Maybe he's got money to invest for his government and he's doing market research. There are problems with that theory though. Why would he do his own research when there are firms who could do a cheaper and better job? Why is the White House involved, if he's just playing the market? And why is he shadowing his contacts before he meets with them? I don't know."

"Why did you put a tail on Can, if the White House didn't want him followed? You wouldn't go that far out on a limb just to please the Bureau."

Stiles looked into the bowl of his pipe, then wrinkled his nose. "You know how these damned politicians are. You have to protect them from themselves, not to mention cover your own ass. It's all 'Do as I say' and Marquess of Queensberry rules until the baby food hits the fan. Then, they'll want a life history on the good Colonel Can, including his mating habits, and they won't care how many fingernails I have to pull to get it. I'm paid to know everything that the Vietnamese are doing and I don't intend to come up short if Can turns out to be a problem." Stiles clamped his teeth hard on the pipe stem for emphasis.

Holloway noted, "Can came here as a U.N. observer. Was anything going on in the U.N. that would have triggered his visit to the States?"

"I don't remember anything of extraordinary significance."

"Any bilateral action involving the United States and Vietnam?"

Stiles chewed his pipe stem and looked at the ceiling. "The only thing that comes to mind is the MIA negotiations in Hanoi." Stiles grunted. "That mission gave me a sleepless night or two."

"What happened?"

"A U.S. delegation was in Hanoi negotiating the investigation of air crash sites and the return of MIA remains from the Vietnam War. Admiral Schaeffer was there from the Company. His interpreter was Dr. Hong, one of our consultants on Vietnam. The second day there, Schaeffer fired Hong on the spot. I had to dig up another interpreter—some cave dweller named Trung—and fly him to Hanoi within twenty-four hours. Schaeffer handpicked him. He looked like the sort of fellow who would break your kneecaps if you didn't pay your bills on time. Worked for the Company in Vietnam. Anyway, it was a hectic few hours in my life. That's why I remember the negotiations."

Holloway asked, "What was the problem with Hong?"

"I don't know and I didn't ask. All I know is that he crossed Schaeffer and Schaeffer froze him out—'graylisted' him. That's a Schaeffer term. It means that we keep the guy on retainer for a while, but never call him."

"Where is Hong now?" asked Holloway.

"He teaches economics at Morgan State University in Baltimore."

"What's Admiral Schaeffer's job with the Company?"

"National All-Source Intelligence Officer," said Stiles, sarcastically.

"I don't recognize that title."

"No reason why you should. Schaeffer dreamed it up after you left. The Director gave him the job of coordinating input from all intelligence community agencies: CIA, FBI, State, Defense, Energy . . . the whole ball of wax. He set up something called the Community Intelligence Staff with himself as czar, and assumed the title of National All-Source Intelligence Officer. It's the same old plot with a new prima donna."

Holloway nodded in understanding. This was an old story. CIA directors since the Kennedy Administration had been trying, without success, to establish control over the intelligence community's collection assets. The theory was that centralized control of collection assets and integration of the products would provide every user with better intelligence. However, those assets were embedded in more than a dozen military and civilian agencies—political fiefdoms—and neither the power of the White House nor the bureaucratic maneuverings of a succession of CIA directors had been able to dislodge them. Schaeffer was evidently the latest in a long line of Company point men who had attempted the intelligence coordination task with high hopes, only to be frustrated and ultimately defeated by bureaucratic foot-dragging and certain legal restrictions.

"That's the old Deputy for Central Intelligence job," said Holloway.

"Right. Before you left the Company, the job was held by that boy-brigadier general with all the degrees and the Coke-bottle glasses."

Stiles and Holloway shared a laugh. "I swear, I don't know where they recruit for that job. Almost every one is an oddball."

"Is Schaeffer cut from the same cloth?" asked Holloway.

"No, no. Schaeffer is a Navy line officer—and an asshole. He thinks he's still commanding a destroyer. His intel knowledge is a mile wide and an inch deep. He got the job because he's the fair-haired boy in the front office. Plays golf with the Director at Burning Tree." Stiles turned the ends of his mouth down and made big eyes. "The Director backs him to the hilt. Cross Schaeffer and you get a rocket ride to our embassy in 'Lower Eastern Slobovia.' We call it the 'Schaeffer Express.' The man has ruined some promising careers."

"What was Schaeffer's role in the MIA negotiations?"

"He got himself appointed to the team as one of the Navy reps. The real reason was personal. His brother was shot down in a Navy jet over North Vietnam in 1968 and has been missing ever since."

"Is that the end of the story?"

"It's the end of my story. Now, it's your turn. Where is Can?"

"I didn't say I would tell you where he is. I said I'd tell you what happened to him."

Stiles bristled. "Don't jerk me around, Holloway."

"Can tried to stick a knife in me on Monday night in Geneva. I had to kill him. I was taken to a police station and while they were questioning me, the body disappeared. Then, someone showed up claiming to be from the American Consulate and drugged me. When I woke up in the drunk tank, I got a tongue-lashing for being disorderly and an invitation to leave the country. How does that grab you?"

It must have grabbed Stiles hard because he turned pale. He was obviously not aware of Can's death.

Holloway continued. "I'm wondering who had enough pull with the Swiss to make a body disappear and clean up the police files on a murder? Only one answer comes to mind: the Company. But you don't know anything about it. I can tell from the look on your face. That means that the Company is running an operation involving Can that they didn't tell you about and you're running one that the Company doesn't know about. What are you up to, Stiles?"

"How I run my desk is my business." Stiles was ash-white.

"Don't get defensive. I just want to know what Can was doing that would make him try to kill me."

"I told you, I don't know."

"Okay, I believe you. Why don't you tell me how your piece of the Geneva action went? Maybe both of us can learn something."

Stiles considered the proposal. He needed information. Someone in the Company was playing in his sandbox without telling him. It was embarrassing to be cut out of the action on a nobody like Can. "Alright. Can was spending time in Liechtenstein and Geneva. I have a friend in the Company at Geneva Station. He has surveillance assets. As a favor to me, he kept tabs on Can during those trips."

"Without the knowledge of the chief of station," Holloway added.

"Yes." Stiles found something of intense interest in the bowl of his pipe and picked at it with his pipe tool. "Last week when the Bureau told me that Can was headed for Geneva again, I notified my friend there. He was following Can and, in the process, stumbled onto another Company surveillance team from Geneva Station. Since my friend's surveillance was not authorized, he broke contact. Of course, he couldn't ask the station chief what was going on because it wasn't his case. He tried to reestablish the surveillance at Can's hotel, but the man had vanished. The hotel staff never saw him leave and he paid the hotel bill by mail and in cash, after his departure."

Holloway could have told Stiles that the surveillance his friend stumbled into was probably targeted at one Edward J. Holloway rather than Nguyen Can, but he thought better of it. No point in showing all of his cards. "Did your friend tell you which Company people were following Can?"

"No," said Stiles, with a touch of irritation. "That would have been a breach of security, as you well know."

Holloway shrugged. "No harm in asking. For your information, there may have been a couple of teams on Can. One had a Marine-looking fellow with long hair. A pair named Braxton and Pinchot may have been on the other team. I don't know if those are real names or work names. When you talk to your friend in Geneva, ask him if he knows those two. I'd like to have a talk with Pinchot, if I'm ever in Geneva again."

Stiles lit his pipe. Through a cloud of blue smoke, he said, "You never did say why you were in Switzerland."

"I was trying to help a widow close out her husband's estate. A banker owes her some money. Maybe Can was haunting the bank and thought I was somebody else." Neither of them believed that.

"There's a lot we don't know," observed Holloway. "If Can was into something important enough to make his body disappear and the Company didn't tell you about it, they obviously didn't want you to know. If I were you, I'd toss that bootleg file on Can into the burn bag and forget I ever heard of him." Holloway stood up to leave. "I'll keep in touch."

Holloway was excited as he drove back to Washington. At last, he had some leads that he could sink his teeth into. As for the bad guys—if indeed there were any besides Can—they were probably still squirreling around, trying to figure out where Holloway was. Although, it was a good bet that they were covering his house. He would have to check on that later. Kruger was at least twelve hours behind him, too far back to do any damage. As for Hugh Stiles, he wouldn't want to expose his rogue surveillance operation to his CIA superiors. Holloway guessed that Stiles would get rid of Can's file and keep his mouth shut. He guessed wrong.

Stiles was gifted in his ability to master Oriental languages. That gift was also a curse that, in Stiles' view, would keep him buried forever in Asian intelligence. After two tours in the Pacific, Stiles and his wife had had their fill of that part of the world. In fact, Mrs. Stiles, who was also with the CIA, had put her foot down. "You'll do the next tour in the Far East without me! I'll quit the Company before I go back there!" That ultimatum held in spades, now that they had a child on the way. Personal preferences aside, Stiles believed that unless he soon got a European posting, his advancement potential would be limited. He did not intend to accept that eventuality without a fight. To date, however, every one of his requests for the Continent had been denied on the grounds that his language skills were needed in the Asian Division. He had reached the point where only one thing could rescue him from the Asia beat and obscurity: a godfather. Unfortunately, he didn't have one. But he had been looking.

In Stiles' estimation, the best godfather to have in the CIA, other than the director, himself, was the DCI's fair-haired boy, Admiral Schaeffer. Never mind that Schaeffer was an asshole. There were lots of assholes in the Company. Schaeffer's attractiveness lay in the fact that he was a very powerful asshole. The admiral had an interest in Asia because of his MIA brother. He also had limited knowledge of intel operations. What Schaeffer needed was his own man in the Asian Division to do his personal bidding, someone who, at the proper time, would be rewarded with a plum job in Europe. Stiles wanted to be that someone.

His problem was visibility. Stiles' duties did not bring him into frequent contact with Schaeffer. Without benefit of routine exposure, he had been unable to cultivate the admiral. Therefore, something dramatic was required to call Stiles to the attention of his potential benefactor, and Holloway had provided the vehicle. How lucky that Holloway had stopped by today. As watch officer, Stiles had access to Schaeffer's office. It would be easy to have security unlock the door. He could slip in and leave a memorandum on the desk— sealed of course— "FOR ADMIRAL SCHAEFFER'S EYES ONLY." The memo would report the essence of Holloway's visit.

Of course, there was no question of telling Schaeffer that the FBI had put Stiles onto Can. If he invoked the FBI, he would have to admit that he knew about the White House prohibition against surveillance of Can. Such an admission might land him in deep trouble. He would have to finesse that part of his report. He would say that an anonymous tipster had put him onto Can. That was a thin story, but serviceable. He would have to take the hit for running a surveillance without Agency approval. That was a calculated risk. He would emphasize that he had enough sense to terminate his little adventure when his friend stumbled across the CIA surveillance of Can in Geneva. Stiles smiled. It was all a bit pushy, perhaps, but would do for a starter. Stiles went to the watch officer's room and fed paper into the typewriter. His fingers hovered over the keyboard for a moment as he wrestled with second thoughts. *What the hell? No guts, no glory.* Stiles began to type.

* * *

The beltway was still crowded when Holloway eased his car into the traffic flow and headed back to Washington. He was pleased at the results of his meeting with Hugh Stiles and for the first time since his return from Europe, he allowed his mind to dwell on Miriam Slayton. He wanted to taste her sweet body again. That thought reminded him that he was entering his third day in his Geneva suit. It was time to check in at home. An hour later, Holloway turned the rented car into the street where his apartment was located and drove slowly toward the house. It was on the left side, near the end of the block. There were townhouses on his right, separated from the street by a residents' parking lot that ran the length of the block. The lot was two rows deep and almost filled. It was 7 p.m. and most of the commuters were home from work. The lot was the logical place for a stakeout, and Holloway looked for one as he rolled slowly towards his house. Two-thirds of the way down the block, he spotted the watcher. He was in a blue Ford on the back row of the lot. Holloway continued past his house and turned left at the end of the block. Two streets away he found a convenience store with a public telephone and called home.

"Thank God!" gasped Miriam Slayton. "Where are you? Are you alright?"

"I'm okay, but I don't have much time." He didn't say that the phone might be bugged. "The front of the house is being watched. I want you to pack a suit, shirt, and some underwear for me and slip out the back. There's a convenience store a couple of blocks west of the house. Do you know it?"

"No, but Donna can give me directions."

"Go to the store and wait. A cab will pick you up in thirty minutes and bring you to me. See you soon." Holloway drove his rent-a-car to a townhouse parking lot one block over from his own and waited. Ten minutes later, Miriam stepped out onto the back porch carrying a suitcase. From the darkness, Holloway watched her walk the narrow stone path between the backs of the buildings and across the lawns toward him. Miriam passed close enough for him to get a whiff of her perfume. She turned left and walked along the sidewalk between the townhouses and the parking lots. Holloway had parked the car at the far end and Miriam was walking towards it. When he was sure she was not being followed, he sprinted along in the wake of Miriam's perfume. As she came abreast of the car, he called her. She turned to be crushed in his embrace. Holloway said, "I got impatient." Miriam smiled at his lie and allowed him to bundle her and the suitcase into the rent-a-car. Holloway drove a fast, twisting route through side streets. When he was sure they had not been followed, he headed for Baltimore.

Three hours later, Miriam Slayton and Holloway lay naked and exhausted on a hotel bed in Baltimore's northeastern suburbs. Holloway said, "I missed you the whole time I was away."

"Why didn't you call?" Before he could answer, Miriam declared, "You were afraid the phones were bugged!" She pushed herself up on one elbow and looked down at him. "That's why you didn't meet me at the convenience store."

Reluctantly, Holloway said, "Yes."

It was an honest answer. Nevertheless, Miriam didn't like it. She rolled away from Holloway and onto her back, pulling the bedsheet up to her neck. "I'm scared, Holloway. Two people I know have been murdered, someone is watching the house, and the phones may be tapped."

They were both quiet for a while. Then Miriam asked, "Was your trip to Switzerland was worthwhile?"

"It may have been very worthwhile for your piece of mind. Do you know what your cousin's blood type was?"

"No," said Miriam with renewed interest. "Why?"

Holloway ignored her question. "Can you find out what her blood type was?"

"I suppose so. I could call Denise's mother."

"Does she live in Kansas?"

"Yes, in Mission.

Holloway looked at his watch. "It's just nine. Call her."

Miriam slipped out of bed and took an address book from her purse. She raised the receiver from the cradle and hesitated. "This is a bit ghoulish, Holloway. Is it necessary?" Tears glistened in her eyes.

"It may help the police find out who killed Denise." Holloway kissed her on the forehead and went to the bathroom to give her privacy.

When he returned several minutes later, Miriam was sitting naked on the edge of the bed wiping tears from her cheeks. "AB-positive," was all she said before she curled up in Holloway's arms.

When she stopped crying, Holloway said gently, "When I left for Geneva last week a man followed me. I took his picture and he tried to stab me. I disarmed him and kept his knife. The FBI lab found fingerprints and human blood on it. The blood was AB-positive. I think he was the one who killed Denise. Tomorrow, I'll mail the evidence to the Kansas State Police and tell them that the FBI has the identity of the killer." *That should make Kruger's day.*

Miriam looked at him with alarm. "Where is this man now!"

"He's dead."

Miriam studied his face. "You killed him."

He would not lie to her, but it was foolish to admit to a killing. "He's dead and you're safe. That's all that matters." He tried to pull her closer, but she resisted.

"What about the people watching the house. Was he one of them?"

"No. Those are some 'friends' I picked up last week. I got into a little trouble in Geneva. It has nothing to do with you. They've been watching the house for several days. If they wanted to harm you, they would have made their move by now. They just want to keep an eye on me."

Miriam looked worried. "Does this have anything to do with my husband's business in Geneva?"

Holloway's jaw muscles flexed, betraying his irritation, but he responded with patience. "Frankly, I don't know why your husband went to Geneva. The man he was seen with has disappeared."

"Those people watching the house, are they CIA?" It was a fearful whisper that Holloway barely heard.

Holloway sat up in bed and took Miriam's face in his hands. "I don't want to lie to you, but you're asking too many questions. You don't have to worry about someone trying to kill you anymore. Now is the time to start living. I want you to do your living with me. Stay in D.C. for a while. Let's get to know each other under normal circumstances." He kissed her on the lips, but she was distracted.

"The man you . . . disarmed in Geneva, did he kill my husband?"

"I don't know, Miriam. Maybe I'll get the answer to that tomorrow."

"You'll tell me, if you find out?"

"If I can, yes."

Miriam curled up against Holloway, her heart pounding. One thought consumed her: *CIA people are watching the house.*

* * *

It was six o'clock in the morning. While Miriam slept in the hotel room, Holloway drove west on Cold Spring Lane. He had deliberately not called Dr. Hong for an appointment. Better to surprise him—and preempt his opportunity to check with the CIA. Traffic was light, and fifteen minutes later Holloway pulled to the curb in front of Dr. Hong's detached two-story house in Morgan Park, a middle class community on a hill just behind the university. He pressed the bell. Hong answered the door in his bathrobe and pajamas. He was a head shorter than Holloway and in his fifties. His full head of straight black hair and impish smile made him look younger.

"Yes?" said Hong blinking sleep out of his eyes.

Holloway introduced himself and said, "I'm from the Company. I'd like to discuss some consulting work you did for us."

Hong hesitated. He was surprised that he was still of interest to the CIA. "Please come in." He led Holloway through a foyer and into the surprise that was his living room. The room was massive. Hong had evidently gutted the second floor so that the room was actually two stories high. A large fan turned slowly in the ceiling, keeping the room airy. The sofa and chairs were arranged in a loose circle around a cocktail table in the center of the brown tile floor, accentuating the illusion of spaciousness. There was no other furniture and the walls were decorated tastefully with Oriental art.

"You are pleased with my home, Mr. Holloway?"

Holloway surveyed the room. "It reminds me of the nicer villas I saw in Vietnam."

"That is why I renovated in this manner, to remind me of home." Hong settled into a chair. "What can I do for you, Mr. Holloway?"

"I'm from the Inspector General's Office at the Company. We've had complaints that Admiral Schaeffer acted in an arbitrary manner when dismissing employees. As part of our effort to settle this matter, I'm interviewing all former employees who were fired or encouraged to terminate their employment, due to the admiral's intervention.

Hugh Stiles told me that the admiral dismissed you during the POW/MIA negotiations in Hanoi. Could you tell me what happened?"

The Vietnamese professor did not let it show, but he was pleased. At last Schaeffer's high-handed ways had gotten him into trouble. "Would you like a cigarette, Mr. Holloway?" Dr. Hong opened his gold case and extended it. Holloway declined. With unrestrained glee, the professor selected one for himself. "An unhealthy habit, but I enjoy it." He lit up and exhaled. The smoke drifted lazily toward the high ceiling. Hong cocked his head to one side. "The context of my termination is relevant. A brief history lesson might be in order."

Holloway nodded his agreement.

"In 1973 North Vietnam signed the Paris Peace Agreement under which American troops were withdrawn from South Vietnam. Article 8 of the Agreement provides for an exchange of prisoners of war, return of the remains of those who died, and an honest attempt to resolve the issue of those missing in action in North Vietnam." With a parenthetical touch of bile he added, "Once again, the communists agreed to anything that would further their politico-military objectives and the West accepted it at face value."

Holloway disagreed. "I don't think we had any illusions about the North Vietnamese. We were just tired of the war and wanted to get out."

Hong gave him a patronizing smile and continued his discourse. "In spite of the agreement in Paris, peace did not come to my country, nor did the communists act in good faith concerning the delivery of the remains of U.S. soldiers and airmen. During the two years between Paris and the fall of South Vietnam, the North Vietnamese communists returned the remains of only twenty-three Americans.

"After the war, the communist government of my homeland had only two major political objectives with regard to the United States. The first of these was diplomatic recognition. This would have conferred legitimacy upon their regime and raised its stature in the community of nations. Second, the communists wanted the United States to pay reparations for war damages or provide foreign aid to help modernize the Vietnamese economy. The United States, of course, was in no mood to grant either of those wishes. At that point, the communists made the decision to stall on the MIA issue until the United States agreed to diplomatic recognition and foreign aid. No substantial progress was made on these issues for several years, in spite of numerous meetings between U.S. and Vietnamese officials. With characteristic ruthlessness, the communists would periodically offer up the remains of a few MIAs to keep public pressure on the U.S. Government to make concessions.

"In 1986, a high-level delegation of U.S. Government officials visited Hanoi to try and resolve the MIA issue. There were people from Defense, State, and other interested agencies. Admiral Schaeffer was along, using a cover identity, to represent the intelligence community. My role was strictly that of trusted interpreter and adviser to Schaeffer.

"The MIA negotiations took place on two levels: the official and the private. In the official sessions, the U.S. and Vietnam discussed the humanitarian aspects of the MIA issue and considered some technical details: the number still unaccounted for, their names, crash sites, recovery of remains, and so forth. My observation was that these official sessions dealt almost exclusively with American concern for the return of MIAs. Previous attempts to mix political issues with the MIA problem had failed. With that in mind, a great effort was made by both sides, in the formal sessions, anyway, to eliminate politics. However, private meetings became the arena for dealing with political issues, which were the primary concern of the communists. That was where I got into trouble with Admiral Schaeffer.

"One evening the communists hosted a cocktail party for the American delegation. It was a pleasant enough affair. Near the end of the evening, one of the interpreters on the communist negotiating team called me aside. After some perfunctory chitchat, he told me that he understood I had connections with U.S. intelligence. I don't know how he knew. In any event, he told me to pass the word along through intelligence channels that Vietnam would drop its demands for war reparations and expedite the return of MIA remains in return for certain considerations."

"What considerations?" asked Holloway.

Hong ground out his cigarette and lit another. "The man told me that Vietnamese intelligence believed that certain assets held by U.S. citizens were the rightful property of the Socialist Republic of Vietnam. He was sure, he said, that it would be politically impossible for the U.S. Government to track down these assets. However, he wondered if the U.S. would allow a Vietnamese agent to pursue the assets in return for movement on the MIA issue. Specifically, he wanted permission for a Vietnamese agent, assigned to the U.N. delegation in New York, to conduct an investigation without hindrance from the F.B.I.

"I asked him what the alternative was and he said that not only would Vietnam continue to press its case for war damages, but that it would go public in the international press with allegations that U.S. citizens were holding Vietnamese assets. Also, there would be no further movement on the MIA issue until the foreign aid problem was resolved.

"Of course, I pointed out that the communists might be painting themselves into a corner by taking such a position, but he insisted that the information be passed along. I informed Admiral Schaeffer that same evening. I also told him that regardless of the impact on the MIA negotiations, I had serious reservations about allowing communist agents to roam the U.S. on what I assumed would be a witch-hunt for former South Vietnamese officials for God-knows-what purpose."

"What did Schaeffer say?"

"He didn't say anything at first. He just listened. But when I got to the part about American citizens holding Vietnamese assets, he became agitated and began asking very detailed questions, all of which concerned the asset issue. Who was holding the assets? What were the assets worth? What kind of assets? I had no answers for him. He found that annoying, then appeared to be relieved. That seemed a bit odd to me, but Admiral Schaeffer is an odd person.

"Again, I questioned the wisdom of allowing the communists free rein. He responded with anger. He told me that it was not my place to make those kinds of judgments. I reminded him that I was the CIA's consultant on matters related to communist Vietnam. He was not impressed and we parted on a rather hostile note. He told me that he would handle the problem and that I was to have no more private conversations with my counterparts on the communist delegation. That was an awkward restriction, but it was my intent to respect the admiral's wishes.

Unfortunately, the very next day, the communist interpreter cornered me at lunch and asked if I had passed on his message. I told him that I would put it in the proper channels when I returned to Washington. Obviously I could not tell him that there was a senior intelligence officer there in Hanoi with us. At that moment, Admiral Schaeffer entered the dining room and saw us talking. I could tell that he was furious, but he never mentioned the incident. Schaeffer was a man of action. Two days later, a new interpreter, my replacement, arrived. The admiral dismissed me and I left immediately for the United States. From that moment on, the Agency had no need for my services. I was kept on retainer for a time," Hong smiled, "—a bribe, no doubt, to ensure my silence—but I was never called for advice. I know that Schaeffer was responsible."

Holloway asked, "Did you hear anything more about the Vietnamese sending agents to the States to look for those assets?"

"No. I was completely out of the Agency's information loop."

"Did you monitor MIA negotiations after you were dismissed?"

"Yes."

"And?"

"The communist Vietnamese continued to produce a set or two of remains of U.S. personnel when it suited their purpose, but no substantial progress has been made."

"Why do you suppose that is, assuming that their agents have permission to operate in the States?"

Hong exhaled a stream of blue smoke toward the ceiling. "Either their agents are operating without permission or they have found the so-called assets they were looking for and are dragging their feet on the MIA issue until these assets are turned over to Hanoi. I think the latter is much more likely."

"You've been very helpful, Dr. Hong. Thank you."

* * *

Admiral Schaeffer strode along a corridor on the first floor of the Pentagon. He wore civilian clothes and carried a stylish gym bag. His work as intelligence coordinator brought him to "The Building" frequently and, on these occasions, he took the opportunity to get in some exercise. Schaeffer pushed through the swinging doors and walked into the sunlight of a windy May morning. After a short walk across the concrete ramp, he disappeared into the Pentagon Officers' Athletic Club, known affectionately by its initials as the "Poe-ack." Ten minutes later, he emerged from the Club's side door in a black and gold Gortex running suit and joined the throngs of runners on their lunchtime jog into Washington. As he ran, the plastic nametag attached to the laces of his right shoe slapped the top of his foot, breaking his concentration. He paused and secured the tag by tucking it between the tongue and laces of his Puma, then loped off in the direction of the Arlington Memorial Bridge.

The lunchtime run had become an accepted Pentagon ritual that started daily at about eleven-thirty, when many officers left their desks for the POAC, and concluded when they returned at one-fifteen or so. The extra forty-five minutes tacked to the lunch hour was tolerated by Pentagon brass in the name of stress reduction through physical fitness. The alternative was to keep stressed-out officers tied to their desks until the Pentagon pressure cooker served them up as heart attack victims. However, the daily exercise regimen had not been a total success. Occasionally, one of "The Building's" thousands of workaholics who smoked like a fiend at his desk and ran like a fiend during his exercise period would drop dead in the POAC locker room after the lunchtime run. Just such a situation had occurred several years earlier. An officer was found dead there in his running suit and without identification. Tragedy was compounded by embarrassment as it had taken a major effort to identify the deceased before the end of the workday. That incident resulted in the rule that all POAC members would wear a plastic nametag like the one that had been slapping Admiral Schaeffer's foot.

The admiral jogged over the Arlington Memorial Bridge, admiring its massive statuary as he went. At the Lincoln Memorial he ran a wide arc around the south side and headed east along the Reflecting Pool to the Washington Monument. By this time he had worked up a good sweat. As he crossed 17th Street, a jogger in blue shorts and a T-shirt sprinted up to the admiral and fell in beside him. It was Hugh Stiles.

"Good afternoon, Admiral."

Schaeffer kept running. "Hello, Stiles. Good day for a run." The two men jogged past the Washington Monument. After they crossed 14th Street, Schaeffer said, "Let's walk a bit."

Schaeffer strolled along The Mall, breathing deeply and enjoying the sights and sounds of downtown Washington. After a while he said, "I wanted you to meet me here because there are too many eyes and ears at Langley."

Stiles bobbed his head in agreement.

"That was a good report you left for me last night. Did you include everything you know about Can and Holloway?"

"Yes, sir."

"What kind of files have you been keeping on Can?"

Stiles was uncomfortable. "Just some informal notes. I thought documentation would be required if Can got into—"

Schaeffer cut him off. "Do you have them with you?"

"Yes, sir. Just as you requested." Stiles reached under his T-shirt and took a sealed brown envelope out of his waistband. Schaeffer stuffed the envelope into a large pocket on the front of his running suit.

"Copies?"

"No, sir."

"Good man," said Schaeffer, pleasantly. "What about your friend at Geneva Station? I assume he has detailed surveillance reports on Colonel Can."

"I only requested summaries: places Can visited and people he contacted."

"I want the complete reports," said Schaeffer. "Get in touch with your friend in Geneva and make the arrangements. Don't tell him any more than he needs to know and be sure he keeps his mouth shut. If there's any problem at all with getting the documents back here, you go pick them up yourself. Take some leave and fly to Geneva. You'll be reimbursed, of course. I'm flying to Latin America tomorrow for ten days. The day after I get back, I want you to meet me right here and put those reports in my hand."

"Aye, aye, sir."

"About this man, Holloway, you were right to bring him to my attention. That took a lot of guts, considering that you had to expose your unauthorized surveillance of Colonel Can." Stiles cringed. "But," continued Schaeffer, "you've got good instincts, good sources, and initiative. I admire those qualities." Schaeffer stopped and turned to Stiles. Gravely, he said, "We've got to find out what

Holloway is up to. And Can, too," added the admiral, for Stiles' benefit. Schaeffer already knew that Can was presently swimming in Lake Geneva and wouldn't be coming up for air. "Let me know if Holloway contacts you again."

Now, Stiles had to make his move. "Shall I send the report through my division chief, Admiral, or directly to you?"

Schaeffer gobbled up the bait. "Report directly to me. No need to bother your chief with this. Let's keep this between us for the time being." At the admiral's lead, they turned and began to retrace their steps. "And Stiles, no more 'EYES ONLY' messages on my desk. They attract undue attention." The admiral handed Stiles a slip of paper. "If you run into an emergency, call this number and leave your first name with the answering service. Someone will get back to you. Questions?"

"No, sir."

The admiral began to jog again, with Stiles trotting at his side. "This might be important. Do a good job with it and I'll take care of you. Keep in touch." Schaeffer accelerated in the direction of the Washington Monument. Hugh Stiles peeled off and headed for his car, which was parked on Constitution Avenue. The man called Pinchot watched him from a Mall bench.

As Schaeffer approached the Lincoln Memorial, he slowed to a walk and stopped next to a tall man carrying a coat over his arm. "Hello, Jules."

"Hello to you," said Jules Vaterman. "How did it go with Stiles?"

"Not good. Holloway showed up at the Agency asking questions about me and Can, and that idiot, Stiles, spilled his guts about the Hanoi trip. He tried to cover his ass with a memo when he realized he was in over his head."

"How much does Stiles know?"

"Not enough to be a problem. I told him to get back to me if Holloway contacts him. I've got a man on Stiles who knows Holloway by sight. If Holloway meets Stiles, we'll have him."

"Your people shouldn't have lost Holloway in the first place."

Schaeffer was irritated. "The guy is smart, Jules. He knew we would be waiting for him when he came back from Geneva. So, he's been staying away from his apartment. Maybe he's tracking some new leads."

"Leads? What leads could he have gotten in Geneva? You told me—" Vaterman realized that he was shouting and lowered his voice to a harsh whisper. "You told me that Ackerman stonewalled him about Dillworth. What leads could he have gotten?"

"Maybe Holloway got something out of Can."

"How can that be? You told me that Can damn near killed Holloway." There was a pause while Vaterman backed away from the attack and took a more conciliatory approach. "Are we overlooking something obvious?"

"Miriam Slayton is an obvious answer," said Schaeffer, angered by the thought of it. "If that bitch sent Holloway just to yank my chain, I'll wring her neck."

In a firm voice, Vaterman said, "You will not wring her neck. Miriam Slayton must be treated with care. She has the glass ball and we can't afford to let her drop it. Besides, I don't think she's behind Holloway. Remember, it was Miriam who told you that Holloway was in Kansas asking about her husband. That's how we found out about him in the first place."

"That might have been a trick," suggested the admiral.

"I don't think so. Before we take any action, we need to know who sent Holloway to Kansas. Who is he working for? A newspaper? Is he a Senate or House investigator? What?"

Frustrated, Schaeffer ran a hand through his iron-gray hair and barked, "To hell with that! This is taking up too much of my time. Meanwhile, we're just sitting around waiting for Holloway to stumble onto something important. I'll have my people take him out on sight and put an end to this."

Keeping to the conciliatory course, Vaterman asked, "Have you talked to the Embassy Man about our difficulties with Mr. Holloway?"

"No. You know he doesn't want to be contacted unless there's an emergency. Might blow his cover," said Schaeffer derisively.

"Well," said Vaterman in that professorial tone that Schaeffer despised, "my assessment is that we are in a crisis which extends beyond the elusive and worrisome Mr. Holloway. Dillworth and Miriam Slayton are in hiding. Colonel Can is dead and, sooner or later, we'll have to deal with the Vietnamese on that issue. We need a plan of action. Perhaps the Embassy Man would like to have some input. I would suggest that you not take any precipitous action until we discuss this with him."

Schaeffer was angry. "'No precipitous action.' Is that how you'd vote?"

"If it came to that, yes, but I hope we're not choosing sides just yet."

Schaeffer cautioned, "Ackerman will vote with me."

"Trung is my man," countered Vaterman. "So, we have a tie and the Embassy Man will have to break it. You can try to force a vote before you leave tomorrow or wait for our Committee meeting to present your case."

"Whatever you say, Jules." Schaeffer wanted to end the conversation.

"Cheer up, Admiral. There is some good news. The Iran-Contra investigation is bypassing us completely." Vaterman headed off in the direction of the Treasury building.

As Schaeffer jogged past the Lincoln Memorial, his thoughts were on damage control, not assessment. *To hell with you, Jules Vaterman, and the embassy man, too. When I get back from Latin America, I'm going to fix the Holloway-Slayton-Dillworth situation. I'll punch a few tickets and we can argue about it at the funeral services.*

CHAPTER 12

They drove toward Washington in silence. Holloway tried to make sense of what he had learned, while Miriam washed away that half-awake feeling with sips of black coffee from a large Styrofoam cup. When they entered the Baltimore Harbor Tunnel, she was alert enough for conversation.

"What did Dr. Hong have to say?"

"Nothing about your husband." The words came out in an unfeeling monotone, causing Holloway to realize that he was very tired. A week of travelling and the previous night's amorous exertions with Miriam had taken their toll. He yearned to be in his own bed—alone.

Miriam looked at him. "Is that your polite way of telling me I have no need to know?"

Holloway gave her a tired smile. "No, sweetheart. It's my way of saying 'no innocent victims this time.' " He put his hand on her thigh. "If you don't know anything, you can't get into trouble."

They emerged from the tunnel into bright sunlight. Holloway moved into the left lane and pressed the gas pedal. He wanted to get home. Miriam was giving him a cold, appraising stare.

"What?" he asked.

"Has it occurred to you that just being with you means trouble for me?"

"What are you talking about?" He slowed the car and took the ramp to the Baltimore-Washington Expressway.

"I'm afraid. I don't want to go back to a house that's being watched."

Holloway gave the matter some thought and his jaw muscles tightened. "Neither do I," he said, angrily.

They pulled off the road at the first rest stop with telephones, and Holloway dialed the chairman of his neighborhood Crime Watch committee. The man, a retired Foreign Service officer, was at home. Holloway talked to him for several minutes and they agreed on how the matter would be handled. Then, Holloway rejoined Miriam for the trip home.

* * *

With Pinchot and his blue Ford now assigned to follow Hugh Stiles, the person know as Tom Braxton was manning the stakeout near Holloway's apartment. He sat in a black Toyota parked on a side street that gave him an excellent view of Holloway's front door. Most stakeouts were boring, and this one was no exception. There was hardly any traffic. In fact, almost nothing had moved on the street since Donna's departure for work at 8 a.m. An hour earlier, an old man had walked by with his dog. Nothing special. Except that the old man, in accordance with Holloway's instructions, had memorized the Toyota's license number and a description of its occupant. Braxton was too absorbed with the morning paper to notice policemen approaching on either side of his car.

The one on the driver's side startled Braxton when he said, "Keep both hands in sight and step out of the car, please."

Braxton did as he was told while he went through a "What-is-this-all-about-officer?" routine, but the policemen had a routine of their own.

"Lean forward and put your hands on the roof of the car." One officer frisked Braxton while the other stood nearby with his hand resting on his holster. Braxton was glad that he was not armed.

"Driver's license and registration?" Braxton handed them over.

"What's your business in this neighborhood, Mr. Braxton?"

"I'm in public relations. I'm here to see a prospective client."

"You've been observed sitting here for several hours. Why haven't you left your car?"

"I did go to his house as soon as I arrived, but he was out. I'm waiting for him to come home." The policemen exchanged skeptical glances. "There's a lot of money riding on this account. I really don't want to miss this guy," explained Braxton.

"Who's your prospective client, sir?"

Braxton had not done enough homework. So, he gave the only name on the street that he knew. "Ed Holloway. Lives right over there." Braxton pointed to Holloway's house.

The second policeman lifted the flap on his holster and rested his hand on the pistol grip. The officer who had been asking the questions removed the handcuffs from his belt and said, "Turn around, Mr. Braxton, and put your hands behind your back."

Braxton did as he was told. "What's the problem?"

"It was Mr. Holloway who complained that you were watching his house. We're going to take you to the station and sort this out."

* * *

After Holloway dropped the rental car off in downtown Washington, he and Miriam took a cab to his apartment in Virginia. On the way home he told her how he had handled the "watchers." To his surprise, Miriam did not appear to be relieved. When they arrived at the apartment, Holloway went straight to bed. While he slept, Miriam prowled the house like a caged cat, more worried than she had been before.

It was eight o'clock in the evening when Holloway awakened to the sound of voices in the apartment. He lay there half asleep until he could identify them. Donna, Miriam, and Dan were having dinner in the kitchen. Holloway struggled into a cotton exercise suit and slippers, and followed his nose toward the origin of the food aromas.

Donna saw him first and her eyes widened in mock surprise. "My God," she exclaimed, "It's alive!"

Holloway shuffled into the kitchen. "It wouldn't make much difference what condition I'm in. You guys are making enough noise to wake the dead." He got jeers from Donna and Dan as he made for the coffee pot. Holloway poured himself a cup and joined them at the table. Miriam smiled, but was withdrawn.

They were having wine and spaghetti, one of Holloway's favorite meals. "Is this a welcome home party?" he asked.

"Actually, no," replied Donna. "It's a meeting. We thought you had died in there and we were divvying up your furniture."

Dan laughed, but Miriam was not amused.

Donna took note and changed the subject, while she fixed Holloway a plate of spaghetti. "We're glad to have you home. Aside from the fact that we didn't know where or how you were, there *is* a business to run."

"Sorry I worried you. I had business that took longer than expected."

Holloway's friends sat in silent expectation while he swirled up a fork of spaghetti and put it into his mouth.

"Well, are you going to tell us about it?" asked Donna.

Holloway gave her a cheerful and simple, "No."

"No? That's all we get for worrying ourselves sick about you?"

"That's all I'm going to say about it." Holloway forked up another portion of spaghetti while they all looked on in disbelief. "Now," he said through a mouthful of spaghetti, "let me ask you a question. What do you know about Admiral Gordon M. Schaeffer of the CIA?"

Donna didn't want to talk about the Agency. She avoided Holloway's eyes and twisted a cigarette into her rhinestone-studded holder.

It was Dan Vogle who started the ball rolling. "If I remember correctly, he was the project manager for the DCI's government-wide intelligence coordination function, the poor bastard."

"What else do you know about him, Dan?"

"Nothing. My bailiwick was computers, remember."

"What about you, Donna?" asked Holloway.

Donna was feeling conflict. She was curious about any new leads Holloway had discovered, but reluctant to be drawn into his dangerous game. With very deliberately movements, Donna took the cigarette holder from her mouth and balanced it on the edge of an ashtray. "I knew Schaeffer."

Holloway waited for her to continue and became irritated when she didn't. "Did you know him in the Biblical sense, or was it a relationship you can share with us?"

Donna glared at him. "Don't get yourself in an uproar, Holloway. I didn't know Schaeffer personally. I heard about him from my co-workers in Research. I'll tell you this much, if Schaeffer was involved in a project, people ran the other way. He came to the Company about the time you left. Knew as much about intelligence as my foot." Donna made a face. "The front office detailed Research to brief him up to speed for his new job. The Research comers were jockeying to get visibility with the new fair-haired boy. As things turned out, those briefings were not the plumbs everyone expected them to be. Schaeffer was a nitpicker, always eager to prove that we didn't know as much as we should. The briefings turned into fencing matches, and Research always lost. Every answer generated two new questions from Schaeffer and he wasn't kind to people who didn't have ready answers." Donna paused to take a drag on her cigarette.

"Schaeffer pummeled us for a couple of months, until he found a new set of whipping boys in the Ops Directorate. By the time those briefings ended, he had earned the reputation of being—and here I quote one of my most respected former colleagues—'a first-rate SOB with a second-rate mind.' " Donna forced a blast of blue smoke out the side of her mouth. "We never understood why he was so popular with the Director, but Schaeffer could do no wrong."

Miriam came to life. "Where does Schaeffer fit into the CIA hierarchy?"

Donna explained, glad for an opportunity to show that she was superior to Miriam in at least one area. "The Director of Central Intelligence has two major responsibilities. One is Director of the CIA. The other is coordinating all government intelligence activities. The DCI has a high-ranking military man or civilian out at Langley as his deputy for running the CIA. Schaeffer is the DCI's deputy for the government-wide intelligence coordinating function. He has an office at Langley, too, but operates most of the time out of an office in downtown Washington."

Holloway addressed Miriam. "Do you know Schaeffer?"

There was the slightest hesitation before Miriam answered. "Yes. Jack brought him to the house several times. I thought he worked at the Pentagon."

"What did Schaeffer and your husband talk about?"

"The same things that everyone in Washington talks about. I don't remember anything unusual."

"Did they discuss the arms-for-hostages deal with Iran or the Iran-Contra money?"

"No."

"What about the Contras?" Holloway pressed her.

"No." Miriam blurted out the 'no' answer faster than she should have. Holloway made a note, but didn't pursue the issue.

"Did you ever hear them talk about Vietnam?"

"No. I told you in Kansas that Jack was careful to keep the details of his work from me." Then, she added caustically, "Isn't that the way you spooks like to operate?" Her eyes locked onto a bewildered Holloway.

Dan Vogle broke the tension. "Coffee anyone?" He began filling their cups.

Holloway broke eye contact with Miriam and turned to Donna. "I understand that Schaeffer is not a career intelligence officer?"

"Lord, no." Donna waved her hand in a dismissal gesture. "He's blue water Navy. Commanded a destroyer in the South China Sea near the end of the Vietnam War. I hear he had only one other intelligence assignment."

"What qualifies him to be one of the DCI's principal deputies?"

"Beats me," said Donna.

Dan Vogle saw Miriam glaring at Holloway again, apparently not thrilled with the conversation. "Well," he said, "this is all very stimulating, but we do have a business to run. If the partners would care to join me in the basement, I will share my progress reports with them. Would you excuse us, Mrs. Slayton?"

Miriam remained in the kitchen to do the dishes while the trio discussed business in the basement and sorted out their tasks for the remainder of the week. When they were finished, Donna asked Holloway, "Will you be working a full day tomorrow?"

Holloway shrugged. "I'll give you half a day, in the morning. That's the best I can do."

Donna uttered a sigh. "The Slayton case?"

"Yeah."

Donna slammed down the project book and stomped off in search of a fresh cigarette.

Dan Vogle was still eager for news. "What happened in Switzerland, Ed?"

"What makes you think I went to Switzerland?"

Vogle smiled. "Miriam told us over dinner. She said you found the guy who killed her cousin." Thoughtfully, he added, "That didn't seem to comfort her much. She's still as jumpy as she was while you were gone."

That disturbed Holloway, too, but he didn't want to discuss it. He gave Vogle a noncommittal, "Humm," and asked if any mail had come for him while he was away.

On her way back from the cigarette hunt, Donna dropped a bundle of letters and messages into Holloway's lap. "Some creep kept calling the office claiming to be your 'friend from Georgetown.' He wants you to get in touch with him right away. Wouldn't leave his number. Our mystery client, I presume?"

Ellis Eaton, Holloway thought. *What am I going to tell* him?

Donna sat down and crossed her legs. "You might as well tell us what you've been up to. We're simply dying of curiosity." She made the statement sarcastic to hide the truth of it.

"I thought you didn't want to be involved."

"I don't," she said emphatically. Then, with eyes blazing and teeth clenched, she hissed, "Now, will you please tell me what the hell is going on?"

Holloway knew that she would pester him until he told her. So, he did. "Jack Slayton had a connection in Geneva that he wanted to keep secret. I went to Switzerland to check it out." *No need to tell them that Sid was there, too.* "I may have stumbled into a CIA cover organization for supplying the Contras—one that hasn't been made public yet."

"You mean an organization in addition to the Secord-Hakim group?" asked Vogle.

"Yes."

Donna bit her knuckle.

Vogle whistled. "That'll blow the Iran-Contra scandal wide open. The CIA claims it had nothing to do with the Contra pipeline."

"Is Admiral Schaeffer involved?" asked Donna.

"I don't know," answered Holloway, thoughtfully. "I connected him and Slayton to another operation. They may have been involved in keeping the FBI from conducting surveillance of a Vietnamese intelligence agent. That same agent killed Miriam's cousin in Kansas and tried to kill me in Geneva." Holloway raised his palms to head off their questions. "I don't know any of the whys, yet."

Vogle wanted to know if Schaeffer and Slayton were connected to The Seven.

"I don't know, Dan. I just don't have enough information to make that connection."

Donna half heard the conversation. She was lost in thought. "Forget about operations," she advised. "Concentrate on people. If 'The Seven' does exist, it's a tightly knit group. You don't plot against the President with people you don't know and trust. Slayton is the key. Find his close friends and you find the conspirators. Go for the commonalities: his chummies in law school, Army friends, and so on. How many of them were in the White House or the Administration with him? That's the approach I would take."

"Is Admiral Schaeffer one of Slayton's old friends?" asked Vogle.

"Good question," noted Holloway. "Let's check him out." Holloway got up and started to pace while he considered method. "Dan, I want you to call the Navy's public affairs office tomorrow. Tell them that you're writing a book on, say, the Navy's role in the final evacuation of Vietnam. Say that you want to look at the evacuation through the eyes of the ships' captains. You need profiles of some of the skippers involved. What we're really after is Schaeffer's history."

Dan Vogle looked puzzled. "Maybe I'm missing something here. The Navy gives out information on its admirals all the time. Why don't I just ask for a profile on Schaeffer and forget the smoke screen?"

"Because, dear boy," said Donna, "whenever you request information about military individuals in sensitive positions at the Agency, such as the one Schaeffer occupies, your name is run through the computer to find out who you are. Schaeffer might even be notified of your interest in him. Would you like that?"

With a sheepish grin, Vogle said, "I think I like Ed's idea better."

Holloway turned to Donna. "I didn't want to ask you, but since Dan brought it up, do you think you could get us something on Schaeffer through your connection at the Agency?"

A cloud seemed to come over Donna. "I could get a resumé of his unclassified file, but I'm not sure I want to use my friend like that." There was an exchange of knowing glances between Donna and Ed. "Are you planning to use your, ah, influence," Donna's eyes dropped momentarily to Holloway's crotch, "to pump Miriam Slayton about her husband's other friends?"

Anger seared through Holloway. He said, icily, "I'll do whatever it takes. Will you?"

Donna closed her eyes and turned away.

Ever the man in the middle, Vogle sat through a few seconds of uncomfortable silence before clearing his throat. "Ahem. Well, tomorrow will be busy. I'm going home and get some sleep. Don't bother to show me out. Just keep on enjoying yourselves." Donna and Ed glared at Vogle's back as he bounded up the cellar steps.

When Vogle had gone, Holloway turned to Donna. "Want to tell me what's wrong?" He was surprised to see tears on her cheeks.

She produced a tissue and dabbed them away, "Too many things happening at once, I suppose. I'm mad. I'm scared. Who was watching the house, Agency people?"

"I think so. They got onto me in Geneva. They're probably trying to find out who I'm working for and what I know."

"And what will they do when they find out?" She stood in front of him, her large expressive eyes reflecting anger and fear. "What will they do then, Holloway?"

"I don't know."

"You don't know?" She brought her face close to his and said in a harsh whisper. "Take a wild guess!"

Holloway sighed. "Is that the only thing bothering you?"

"No." Her voice was firm. "I want you to close the damn heating vent in your bedroom. When it's open, your mating activities can be heard all over the house."

Holloway left Donna and went upstairs to his apartment. It was quiet when he entered. Miriam was asleep. Having napped since the afternoon, Holloway was wide awake and eager for action. It was a little before ten, still early enough for a conference with Sid Mitchell.

* * *

Mitchell lived on City Line Avenue in a two-story fixer-upper. He let Holloway in and led him past a plastic bubble of dust and building materials that was being converted into a living room. "The contractor is making a career of remodeling the place. C'mon upstairs. You can watch me pack."

"Where are you going?" Holloway asked, tromping up the steps to Mitchell's bedroom.

"I'm accompanying the First Lady to New York."

"When do you leave?"

"Day after tomorrow. I'll be back by the end of the week."

Holloway was disappointed. He had hoped that Mitchell would be available to help him with the Slayton case. He sat on the edge of the bed while Mitchell expertly folded clothing into two suitcases lying open on the floor.

"What brings you out at this time of night?" asked Mitchell. "Now that you've reclaimed your street from the CIA, I thought you'd be at home attending to domestic matters with Mrs. Slayton." Sid winked and treated his friend to a sly smile. He had been drinking. There was an empty whiskey glass nearby.

"Things are not going as well as I had hoped with Miriam," Holloway confessed.

"And you came here to seek the counsel of a man more experienced in these matters, a man older and wiser than yourself?" deadpanned Mitchell.

"Go to hell, Sid."

Mitchell laughed. "Okay. Okay. What's the problem?"

"When I told Miriam that the Vietnamese who killed her cousin was permanently out of the way, I thought she would be relieved. That didn't happen. She's still scared to death, and not terribly happy with me."

Mitchell shrugged. "She's got a right to be scared. That Vietnamese was out to kill her, not her cousin. If I was in her shoes, I wouldn't rest easy until I knew why."

"That's the other side of the problem," complained Holloway. "I can't find out what the Vietnamese guy was up to unless I keep digging into Jack Slayton's past. Miriam doesn't want me to dig."

Holloway rambled on, the dam of his pent up frustrations broken. "Donna is irritable, too, and giving me more grief than usual. One minute she wants to know all about the Slayton case. The next minute, she doesn't want any part of it. She even cried tonight." Holloway threw up his hands and began pacing around the suitcases.

Mitchell dropped the shirt he was trying to find a place for and cleared a seat for himself on the cluttered dresser. He watched Holloway pace for a while and said, "You don't know, do you?"

"Know what?"

Mitchell hesitated. "Donna is very worried about you and this Slayton thing." Holloway didn't react because this was not news to him. Mitchell took a deep breath and tried again. "Let me put it another way. Donna loves you."

"What!"

"She's had the hots for you for a long time. She wouldn't tell you while you were mourning your family. After that, you started chasing women and she wanted you to get that out of your system. I'm sure that some of her strange behavior is the result of Miriam Slayton sleeping upstairs in your bed."

"Aw, come on, Sid. Are you sure?"

"Donna calls me at least twice a week to talk about you. She made me promise not to tell you, but that was before Miriam arrived on the scene. Now, it's cruel for Donna to be in that situation. You need to fix it. She won't. She wants to win you 'fair and square,' whatever that means."

Sid pushed himself off the dresser and continued packing. "You and Donna are a lot alike, you know. Everything has to be done according to your own uncompromising personal codes." Mitchell waved his arm in a grandiose gesture. "Let truth, justice, and fair play prevail." He had been drinking quite a lot.

"What else is on your mind, Ed? You didn't come over here just to get my advice on women."

"When we were in Geneva, Jessica Talbot told us that the Pentagon wouldn't give her the service records for Dillworth and Ackerman. I want those records, Sid. You can request them through the White House and nobody will ask questions. I want Slayton's records, too, and whatever any other agencies have on the activities of Vietnamese intelligence agents in the United States for the past five years. Can you get that for me?" Holloway braced himself for massive resistance.

Instead, Mitchell said, "Sure." He picked through the clutter on his dresser, found a set of keys, and motioned for Holloway to follow him across the hall to his office. Mitchell unlocked his desk and took out several stacks of photocopies. "This is the goods on Dillworth, Ackerman, and Slayton: service records, background investigations, newspaper clippings on Slayton, the whole shebang. If it ain't here, I couldn't get it without making a fuss. I didn't ask the CIA for any records. If WorldCorp is their front, a request would have sent up the red flags. You can take this stuff home in that box over there."

Holloway smiled and shook his head. "In addition to being a miracle worker, you're also a mind reader."

Mitchell waved off the compliments. "I knew you'd ask for these. They're yours. Burn 'em when you're finished."

"I appreciate this, Sid, but I'm surprised. What's the deal?"

"No deal. Let's say you caught me in a generous mood."

"As long as you're feeling generous, how about getting me some information on a Vietnamese named Buie Trung. He runs East Asia Imports, a string of expensive gift shops in the Baltimore-Washington area. Trung has recent CIA connections and maybe some old ones. Run his name by Immigration, the FBI, and State Department intelligence."

Mitchell gave him an exasperated look. "How do you spell the name?" Holloway told him. "Why don't you just put me on your payroll as a full-time employee?"

"I already have. You're in charge of my Dead Cat Bureau." Holloway laughed.

Getting the records on the WorldCorp gang improved Holloway's disposition. Now, he was in the mood to handle another difficult problem. He checked his watch. It was not too late. "Sid, can I have some privacy here? I need to make a call." Mitchell went out, shaking his head and mumbling about the brass of some people. Holloway closed the door and telephoned Ellis Eaton.

It was a short conversation. No, Holloway had not disturbed Eaton. Yes, he could come by for a brief meeting.

Holloway picked up the carton of photocopies and carried it downstairs. Sid Mitchell was in the kitchen pouring himself another drink. "Have a nightcap," he said.

Holloway waved off the alcohol and found a cola in the fridge. Straddling a chair opposite Mitchell, he said, "I'm surprised that you didn't give me an argument about these records. I thought you had washed your hands of Slayton and WorldCorp. What made you change your mind?"

"I gave your little witch hunt a lot of thought on the flight back from Geneva. My business is protecting the First Family. If there is a conspiracy against the President and I didn't help you uncover it, I wouldn't be doing my job. Inaction might even be considered . . . treason." Mitchell winced at the sound of the word and took a drink.

"Suppose," he speculated, "you find that WorldCorp is a CIA front to supply the Contras. Then what? Have you given any more thought to what you would do with that information?"

Holloway looked at his friend sideways. "This isn't another 'dead cat' lecture, is it?"

"No. This is the one about politics and intelligence. But first let me tell you my bias about the Iran-Contra scandal. Personally, I don't give a damn if the President traded arms for hostages. He did exactly what I would want him to do if *I* was chained to the wall in some Beirut shithole." Mitchell's voice grew louder and Holloway noticed the alcoholic gleam in his eyes. "And I don't care if the Contras were financed by ripping off the Iranians, or by the CIA, or by Ollie North selling White House furniture at a fucking flea market. I'm just glad that somebody had the balls to deal with communism in Central America."

Mitchell pulled at his drink, which seemed to subdue him a bit, and resumed his lecture in a more conversational tone. "This is a sick, damned town, Ed. The Iran-Contra mess is a product of a gutless, meddling Congress. They have eighteen months to get a budget passed. That's their job. Do they ever pass one on time? Hell no. Why? 'Cause they're busy doing the President's job in foreign policy. They're doing the CIA's job in covert operations. And they do all that about as well as they pass budgets." He uttered a weak laugh. "Well, now you know where I'm coming from. That's my own unsophisticated, personal, damned view."

"So, what's your point, Sid?"

"My point is that there are powerful people in Washington who think that the CIA should be out of the covert operations business altogether. If WorldCorp turns out to be a CIA front for the Contras, that fact will be used to bash the Agency and the President. Congress would have an excuse to go after the Agency's covert actions capability, maybe even chop the Agency into several smaller ones. At best, the CIA would be right back where it was seven years ago— flat on its ass. That can't be good for the country, Ed, and I don't think that's what you really want."

Holloway was puzzled and irritated, "What do *you* want, Sid? First you give me these records. Now, you're giving me reasons not to look at them."

Mitchell leaned across the table, suppressing his own anger. "Damn it! Did I say, 'don't look'? I just want you to know what the stakes are. If it gets out that the CIA was supplying the Contras through WorldCorp, there will be a political bloodletting like you've never seen. You'd better be able to live with the fallout that you generate. Besides, you should give some thought to your own future. You were lucky in Geneva. There are still a few CIA hoods who would cut your throat on the Capitol steps at high noon if they knew where your investigation was headed. And what about your business? You've got a lot of hard-liners on your client list. Drop a dime on the Agency and they'll drop you like a hot rock. You know that." Holloway did know it. "It took Donna years to build that business. If you don't care about yourself, think of her."

* * *

Holloway did think about Donna, all the way to Georgetown. Donna in danger of losing some business? Quite possible. Donna in love with him? Doubtful. Sid always exaggerated when he drank. Still, there was merit in what he said about the political repercussions. Bottom line: he had the WorldCorp records. Unfortunately, Sid's comments had complicated his life and a visit with Eaton would probably not simplify it. Holloway rang his employer's doorbell.

Impeccably dressed as usual, Eaton opened the door with the gravity of an undertaker. "Good evening, Edward." Holloway almost laughed. "You've been out of touch for a while." The statement was meant as a reprimand.

No relief here, thought Holloway. "A personal problem came up. I had to take care of it."

"Nothing serious, I trust?" Eaton led the way to his study.

"No, nothing serious, just time consuming."

"I called your office several times," said Eaton, lowering himself into his desk chair as he gestured for Holloway to sit on the couch.

Holloway noted that Eaton did not offer drinks. This meeting would probably be short and unpleasant. "Did you want anything special or just a progress report?" asked Holloway.

Eaton leaned forward, hands clasped like a priest. "I was hoping for a *final* report. When you returned the Tower Commission documents, I assumed that your inquiry was completed."

Holloway tried to sound casual. "I've got a few loose ends to tie up. I'll have something to you in a couple of weeks."

"Two weeks. That's out of the question. Unless," Eaton raised an eyebrow, "you have some evidence that 'The Seven' exists?" Holloway did not respond. "Do you?"

"No."

"Well, then, what's the holdup?"

"I'm just being thorough. You do want me to be thorough, don't you?"

"Yes, yes, of course." Eaton waved impatiently. "But speed is also essential. I made that clear at the outset. The President is under tremendous pressure from Congress, the media, and even his political supporters to get to the bottom of this Iran-Contra business. He's trying to stay out of the fray as much as possible until he has the results of your inquiry, among other things. It's essential that he know if there is any truth to Slayton's allegations before he moves decisively. The President has asked me repeatedly about this matter. I can't continue to put him off. It's getting to be an embarrassment. I need your conclusions now."

"And I need two weeks," said Holloway, stubbornly, but he knew that he would not get them unless he gave Eaton something in return. "I have a few new leads to check. If they turn out to be dry holes, the inquiry is finished."

Eaton looked at him suspiciously. "What sort of leads? Did you find something in the Tower Commission documents?"

"I have another source."

"Edward, this is no time to be mysterious. I'll see the President tomorrow. He will want something to justify any further delay. What, specifically, are you working on and who is your source?"

"I came across documents that might identify some new Iran-Contra players. I need time to evaluate them. My source wants to remain anonymous."

Eaton looked incredulous. "Surely, you trust me with your source's identity."

"It's not a matter of trusting you, Ellis. I gave my word."

Eaton sat back in his chair, eyeing Holloway with cold detachment. "And what must I say to the President tomorrow—'Trust me'?"

"Why not?"

* * *

While Ellis Eaton was saying an unhappy farewell to Holloway in Georgetown, Admiral Schaeffer was at Fort McNair, on the other side of the city, with a visitor of his own. The admiral strolled along the grassy banks of the Potomac with Tom Braxton. Braxton had just been released from custody after a day of fruitless interrogation by the Alexandria Police Department. The admiral was unhappy. He had to interrupt preparations for his trip to Latin America in order to arrange an after-the-fact alibi for Braxton. A CIA proprietary firm had been located to back up Braxton's public relations story with a convoluted tale of mistaken identity involving "another Mister Holloway." Fortunately, the police had accepted the explanation, but the problem of dealing with Holloway remained. And, of course, there was Braxton, who, in the admiral's view, was not only blown but stupid.

Schaeffer was irate. "How the hell could you let yourself be caught outside of Holloway's house without even a believable cover story, for Chrissakes?" The question was not meant to be answered. Schaeffer already knew the details of the disaster.

"Not only did you blow the surveillance, but you called attention to Holloway. If something happens to him now, the police will remember you. This is not shipshape." The admiral looked out over the Potomac at the lights on the far shore. "Not shipshape at all."

Braxton tried to redeem himself. "I gave it some thought on the way over. We can bug his house and office. That should be no problem."

The admiral regarded his visitor with disappointment. "And, of course, Holloway wouldn't be expecting us to do anything like that. Man, that's exactly what he'd look for. Listen, you're dealing with a very capable operator here. You should have realized that when Holloway got away from you in Geneva. He knows the drill! I expect you and Pinchot to come up with something clever." The admiral gave the problem some thought. "What about that shopping center near his home? It has a high rise office building. Rent an office and get some cameras up there. Do the same thing at his office. I want to know who Holloway talks to. And find a way to track his movements. No more sitting outside of his house. Use several cars. Cruise the neighborhood. See Trung and get whatever resources you need—cars, people, helicopters—but I want Holloway covered."

"You've got it, sir. Anything else?"

"Yes. This is your third shot at Holloway. Don't screw it up."

Braxton departed and Schaeffer went home to call Switzerland. A sleepy voice answered, "Ackerman."

"This is the sailor."

"Yes?" said Ackerman with a new level of alertness.

"You had a visitor last week." Schaeffer was referring to Holloway. "Remember that we were concerned about his health?"

"Yes."

"He's been diagnosed as terminal. I'd like you to be here in ten days to help with the final arrangements."

"Can't Braxton or Pinchot handle it?"

"I don't think they are up to it. Braxton was keeping an eye on our sick friend and botched it. Come prepared to issue his severance pay." Personally, the admiral liked "terminate with extreme prejudice," but that terminology was passe.

There was a long silence on Ackerman's end. "Is this absolutely necessary?"

"Braxton was picked up by the police. I secured his release at great expense. He's a liability we cannot afford."

"Alright. I'll handle it."

With that out of the way, Schaeffer moved on to his other concern, the whereabouts of one Randolph Dillworth. "Have you located our missing partner yet?"

"No. We're checking private hospitals and clinics that treat his condition. It's slow work. People who patronize those places don't want it known. The institutions take elaborate precautions to protect the identities of their patients. It's costing us a fortune."

"He might have written down everything he knows by now," cautioned the admiral. "I don't want to deal with another letter-to-be-opened-in-the-event-of-my-death."

"Don't worry. We'll take care of it."

"I'll depend on you to do just that. Be here in ten days."

* * *

Holloway had stopped off at Lenny's for a drink. It was well after midnight when he arrived home. The street was empty and the lights were off in both his apartment and Donna's. He locked the WorldCorp photocopies in the basement vault and went up to his apartment. Miriam was sleeping. Holloway removed his clothes and slipped between the sheets, snuggling up to her back. He put an arm around her and cupped one of her breasts in his hand. Without waking, Miriam moved back against him. She was naked. The smell and feel of her aroused him. He wanted to make love, but remembered Donna sleeping in the room below. *Damn you, Sid Mitchell. Why did you pick now, of all times, to tell me about Donna's feelings? This is not fair.* That was Holloway's last thought as he drifted off to sleep.

* * *

Miriam came fully awake in an instant, heart pounding in response to some real or imagined danger. She had been dreaming about the death of her cousin. Lying perfectly still, Miriam peered into the darkness, half expecting to see Admiral Schaeffer standing over her with a garrote. As her eyes adjusted to the dark, she realized that the room contained no such threat.

In time, Miriam accepted the fact that her unease grew out of haunting questions. For the first time since she had placed herself under Holloway's protection, she pulled those questions out of the shadows of her subconscious for careful examination. Had Admiral Schaeffer sent the Vietnamese to kill her in Kansas? If so, why? He had nothing to gain by her death. In fact, he had something to lose. It didn't make sense. She decided that Schaeffer had not sent the Vietnamese. That would have been just too bizarre. Who could it have been? Did it matter? She decided that it did not. Because if Schaeffer was not trying to kill her, that put a whole different light on her situation. At that moment, she realized that she no longer needed Holloway's protection. She might even need protection *from* him. Without knowing it, he was trying to bring the world down around her.

Holloway. She turned and appraised him. A good man and a good lover, but he was the wrong man at the wrong time in her life. What should she do about him?

The clinking sound outside interrupted Miriam's thoughts and frightened her. She strained to hear it again, but there was only the wind. The luminous dial on the clock told her that it was a little after three. Something drew her to the window. She eased out of the bed and peered through the venetian blind. Holloway's car was in the shadow of a large tree. Miriam thought she saw a movement near it, but couldn't be sure. She watched for a long time, but saw nothing. Maybe it had been her overactive imagination. Miriam's body was covered with goose bumps. She slipped back into bed and drew warmth from Holloway's sleeping form, but could not sleep. There in the darkness, Miriam decided how she would handle Holloway and Schaeffer.

CHAPTER 13

Miriam Slayton fidgeted impatiently until Holloway left for work. As soon as his car had cleared the parking space in front of the house, she packed her clothes and made a series of telephone calls. Unfortunately, she was unable to connect with her party. A useless secretary here and an answering machine there only heightened her anxiety. When it became apparent that she would be unable to make contact with Admiral Schaeffer before Holloway returned for lunch, she unpacked and steadied her nerves with a brandy.

Meanwhile, Holloway, after spending the early morning with a client in Chevy Chase, had driven to the mall which housed Dan Vogle's computer shop and the office of Holloway Security Consultants. Donna's greeting was subdued and she quickly returned to her work. As Holloway plodded through his own in-basket, he realized that the constant chatter he had come to expect from Donna had been replaced by long periods of silence. Occasionally, he looked up to find her staring at him. Caught in the act, she would ask a question about the business and promptly break contact. As morning turned to afternoon, Holloway thought he saw in Donna's large, expressive eyes a loneliness that he had not previously recognized. It crossed his mind that, in recent months, as his own social life had become more active, his interest in Donna's had waned. Not that she was his responsibility. After all, she was an attractive woman who got her share of offers, which she selectively accepted. But Holloway knew that there was no "Mr. Right" in Donna's life, nor had there been since the death of her husband. The nearest thing to a steady was a long-running, but intermittent affair with Joe—or was it John—Somebody, who worked in Central Cover at the Agency. Holloway tried to put Donna's love life out of his mind, but when he said goodbye at two o'clock and headed for home, he felt a vague, though illogical guilt about his partner's predicament. *Guilt without sex,* he thought. *Ain't that a kick in the head?*

When Holloway arrived in the apartment, Miriam gave him a peck on the lips. "I expected you around noon," she said, but there was no disappointment in her voice. His late arrival had given her time to get her clothes put away. Holloway took his lunch with Miriam, then pleaded the demands of work and went to the basement to deal with WorldCorp photocopies. Several hours into the job, he received a phone call from Sid Mitchell.

"Ed, here's a rundown on your Vietnamese friend, Buie Trung. He was evacuated from Vietnam during the last days of the war. According to the Immigration and Naturalization Service, he was granted resident status under a special category for the protection of Vietnamese who worked with U.S. intelligence forces. Guess who sponsored him?"

"Schaeffer?"

"Nice try, but no cigar," said Mitchell. "It was Dillworth. You owe me, pal. Don't forget to water my plants while I'm gone." Mitchell rang off.

While Holloway was considering this new information, Donna arrived and went to her apartment. For reasons which he didn't quite understand, Holloway wanted to avoid her company and suggested to Miriam that they go out for dinner. She hesitated. Holloway smiled. "Don't look so worried. I'm buying." They both laughed. For Miriam, it was a welcomed release of tension.

"Let's take a cab," she suggested, "so that we can drink lots of wine." She winked and took his arm. The only thing Miriam wanted less than being seen with Holloway was a ride in his car. The memory of that shadow near it in the wee hours still gave her goose flesh.

The restaurant had a cozy nook where they drank good wine, ate chateaubriand, and talked about everything and nothing.

When Holloway was slightly under the influence of the wine, Miriam began to probe. "Well, are you ready to talk?"

"About what?" asked Holloway, puzzled.

"You."

"I've been talking about myself all evening. I was boring."

"You spoke of Holloway, the boy and husband. What about the man?"

"What do you want to know about Holloway, the man?"

"Anything," she said, with a shrug that belied her interest. "What did you do in the war?" Miriam could not have cared less about what Holloway had done in Vietnam, but war was stressful and stress revealed a man's character. That was a lesson she had learned during those last difficult months with her late husband.

"I don't particularly like talking about the war," admitted Holloway.

"Then tell me how you became a spook."

"I don't like talking about that either," said Holloway.

She pouted. "Can't I know something about the man whose bed I share? You asked me to stay with you so that we could get to know each other."

"I did say that, didn't I?" Unable to avoid the subject, he was determined to tell her in the bluntest terms, hoping to turn her away from the subject.

"The war," he sighed. "I was in the infantry. My outfit went to Vietnam in '65. We saw a lot of action. 'Kill a commie for Christ' was the battle cry of the time, and I got my share." There was neither pride nor remorse in the statement. "I earned a couple of medals for bravery in the process and I spoke fluent Vietnamese. I suppose that combination brought me to the attention of the CIA. I was called to Saigon for an interview. The next thing I knew, I was in the spook business."

"What did your unit do?"

"Our job was to eliminate the Viet Cong infrastructure in a certain group of villages. We killed anybody who could be identified as Viet Cong."

"Do you regret killing those people?" asked Miriam.

"No."

"What about killing a commie for Christ? Wasn't that a morally ambiguous act?"

Holloway gave Miriam a look that made her uneasy. "I didn't kill commies for Christ. I killed them because they needed killing." Holloway took a swallow of wine. The conversation was wearying him and he wanted to end it. "In Vietnam, there was one rule: losers die. There wasn't much time to consider moral ambiguities."

He made a show of looking furtively over his shoulder, then whispered, "Let's get out of here. I hear that this joint has been infiltrated by Viet Cong and you know how they can spoil a romantic evening. Dessert at my place?"

"Great idea," replied Miriam. There would be time for another morality talk before she had to make her call.

Dessert consisted of strawberries over ice cream with a dash of Grand Marnier, followed up with anatomical explorations of a recreational nature. They were both breathing heavily when Holloway disengaged to close a heating vent above the bed. Miriam pushed herself up on an elbow and asked, "What is it with you, Holloway? Whenever you want to make love, you close that damned vent. Is this some new sexual fetish?"

Holloway slid into bed beside her. "Not too long before I met you, I sacrificed an occasional virgin on this very bed and—"

She interrupted him with a derisive, "Hah. The only virgins you've had in this room have been on Christmas cards."

He ignored her comment. "During the sacrifice, the gods would suck the lucky maiden's spirit out of her body and up through that vent. I haven't made any sacrifices lately," he confided. "The gods will be angry. If I leave the vent open, they might even snatch you."

"Your deities must be all male to forego a virgin with such ease." She gave him a playful punch in the ribs. "Seriously, what's with the vent?"

Holloway's smile faded. "The sounds in this room carry down into Donna's bedroom through the heating duct. I close the vent for privacy."

Miriam threw her head back onto the pillow and laughed a deep, throaty laugh that was not nice.

It was after one in the morning. Miriam lay awake regretting the after-dinner coffee. Holloway's consciousness was making small steps toward the abyss of sleep, its progress slowed by a dull throb behind his eyes, the penalty for too much wine. He wanted to get up for an aspirin, but Miriam's hands were irresistibly massaging his back.

Softening me up. For what? And where was she coming from at dinner with all that talk about moral ambiguity? The questions faded as Holloway's mind moved closer to the abyss.

"Tell me something," Miriam said softly.

It was a long time before Holloway spoke and in the moments that passed before he asked, "What?," he wondered if women were taught to start conversations at a man's most vulnerable moment: just as he is about to go to sleep. *And where is the perverse son-of-a-bitch who made the rule that men go to sleep after sex and women talk? Probably asleep somewhere,* Holloway thought bitterly.

"Suppose," said Miriam, "that what the papers are saying about my husband is true? Suppose . . . he did lie to Congress about sending arms to Iran and the Contras? What if he did it for the good of the country and not for personal gain? How would you feel about what he did?"

Holloway fought being dragged away from the abyss. Something noncommittal might end this. "I don't want to judge the man."

"Just tell me what you think," Miriam insisted.

"I think he should have told the truth and taken his lumps."

"Your attitude about the truth is surprising. I thought a spook's watchwords were 'plausible denial.' "

" 'Plausible denial' is never having to say you screwed up. Those are a politician's watchwords. Sometimes it's best for everybody if you admit that you made a mistake and walk away. I wonder why so many people in Washington don't understand that? Why do they lie and hang on?"

"To keep the power."

"I never found anything that I wanted that much." There might have been a hint of regret in his voice.

Miriam took another approach. "What do you want out of life?"

Holloway was torn between a serious answer that might keep the conversation going and a light one that would end it. The serious one escaped before he could stop it. "When everything else is gone, I want to be able to look in the mirror and see an honest man." He wanted to add "more or less" in deference to acts for which he could not forgive himself, but only a fool spoke of such things, and certainly not when half asleep.

Miriam was quiet for a time. "What will your report say about Jack?"

Is that what all the talk has been about this evening, what's in my report? "I don't know. If I don't find something in the next few days, I'll turn in a blank page and a bill for my services." He was only half joking. "By the way, do you know a man named Randolph Dillworth?" Miriam tensed.

"No."

"What's wrong."

"I . . . I was thinking about the man who killed my cousin, Denise." Miriam started to weep and Holloway put his arm around her shoulders. It was a while before she felt like talking again. By then, Holloway was snoring.

*   *   *

There was a plan for closing out the Slayton case. Holloway was to spend afternoons culling out the useless documents from those provided by Sid Mitchell. Dan Vogle would feed the remainder into the computer. All documents were to be in the data base by Friday. Printouts of items common to two or more dossiers would be produced for review by Dan, Donna, and Ed on Saturday afternoon. That gave Holloway one week to follow up any new leads and prepare his report to Ellis Eaton. A week was not much time, given the fact that these activities had to be integrated with their other consulting business.

Meanwhile, Miriam had given up trying to contact Schaeffer until his return from Latin America and resigned herself to the role of Holloway's erotic plaything. Besides, his apartment was a good place to lay up until she was sure about Schaeffer, and she was not in the mood to relocate. The anxiety of not knowing which direction her life was taking and Holloway's romantic attentions drained her energy. She would have to take a long vacation by herself when the situation stabilized.

Saturday came and with it a welcomed rest for Holloway and his associates. Sid Mitchell was still in New York. Admiral Schaeffer was winding up his Latin American tour. Five blocks away in the shopping center high-rise, Braxton watched Holloway's house through the lens of a powerful tripod-mounted telescope next to an equally powerful camera that recorded the comings and goings at the Holloway residence.

It was seven-thirty. The morning rain was steady and would last all day. The house was quiet. Still exhausted, Holloway forced aside the comfortable cloak of sleep. He was far behind schedule on the Slayton case and it nagged at him. He turned to Miriam. She was lying on her stomach covered with a sheet that rose and fell with the regular rhythm of her breathing. Holloway eased out of bed, slipped into his exercise suit, and went to the basement.

Donna was already there sitting at the table in a flannel bathrobe and house slippers. She didn't look up from her reading when Holloway came down. The Mitchell files were spread out on the table in front of her and a half empty cup of coffee was getting cold at her elbow. The coffee drew Holloway to the sideboard, where he filled a cup for himself. Donna had anticipated his arrival. There was a small plate of Scottish short breads—his favorite snack—next to the pot. He took several and joined Donna at the table. Her eyes darted over the page in her hand, taking no notice of him.

Holloway looked first at the papers, then at her. "I'm confused."

"That's not exactly a revelation, is it?" asked Donna. Her eyes stayed riveted on the photocopy.

He tried again. "I know that I'm starting to sound like a broken record, but aren't you the lady who didn't want anything to do with the Slayton case?"

"If you don't read this stuff soon, you might as well throw it in the trash. You've got exactly eight days before your final report is due to our mystery client." She looked sideways at him. "Is it the President, Ed?"

"Thanks for the shortbread." He ate one.

Donna applied the needle again. "Did you come down to work or are you here on a tourist visa?"

Holloway refused to hear her. He let his head loll over the back of the chair and looked up at the ceiling. "God, I'm tired."

"Must be rough. Another night at hard labor with the bereaved Widow Slayton, I hear." Donna stared at him with a cold intensity.

"You forgot to close the damn vent." After a while she suggested, "Why don't you go back to bed. These files are in the computer and the intersects are running now. It'll be a while before the printouts are finished. You're not worth a fig when you're tired. If you can't get any sleep in your own bed, lie down over there." Donna made a quick, angry gesture toward the couch and sent the coffee mug at her elbow crashing to the floor. "God damn you, Jack Slayton!" she said.

Miriam could not be sure if it was the crash that woke her or the angry mention of her late husband's name. Whatever it was brought her wide awake in an instant. She lay there, listening to the muffled voices of Donna and Holloway. There was the sound of broken crockery being swept up and dumped into a trash can. Miriam looked up. The sounds were coming from the heating vent that Holloway had been too tired to close the preceding night. Those conduits did carry sound. Her curiosity was aroused. She stood on a chair and pressed her ear to the vent.

In the basement, Donna tidied the table in preparation to leave.

Holloway was stretched out on the couch with his eyes closed. "What time did you say that printout would be finished?"

"Go to sleep, I'll call you," Donna promised. She paused before starting up the steps, her hand gripping the wooden banister. "Dan will be here in a while. He called late last night to say that he has something hot on Admiral Schaeffer." In a bitchy voice, she added, "He didn't want to bother you. I suppose it's alright to bother me, since I don't have a . . . houseguest."

"Great! We can all sit around the table together and trade nasties."

Up in Holloway's bedroom, Miriam moved away from her listening post at the heating vent.

It was early afternoon when Holloway emerged refreshed from his nap. The computer was silent, and three identical printouts had been placed on the table in front of three chairs. A plate of sandwiches and a thermos of what turned out to be soup sat next to one of the printouts. A file card propped against the thermos contained a note in Donna's distinctive scrawl: "For the Sleeping Ugly!" The lady herself was sitting in a corner rocking chair reading photocopies from the Mitchell files in a box at her feet.

Holloway sat down to the soup and sandwiches. "Thanks again," he said, waving half a sandwich at Donna. "D'ja see Miriam this morning?"

"We ate breakfast together and she went back to bed. A headache, she said. Lord knows it's about time. Now, maybe *I* can get some sleep."

Determined that Donna would not provoke him, Holloway ate in silence and leafed through his printout. In an hour, he had worked through the document, circling the promising leads and scribbling questions in the margins. Donna rocked, read, and said nothing.

Holloway had completed the review of his printout when Dan Vogle arrived and went through his habitual drill of ringing the bell and then letting himself in with the key that Donna had provided. Vogle bounded down the cellar steps, sporting a wet trench coat and a bucktoothed grin. "Sorry I'm late. Spent the morning at the Naval Historical Center in D.C. Got some good stuff on Admiral Schaeffer. You're gonna love it!" He hung his dripping coat under the steps and came to the table. Seeing the printout in front of him, Vogle flipped the pages quickly and observed, "Looks like my program worked. Well, let's get down to it. What are you looking for?"

Donna sat back in her chair, arms folded under her large breasts, her Roman nose jutting into the air, looking for all the world like a salt-and-pepper-haired Sphinx.

Holloway noted her lack of enthusiasm. "This is the point of no return, Donna. We have to discuss the details of the Slayton case. If you don't want to know any more, now's the time to go upstairs."

"Let's get on with it," said Donna. "I read the photocopies before I fed them into the computer, and I read the printout while you were sleeping. I probably know more about these people than you do."

Holloway reviewed with them everything that had happened so far, except that Ellis Eaton was their client, his suspicion that Jack Slayton had been murdered, and the blue capsule in the apartment where Slayton had expired. He also conveniently forgot to tell them that Sid Mitchell had accompanied him to Geneva.

"So, what I'm looking for here," Holloway said, tapping his printout, "are some facts that link Slayton, Schaeffer, Dillworth,

Ackerman, Trung, and WorldCorp. I think these people could be part of 'The Seven,' assuming that Slayton didn't make up his conspiracy. Let's go over the files on each man and see if we can connect these people to each other or to WorldCorp. Then, maybe we can find out what they're up to.

"Donna, why don't you start out with a rundown on Dillworth and Ackerman. I'll go second with Slayton and the Vietnamese. Dan, you and Donna can both pitch in on Schaeffer."

Donna unfolded her arms and picked up a piece of lined paper containing her notes. "Dillworth, Randolph T. Born: Dallas, Texas, 1933. Raised there. Admitted to Texas A&M in 1959 and majored in Accounting. Dropped out a year later in June 1960. He spent the next year working as a bank teller in Dallas and acquired a wife, LuAnn, and a daughter, Stacy. The following year, Dillworth was drafted into the Army." Donna consulted a photocopy of the man's Enlisted Qualification Record. "He received extensive intelligence and language training, and afterwards spent a year, '63 to '64, on Okinawa with Special Forces.

"In January 1964," Donna continued, "Dillworth went to Saigon as an intelligence sergeant with the Military Assistance Command, Vietnam, Studies and Observation Group, whatever that was."

"MAC-V-SOG," Holloway informed her, "was a cover unit for covert operations. Before 1964, the CIA had financial and advisory responsibility for covert operations conducted by South Vietnamese military forces. In April 1964, MAC-V-SOG took over those responsibilities and was the headquarters for long-range reconnaissance patrols and covert raids into enemy-held territory, including countries bordering on South Vietnam. Sounds like Dillworth was part of the Army transition team that took the handoff from the Agency. A job like that would have put him in the right place to make good Agency contacts."

Donna continued to review Dillworth's record. "After eighteen months with MAC-V-SOG, Dillworth had a series of routine stateside courses and assignments, most of them at Fort Bragg, North Carolina. He returned to Vietnam in late 1973 and was assigned to the Defense Attaché's Office at Tan Son Nhut Air Base in Saigon with detached duty to the Vung Tau POW Detention Center as an interrogator and liaison sergeant. Dillworth remained in that job until he was evacuated to the States in April 1975, just days before South Vietnam fell to the communists. Two months after he left Vietnam, Dillworth asked for and received an honorable discharge at the rank of sergeant first class. That's it."

Dan Vogle ran a hand speculatively over his chin. "Odd that a sergeant first class, with six years to go for retirement, quits the Army in a recession year. He must have had something going for himself."

"He did." Holloway shared the information that Jessica Talbot had given him in Geneva. "Six months later, he showed up in Switzerland as an eighty-thousand-dollar-a-year investment advisor to the group that was putting WorldCorp together. By the end of 1976, WorldCorp was a going concern with Dillworth as chief of security." Holloway addressed Donna. "Is there anything to suggest that he was qualified for either of those jobs?"

Donna consulted Dillworth's records. "Nothing here to indicate that."

"If WorldCorp is a CIA front, is there anything in Dillworth's record to suggest that he could have qualified for chief of security?"

"Not a chance," replied Donna. "A job like that is a plum. It would have gone to a senior counterintelligence type."

"Then why would anyone give him two jobs that he's not qualified for?"

"Blackmail?" suggested Vogle.

Holloway was inclined to accept Jessica Talbot's theory that Dillworth had come to Geneva to keep an eye on WorldCorp's Swiss front men, but he kept that belief to himself.

Moving on, Donna identified the Dillworth-Ackerman intersects. "Both were in Vietnam at the same time, but assigned to different locations. Dillworth was on the SOG staff in Saigon. Ackerman was an infantry soldier, working out of Tay Ninh. Both of them worked as security chief at WorldCorp.

"The solid intersect is between Dillworth and Jack Slayton. They served together in several units, even in the same sections, and left Vietnam on the same day. The chances of them not knowing each other are zero."

"No question about that," agreed Holloway. "I'll cover their association in detail when we get to Slayton." He made a note on his printout. "Anything else? No? Then, tell us about Ackerman."

Donna produced a second pile of photocopies, her handwritten notes clipped to the stack. The Ackerman file was thin compared to Dillworth's. "Two years older than Dillworth. Born and raised in Pocatello, Idaho. Farmhand. Enlisted in the Army in 1961. Served two consecutive one-year tours in Vietnam with the Special Forces at Tay Ninh. Left the service with a less than honorable discharge in 1963. No evidence in his military record of a connection with anyone else in this case. This note was stapled to Ackerman's service record." Donna passed copies to Dan and Ed. "Any idea where it came from?" she asked. "There's no date or signature."

"A reliable source," said Holloway. Sid Mitchell was definitely reliable.

The note read:

Ed,

Not much on this character, as you can see. His name did pop in the computers at the Customs Service, Drug Enforcement Administration, and Interpol, but their real juicy stuff is old. Here it is in a nutshell. Two months after his discharge from the Army, Ackerman returned to Vietnam and operated out of Saigon as a hired gun and smuggler. Cargo: drugs, guns, and gold. Speculation is that he left South Vietnam in 1975, just before the communists took over. He disappeared for a year, then surfaced in Thailand. From 1976 until he replaced Dillworth in Geneva, Ackerman operated businesses in Bangkok, Hong Kong, and Taiwan. These included a travel agency and an import-export company. They all appear respectable, but do make nice covers, if you smuggle for a living, or spy. He has no background in security. Don't know how he got the top spot at WorldCorp. That being the case, there must be an unknown side to Mr. Ackerman.

Dan Vogle tapped the note with a forefinger. "Notice the post-Vietnam pattern. Both Dillworth and Ackerman dropped out after the war and showed up in a foreign country months later as prosperous businessmen."

"Let's move on to Slayton," suggested Holloway. He skipped Slayton's early life and picked up where he entered the Army.

"Commissioned through ROTC into the Military Intelligence Corps. Attended basic courses for intelligence, airborne, and Special Forces officers, followed by a tour at Fort Bragg. In 1963, he was posted to Okinawa." Holloway looked up. "This was the first intersect with Dillworth. They were assigned to the same unit. Slayton was transferred to Saigon in January 1964 for an assignment with MAC-V-SOG."

Holloway continued, reading from Slayton's qualification record. "After his first tour of duty in Vietnam, Slayton returned to the States for a tour of duty as an instructor at the Intelligence School. He attended the strategic intelligence course followed by a tour at the Pentagon. Finished two years of night school courses at law school." He skipped down the file. "Returned to the Special Warfare Center at Fort Bragg, bringing him to intersect number three with Dillworth. They worked in the same unit and returned to Saigon for five months of temporary duty in 1971. Slayton and Dillworth were in the same unit until 1973. That year they both returned to Vietnam. Dillworth went to Vung Tau. Slayton was assigned to the Defense Attaché's Office at Tan Son Nhut, but detached to the embassy as an 'intelligence coordinator' working with the Vietnamese Army."

"Sounds like double-talk for a CIA assignment," observed Donna.

"That's what I think," agreed Holloway.

Holloway continued. "Both men left Vietnam on the same day." Holloway put the military records aside and picked up Slayton's White House resume. "After law school, he spent two years as an aide to Senator Greene, then went to the Pentagon. He held a variety of jobs at Defense and came to the National Security Council in '81. Slayton was on the fast track until the Iran-Contra scandal derailed him."

Donna pursed her lips. "I don't think so. Have you taken a close look at the jobs Slayton held in the Pentagon?" She unfolded a large organizational chart of the Defense Department and spread it on the table. "Look here. Slayton had been working in high level government for ten years. He had excellent experience and connections. He should have been at least an assistant secretary of defense.

"But look at the jobs he's held." Donna pulled a pencil out of her hair and went over the organization chart checking off the positions as she talked. "He started out as a rising star, getting jobs of increasing importance. All of a sudden, he starts moving sideways.

Note that he never makes a complete break with operational intelligence to move into a purely policy-making position. Here," her pencil stabbed at the chart, "he even went backwards. For the rest of his time at the Pentagon, Slayton's career moved sideways faster than it moved up. Why?" She looked up from the chart to meet their questioning eyes. "And why, with all his experience and his political connections, did Jack Slayton end up as a third stringer on the National Security Council?" Donna turned down the edges of her mouth and shook her head. "Something's not right here." She tossed her pencil on the chart, sat down, and folded her arms. "Did he run out of steam, or did he plan his career that way."

"And if he did, why?" asked Holloway.

The discussion moved on to the Vietnamese, Hong and Trung, Schaeffer's interpreters for the Hanoi MIA negotiations. The name Trung struck a familiar cord with Dan Vogle. While Holloway described the strange circumstances which prompted Schaeffer to fire Dr. Hong and replace him with Trung, Vogle went to his trench coat pocket and removed a large, soggy government envelope that had been folded in half. It contained several damp photocopies. Dan returned to the table, reading them on the way. He reluctantly tore his eyes away from the papers when he heard an impatient Holloway say, ". . . that is, if you're really interested in this, Dan."

Vogle gave Holloway a reassuring smile. "I'm listening. Got a hammerlock on every word." But as soon as Holloway started talking again, Vogle returned his attention to the photocopies. His finger slid down the page until he found the name. "Gotcha!" Only when he saw Donna and Ed staring at him did he realize that he had spoken aloud.

"Just what is it that you've got?" asked Holloway.

Vogle gave them his broadest, bucktoothed grin. "I've got Buie Trung and I can connect him to Schaeffer, Dillworth, and Ackerman."

Donna gave him a disgusted look. "Well, why didn't you say so, for God's sake?"

The grin did not go away. Dan Vogle was pleased with himself. "I didn't have time to read the whole file on Dillworth and Slayton last week, but I did scan their military assignments and noticed that both men were evacuated from Vietnam on the same day. Then, I remembered Donna saying that Schaeffer commanded a destroyer off Vietnam during the evacuation. A lot of people were flown out of Saigon by helicopter and put aboard Navy ships for the trip back to the States. It was a long shot, but I wondered if Slayton and Dillworth had been evacuated on Schaeffer's destroyer. So, when I went over to the Navy Department to get Schaeffer's service bio, I thought I'd do a little research to find out if his ship was involved in the evacuation. It was. A Ph.D. over at the Naval Historical Center is writing a history of the Navy's role during the fall of South Vietnam and he had lots of documents from Schaeffer's destroyer. I spent last night and this morning at the Navy Yard going through the stuff. Guess what I found?" Dan was beside himself with excitement now. "A manifest of people who had been flown out to Schaeffer's ship. Trung, Dillworth, and Slayton were on the list." Vogle was grinning as he handed the damp photocopy over. So was Holloway, when he read it.

Donna said, "That's good work, Dan." She was thinking that the truth can set you up as well as set you free.

"You ain't heard nothing yet. You think Slayton's career in the Pentagon smells peculiar? Listen to this. During the entire trip from the South China Sea to the port of San Diego, Slayton, Dillworth, and Trung were in quarantine with a 'fever of unknown origin,' according to the ship's medical records. Miraculously, their fevers cleared up as soon as they hit the California coast. They never went near a hospital. Now there's a boat people story that sounds fishy."

Donna groaned at the pun. "What do you think happened to them?"

"I think these guys were hiding out in sick bay."

"I wonder why," mused Holloway.

Dan Vogle was out of answers.

Donna spoke reluctantly, saying what had to be said, against her better judgment. "Since we're looking for conspiracy, there's another possibility. Suppose that Slayton, Dillworth and Trung were not on Schaeffer's destroyer? What if Schaeffer falsified the manifest to give them an alibi?"

"And," Vogle added, "told the doctor to make phony entries in the medical records. Oh, Donna, I like this," he said, rubbing his palms together gleefully.

"Did you get the doctor's name?" asked Holloway.

"Last page. Lieutenant Commander Reid."

"Dan, I want you at the Navy Bureau of Personnel first thing Monday morning. Find out where Reid is and go get his story. I think we're onto something!"

Upstairs in Holloway's bedroom, Miriam Slayton had heard enough. After an hour of eavesdropping on her lover and his two companions through the heating conduit, her legs were cramping. She sat on the edge of the bed and massaged them. "Yes, my darling," she said, softly, "you are onto something."

Dan Vogle left with marching orders to find Dr. Reid. Holloway locked the vault and sat down at the table. "You were good today, Donna."

"Yes, I know." She didn't look up from her reading.

"You're worried about me, aren't you?"

"About us—and Dan—yes." This time she looked at him.

"Our situation might be less stressful if we knew what WorldCorp is or isn't."

Donna analyzed the statement. "The indirect approach is not your style, Holloway. Say what you want." They both knew.

"I'd like you to ask Joe What's-his-name—"

"Grisby," she corrected him. "Joe Grisby."

"I'd like you to ask Joe Grisby about WorldCorp."

Donna put down the magazine and looked at him, her head cocked to one side. "Should I just barge into the Central Cover Division at Langley and ask him if WorldCorp belongs to the CIA? Or maybe I should set a honey trap and ask him in *flagrante delicto*?"

Anger flashed through Holloway. "I don't give a damn if you ask him in Swahili!" Donna watched with bitter amusement while he got himself under control. "Forget it," he said. "It was a bad idea."

"Not a bad idea, just bad timing. Joe and I are no longer an item. I would have to use him . . . for you. He couldn't tell me if WorldCorp is a cover, anyway."

"He could tell you if it wasn't."

She changed the subject. "You lost your objectivity today."

"Maybe so, but I want to hear Dr. Reid's explanation."

"I'm not talking about Reid. When you briefed us on Dillworth, you talked about his family. Why didn't you tell us about Slayton's family? Didn't he have children? I wonder who's looking after the little dears while mother is . . ." Donna looked at the ceiling and went back to her magazine.

"Miriam's kids are in boarding school," explained Holloway, and he was getting tired of her sniping. "Look, Donna, would it be better if I moved out?"

"Of course not. Who would I argue with? Besides, your lady friend will probably be moving on soon. I haven't noticed her marking off territory."

"What are you talking about?"

"When a woman plans to stay in a man's house, she declares her intent by marking off her territory. It could be something as subtle as putting out a vase of flowers or as obvious as rearranging the furniture. I haven't seen any markers in your place, Holloway. Have you?"

* * *

There are thousands of underpaid GS-3 government clerks in Washington who have access to data of potential value to any number of private individuals. The lady who could satisfy Dan Vogle's need for information was a thirtyish, overweight woman under a pile of frizzy hair. She wore a shapeless blue dress and her shoulders were draped with a white sweater that had seen better days. By noon, Dan had traded her a hundred-dollar bill for a history of Lieutenant Commander Jefferson Reid.

He had resigned from the Navy in 1976. Dan had no phone numbers, but he did have two addresses. The first was Reid's Maryland home of record when he joined the Navy and the second was his San Diego residence at the time he resigned.

Neither directory assistance in San Diego nor the California State Medical Association were able to located Dr. Reid. Maryland's medical association was no help either. Vogle struck pay dirt when he visited Reid's home of record at the time he joined the Navy.

The Reid family home in Glen Burnie, Maryland was an aging wooden building on a rural back road. The porch was spotless, and well-tended flower boxes attached to the railing indicated that someone was interested in upkeep. There was no bell. The storm door rattled when Vogle pounded it. The woman who opened the inner door was in her late sixties. She was tall and thin with gray hair swept back into a pony tail and held in place by a red rubber band. Vogle saw a deep sadness in the eyes that looked out at him through the glass pane of the storm door.

"Can I help you?"

"I hope so. I'm looking for Dr. Jefferson Reid."

"What do you want with Jeff?"

"He treated some friends of mine during the evacuation from Vietnam in 1975. They asked me to stop by and pay their respects."

The shrill whistle of a kettle erupted from the back of the house. The woman glanced in the direction of the sound and turned back to Vogle. "I'm Mrs. Reid, Jeff's mother. Come in and have some tea." It was more a command than an invitation. She lifted the latch on the storm door. There was no foyer. Vogle stepped directly from the porch into a small, neat living room. The couch against the far wall was flanked by two overstuffed chairs. Mrs. Reid directed him to one of them. "Please, sit down Mr. . . .?"

"Vogle. Dan Vogle."

Mrs. Reid removed a basket of wax fruit from the cocktail table to make room for the tea and disappeared toward the sound of a whistling kettle that was threatening them both with permanent brain damage.

Vogle inspected the room. Its true center was the wall to his right at the far end of the couch. Above the modest fireplace, the mantel and wall were a well-kept shrine to a boy who had reached the flower of manhood in a Navy uniform. Vogle went to the fireplace and examined the centerpiece of the display, a large photograph of a Navy officer. The inscription read: "Happy Mother's Day. Love, Jeff." That picture was surrounded by many smaller ones of various sizes and shapes taken at different times in the life of the subject. Several documents hung on the wall above the pictures: diplomas, Reid's commission as a Navy officer and—Vogle was surprised to see—Reid's medical degree.

Mrs. Reid returned with her tea service on a silver tray. "Have you ever been to England, Mr. Vogle?"

"No, but I'd like to go someday."

"Jeff gave me a trip to England once," she said, arranging the cups and saucers. "I developed a taste for tea in the afternoon there. It's such a civilized tradition." She smiled, remembering a happier time, and set a plate of rolls near Vogle's cup. "Cream and sugar?" She poured the tea.

"Lemon, please."

"That's the way I like it, too," she said.

They sipped and Vogle looked at the mantel. "Is that Dr. Reid?"

"Yes."

"Does he live here?"

"No. Have a sweet roll, Mr. Vogle. The English call them scones. Sounds like the name of a shellfish, don't you think?" She smiled.

Vogle had the feeling that Mrs. Reid didn't want to talk about her son, but he had a job to do. "Could you give me Dr. Reid's address?"

She appeared not to hear him. "You say Jeff treated your friends during the war? Tell me about it . . . please."

"For several days, they were seriously ill with a fever. Your son cured them," Vogle said, hoping that he was telling the truth.

Mrs. Reid smiled to herself, her thoughts obviously elsewhere. Slowly, the smile disappeared and she looked at Vogle with the same sadness he had seen at the storm door. "Were you in the war?"

"I was too young."

"Consider yourself lucky," snapped Mrs. Reid. "I had a husband and three beautiful children. They were all corrupted by that terrible time." The hardness in her voice disappeared as quickly as it had come. "All corrupted," she added, "except Jeff. And even with his good intentions, he destroyed us. It was the times, those terrible times."

Vogle felt awkward, like a person who had stumbled into a conversation that he was not supposed to hear.

Mrs. Reid paused to regain her composure. "I apologize, Mr. Vogle. You came looking for my son and I brought you in under false pretenses. I'm lonely." She looked at the mantel. "I don't have many visitors these days. My friends were driven away long ago by my bitterness. And my family . . . well, they caused the bitterness.

"The sixties and seventies were years of war, promiscuity, and drugs. All three destroyed my family. My youngest son and daughter were involved with drugs. My husband and I were going broke and crazy trying to save them. Jeff had to go off to the Navy after medical school, just when we needed him most. When he left the service and went into private practice, we told ourselves that we had at least one success story in the family. Then, Jeff died and we were devastated."

"I'm terribly sorry, Mrs. Reid. I wouldn't have bothered you if I had known." Then Dan's wheels began to turn. "How did he die?"

"A heart attack. He was so young." She shook her head. "We thought that nothing worse could happen to us. Then, the insurance money came. Two hundred thousand dollars. Jeff made me the beneficiary. We had mortgaged everything to get the children through drug cures and support them. My husband wanted the money to pay off his business debts and my children needed money for their drugs. They pestered me day and night. Finally, they just wore me down. I put a little money aside for myself, paid off the house note, and divided what was left between the three of them. In less than six months, they all left me."

"I'm sorry, Mrs. Reid." Dan searched his heart for words of sympathy that did not sound inadequate. Finding none, he changed the subject. "Do you know if your son had dealings with a firm called WorldCorp? It's in Geneva, Switzerland."

Mrs. Reid took a deep breath and focused her memory. "No. I don't think my son was ever in Europe." Then, less certain, she added, "I didn't know much about Jeff's business affairs. I s'pose he did have dealings with somebody over there. His insurance money came from Europe."

Within minutes, Dan Vogle took his leave of Mrs. Reid. He found a pay phone and called the clerk at BuPer who had given him Mrs. Reid's address. She accepted a new assignment and arranged to meet him after work and exchange the fruits of her labors for two fifty dollar bills. As soon as Dan received the information, he telephoned the home of a sailor in Georgia.

By six o'clock, he got a call through to Holloway at home. "Ed, I talked to Commander Reid's mother. Reid got out of the Navy in 1976 and died of a heart attack two months later."

"How old was he?" asked Holloway.

"Thirty-four!"

"That's young for a heart attack." He considered their next move. "Dan, I want you to find Reid's medical assistant on that destroyer. See if he knows anything about Slayton and the others being in quarantine."

"I've already located him . . . in a veteran's cemetery in Augusta, Georgia. I called his widow a few minutes ago. She told me that her husband died on shore leave in the Philippines one week after Dr. Reid's death."

"Cause of death?"

"Heart attack."

Holloway thought of Slayton's heart attack. "That's quite a coincidence."

"Add one more. Both Reid and his assistant were insured for two hundred thousand dollars by the same company, Grosshandel Versicherungen in Liechtenstein. If I remember my geography, Liechtenstein is right next door to Switzerland."

Holloway wanted to call Jessica Talbot immediately, but it was almost 2:00 a.m. in Geneva. He would have to wait. Since Miriam was out of the apartment for a change, Holloway decided to take a nap. He got his alarm clock and stretched out on the living room couch. As Holloway drifted off, he felt uneasy. It was unusual for Miriam to be out of the apartment alone. Then, he dismissed his concern. She had been cooped up there for too long. It was healthier for her to stop hiding and get out more. As he had told her so many times, if anyone wanted to harm her, they would have done it by now.

The buzz of the alarm woke Holloway at 2:30 a.m., 8:30 a.m. in Western Europe. He checked the bedroom. Miriam was still out. He dressed, took all of the quarters from the change box on his dresser, and walked to a pay telephone near his house. The operator put him through to Jessica Talbot in Geneva.

"Good morning. Jessica Talbot, HAD."

"Ms. Talbot, this is Ed Holloway in Washington. When I visited Geneva a couple of weeks ago, you briefed me on WorldCorp."

"WorldCorp." The word triggered a series of electronic events in a windowless room off the Baltimore-Washington Expressway. Minutes later, a high-speed printer began to zip across the page.

Page 1

CLASSIFICATION: SECRET
CODE WORD: MIDAS

SUBJECT: TRANSATLANTIC TELEPHONE INTERCEPT 0308,
DATE: 23 April 1987
ORIGINATOR: Holloway, Ed, public phone 20571, Alexandria VA.
RECIPIENT: Talbot, Jessica, Hidden Assets Division, U.S. Treasury Dept, Geneva, Switzerland.
TIME INITIATED: 03:08 hours (local) TERMINATED: 03:14.
CONTENT:
TALBOT: Good morning, Jessica Talbot, HAD.
HOLLOWAY: Miss Talbot, this is Ed Holloway in Washington. When I visited Geneva a couple of weeks ago, you briefed me on WorldCorp.
TALBOT: I remember, Mr. Holloway. What can I do for you?
HOLLOWAY: I drew a blank trying to locate Dillworth. So, I've been approaching my problem from a different angle. I thought you might help me trace a lead.
TALBOT: I'll try. What's the lead?
HOLLOWAY: An insurance company, Grosshandel Versicherungen in Liechtenstein. I need to know if Grosshandel is a WorldCorp subsidiary.
TALBOT: Hang on. I'll check the file.
Pause for 54 seconds.
TALBOT: Your information is good, but outdated. Grosshandel was set up in May of 1975 as a privately held insurance company by a Swiss lawyer who is now on the board of directors at WorldCorp. Grosshandel was acquired by WorldCorp in December 1975 and went out of business in September '76. I have no idea what the paper shuffle was all about.

Holloway knew. The company had gone out of business immediately after paying death benefits to the survivors of Dr. Reid and his assistant. Now, everyone involved in the Slayton case was tied to either Schaeffer or WorldCorp or both. He was getting close, very close, but to what? Holloway smiled grimly and trudged through the early morning chill to his apartment. There would have been no smile for him had he known that "WorldCorp" was among the thousands of key words that the National Security Agency computers had been programmed to search for as they screened certain designated telephone communications.

The duty officer in the NSA Intercept Center read the transcript of Holloway's conversation with Jessica Talbot and called up the distribution instructions for MIDAS intercepts on his computer. This was hot traffic! Only two men in the government were MIDAS cleared. Both were at the CIA. The primary addressee was Admiral Schaeffer, but the log indicated that he was out of town. The backup addressee was ill and temporarily removed from the distribution list. The NSA duty officer picked up the telephone for the direct, secure line to his counterpart, the watch officer at the CIA.

"I've got MIDAS traffic for Admiral Schaeffer. The log says he's out of town. I need instructions."

"He's back. Send it over in the distribution pouch. I'll see that he gets it in the morning."

"Can't do that. The material's not supposed to leave the building unless Schaeffer gives the okay."

The CIA watch officer looked at the operations center clock and swore.

"You want to translate that?" asked the NSA man.

"Sorry, that wasn't meant for you. Schaeffer just got back from a trip at midnight. I'll have to call and get him out of bed. He's gonna be pissed."

The NSA duty officer chuckled. "Life is a bitch and then you die."

CHAPTER 14

<u>Washington. D.C.</u>

At 6:30 the next morning, Jules Vaterman was a breakfast guest at Admiral Schaeffer's Fort McNair residence. Schaeffer sipped coffee while Vaterman read the transcript of Holloway's conversation with Jessica Talbot.

"Where did this come from?" demanded Vaterman, the worry lines in his forehead a little deeper.

"A messenger just brought it in from NSA. I had them monitor the pay phones near Holloway's office and apartment." Schaeffer put a match to the transcript and watched it turn to ashes in his plate. "I'll deal with Holloway. The Talbot woman works for you, and she's getting to be a pain. Last year, when she tried to get the Swiss to investigate WorldCorp, you told me that you had shut her down."

"I had, and I haven't heard a peep out of her since."

"It's damned obvious that she's back on the case. Why was she briefing Holloway about WorldCorp?"

Vaterman put down his coffee cup. "I don't know. Miss Talbot has political ambitions. Perhaps she's trying to make a name for herself with this WorldCorp thing. I can handle her. She's due for reassignment to the States. If I dangle a juicy job in front of her, she'll forget WorldCorp. Holloway is another story. He seems to know a lot about our business. Where does he get his information?"

"He's got a pipeline into the Pentagon. Someone gave him military records on Dillworth, Slayton, and Ackerman. He made the connection between those three, my ship, and Dr. Reid. Otherwise, why would he be asking about the Liechtenstein arrangement?"

"Does he have any information about me?"

Disgusted by Vaterman's self-concern, Schaeffer said, "No, Jules. So far, everybody else's ass is hanging out. You and the Embassy Man are safe . . . for the moment."

While Schaeffer spread jam on his toast, Vaterman considered their problem. "This Holloway threat calls for a Committee meeting."

"This does *not* require a meeting. It calls for action. Now! Besides, we can't have a meeting until Ackerman gets in from Europe next week. We've already waited too long to deal with Holloway."

"And we still don't know who he's working for?"

"No," said Schaeffer.

"Perhaps we can buy him off," Vaterman suggested.

"No, but I have another idea." Schaeffer explained it in detail.

"It's messy," observed Vaterman, daintily rubbing the toast crumbs from his fingertips.

"It'll work," retorted Schaeffer.

* * *

In the Southeast Asia Section at CIA headquarters, Hugh Stiles chewed his pipe stem and tried to assess the impact of his relationship with Admiral Schaeffer on his career prospects. The telephone buzzer ended his speculation. Schaeffer was on the line.

Without greeting, the Admiral said, "Take an early lunch. We'll jog The Mall at 1030 hours. Meet me at the same place."

"I'll be there, sir."

At 10:15, Admiral Schaeffer jogged west along The Mall in his black and gold warm-up suit. As he approached the Museum of History and Technology, he turned right and ran across Madison to Constitution Avenue. The red Porsche 944 was parked at the curb facing east. Schaeffer walked over to the car and slid into the passenger seat. The man behind the wheel was a well-dressed

Vietnamese-American. He was balding in his middle age, a result of several stressful sidelines to his import business.

Schaeffer greeted him with, "Hello, Trung."

"Good morning, Admiral. How may I be of service?"

"A man named Holloway has shown an interest in the medical staff who treated you and the others during your evacuation from Vietnam aboard my ship. He's asking about Grosshandel Versicherungen." Trung gave Schaeffer a worried look; his thumbs began nervously stroking the steering wheel. "We'll have to deal with him, of course," said Schaeffer, looking down Constitution Avenue at a group of tourists trying to cross in the middle of the block. "By 1700 hours this evening I need three keys of coke, some wholesale paraphernalia—scales and such—and ten thousand in small bills, nothing over a fifty. Can you manage that?"

"Yes."

"I also want a man standing by equipped to open a vault."

Trung extended his arm and a French cuff with gold link emerged from the sleeve of the silk suit coat. He twisted his wrist and gave the Rolex a skeptical glance. "By five o'clock?"

"That's right."

Trung took a deep breath. In all his years of working with Americans, he had never gotten used to their tendency to want things "yesterday." "I do my best."

"Your best has always been good enough. Call me when everything is in place. I'll give you instructions then." Schaeffer opened the car door. "By the way, Miriam Slayton has reappeared. She called me late last night with the same proposition."

"That lady bad luck," said Trung, with a frown.

"Yes, she is." Schaeffer got out of the car, closed the door, and jogged off toward the Washington Monument.

As Schaeffer crossed 17th Street, Hugh Stiles fell in beside him. The admiral said, "Hello, Stiles. Heard anything more from Holloway?"

"No, sir."

"I want you to call him. Make an appointment at his home for seven this evening. Be sure his partners, Dan Vogle and Donna Goodwin, will be there. Tell Holloway that you want to discuss Dr. Reid."

"Who is Dr. Reid?"

"Holloway will know."

Stiles felt a stab of disappointment. Foolishly, he had hoped to be taken into Schaeffer's confidence immediately. "What do I say at the meeting?"

"Nothing. I'll send a couple of people along with you. They'll do the talking; you just make the introductions. Don't tell Holloway that the others will be coming. Let's have surprise on our side, shall we?" Schaeffer slowed to a walk, then stopped and turned to his jogging companion. "Hugh . . ." Stiles warmed to the sound of his first name on the Admiral's lips. "Not a word to anyone at Langley about this."

"Aye, aye, sir."

* * *

It was one of those rare days when all three partners were in. Dan Vogle was manning the computer store. Holloway arrived at the office late in the morning after visiting a client. Donna was already there working on a consulting project and in what Holloway had dubbed her "neutral-to-hostile mood." She waved a note at him as he entered. "Someone named Hugh Stiles just called." Holloway was surprised. "He wants to come by the house tonight to discuss Dr. Reid with all of us. I presume this is about Dr. Reid of the Slayton case. I told him that he could discuss it with you and Dan." She had more to tell him, but needed time to work up her courage and her anger.

Holloway went to his desk and sat down and, for the next hour, Donna monitored his progress—or the lack of it. He made trips to the coffee pot and the window, unable to concentrate. Donna jammed the pencil into her hair and sat back. "What's eating you?"

"Nothing." He didn't look up from the paper he was reading.

"Your 'nothing' is costing us. You haven't hit a lick of work since you got here."

Donna waited for an answer, while Holloway hoped she would forget the question. Instead, she sat patiently, with folded arms, waiting.

Finally, he said, "Miriam didn't come home last night," still not looking at her. "She took her clothes." Holloway went to the window again and stared out at nothing in particular.

"Did she go back to Kansas?" Donna tried to keep the relief out of her voice.

"I don't know where she went," Holloway admitted.

News of Miriam's departure bolstered Donna's courage. "I was out late last night myself." Her announcement had a distant quality.

"Oh?" Holloway turned from the window, thankful that she had changed the subject. "What were you up to?"

"I had a date with Joe Grisby from the Company." Holloway's smile faded to interest. "He told me that WorldCorp was not CIA."

"I owe you one."

Holloway flopped into his desk chair.

Donna's eyes followed him. "Don't minimize the debt, Holloway. I lied to Joe to get that information and I slept with him as payment. He knows it. I know it. Now, you know it. I did it to make sure that you were not in trouble with the Company." Bitterly, she added, "There wasn't enough water in the shower to get clean this morning." Her eyes blazed with anger. "Now that Miriam Slayton is gone, there's no reason for us to be involved in her husband's affairs. I want you and Dan to stop playing Sherlock Holmes and end this Slayton mess. As for me, I don't like working for people I don't know. So, write the damned report, collect the fee, and call it a day. And I don't want any part of your meeting tonight with Mr. Hugh Stiles."

"But Donna, you don't understand— "

"No!" she shouted. "You don't understand! The Slaytons, dead and alive, have put a real strain on all of us, the business, and my self-respect. I want you to stop mooning over Miriam Slayton and close the Slayton case today or this partnership is finished."

They looked at each other until the phone broke the spell.

Donna answered and said, "It's for you." She left the office as Holloway picked up the extension.

The caller was Miriam Slayton and the conversation brief. Miriam said she had left the apartment to get away from the ghost of Jack Slayton. Holloway's work, she said, not only maintained her late husband's presence, it was keeping her and Holloway apart, and it was dangerous. Had he forgotten the Vietnamese and those people watching the house? She was afraid to go out. She could not live like that. Of course, Holloway understood. He would take a couple of weeks off. To hell with work. They would go away. Miriam declined. That wouldn't work, she said. Why? It just wouldn't. She needed time to herself. Where? Someplace new. He pressed her. Would she be in touch later? She didn't know. Caught up in the desperation of the moment, he made his move and did it badly. "I thought we felt . . . strongly about each other."

Near tears, Miriam admitted that she could love him, ". . . but not now. 'Now' is just too complicated. We want different things." What things? But he couldn't ask the question because Miriam was sobbing through her goodbye. Then she was gone.

A great depression overcame Holloway. In his mind's eye, his life separated into five great failures: Vietnam, Europe, Afghanistan, his marriage, and now Miriam. Perspective would have told him that Miriam's entry and exit represented a tiny fraction of his life, but perspective is not the handmaiden of tragedy. He sat for a long time, trying not to think or feel.

Donna's voice brought Holloway out of his trance. The telephone receiver was still in his hand and making odd noises. He slammed it into the cradle.

"Has she gone for good?" Donna asked, in her neutral voice.

"Probably." Hollow looked around the room for anything but Donna's eyes. His gaze fell on the clock. "I'm going to Lenny's."

"Are you coming back today? Remember, my car's in the shop. I need a ride home." Holloway removed his car key from the ring and tossed it on her desk. Donna's neutral voice turned a shade sympathetic. "I can take a cab."

"No. I'll take a cab. I don't plan to be in any shape to drive."

He was almost out of the door when Donna asked, "What about the meeting with Hugh Stiles?"

"Cancel it."

Donna felt a tremendous sense of relief. The big issues in her life had been resolved, and she took a silent oath to have absolutely nothing more to do with the Slayton case. After Holloway departed, she went to the computer store and told Dan Vogle as much. To make her point, she gave him the note on the evening meeting with Hugh Stiles and told him that Holloway wanted it canceled. Vogle balked. After all, he had unearthed Dr. Reid, and that entitled him to hear what Stiles had to say. Through clenched teeth, Donna ordered, "Cancel it!" But pride of ownership can prevail over orders, and Dan Vogle owned Reid, lock, stock, and Liechtenstein.

* * *

Holloway didn't go directly to Lenny's. He drifted aimlessly through downtown Washington and arrived at the bar around four. That time of day at Lenny's was like the calm before the storm. Those who took a late lunch were long gone, and the after-work onslaught had not yet begun. Lenny's was as quiet as it ever gets during business hours. Holloway took a booth and ordered his drink. The big crowd came in a little after four-thirty. Veronica, the woman Holloway had been admiring from afar before Miriam came into his life, entered and opened court at the far end of the bar. Holloway was nursing his second gin. By six o'clock, he had stopped counting and had almost forgotten that Veronica was on the same planet. Her crowd of admirers had thinned as customers left for the commute home or moved into the dining room.

The proprietor of Holloway's favorite bar and restaurant was Otha Leonard, alias "Lenny." A good-natured man, Lenny liked to glad-hand his patrons, but had the discretion to remain in the woodwork when assignations were being arranged or in progress. Many of Lenny's customers were regulars whom he cared enough about to offer occasional advice and assistance. He took particular delight in playing Cupid.

Holloway was draining his glass when Lenny approached.

"How are you, Mr. Holloway?"

"How do I look, Lenny?"

With characteristic diplomacy, Lenny sidestepped the question. "Sometimes it's not how you look, it's how you feel. Considering the amount of gin you've been putting away, I guess you're not feeling any pain. How about a little food to suck up a some of that alcohol? I got rib-eye steak that's as tender as a mother's love." Lenny made a smoothing movement with his hands and flashed his big smile. Holloway agreed and Lenny passed the order to his wife. Turning back to Holloway, he observed, "Only three things make a man drink like you're drinking: work, women, and money."

"What else is there?"

"Nothing," said Lenny, grinning. "You heard it here first."

Holloway chuckled in spite of his gloomy mood. "Let me buy you a drink and tell you about women."

"The drink sounds like a good idea, but if you knew anything about women, you wouldn't be sitting there ruining your liver." They had a good laugh.

"Seriously," said Lenny, "I'd love to join you but . . .," he nodded toward the arriving dinner crowd. "A few weeks back, you were asking about Veronica. She's at the bar now. Why don't you buy her a drink? She'll listen to your story. Man, in this town, nobody's harder on one woman than another one. We got the numbers on our side." He winked.

"Thanks, but I've had all the women I can stand for one day." Lenny moved on, working his way around the room until he got to Veronica. He whispered something into her ear.

* * *

While Holloway ate his steak, Donna was having dinner with Dan Vogle in her apartment. Her mood was on the upswing now that she was sure WorldCorp was not a CIA front, which meant that Holloway was not in trouble with his former employer. The fact that Miriam was out of her life was icing on the cake. Vogle, on the other hand, was somber. He was wondering how Donna would react when she discovered that he had not cancelled the meeting with Hugh Stiles. He would know soon enough.

The bell rang while Donna was washing dishes, and Dan opened the door to three strangers. One of them introduced himself. "Good evening. I'm Hugh Stiles. You must be Dan Vogle." Stiles stuck out his hand. "These are my associates," he said, nodding in the direction of Trung and Braxton, each of whom carried a large briefcase. "We have an appointment with you and your partners."

Instinct told Dan to slam the door. He had expected one man. There were three, and two of them looked like muscle.

Braxton saw Vogle hesitatate, and attempted to reassure him. "We're here to discuss Dr. Reid. I have documents that might interest you." He hefted his briefcase.

Dan Vogle made a decision, and it was the wrong one. "Come on in."

Donna came into the hall. "Who is it, Dan?"

Stiles answered her. "Mrs. Goodwin?" Donna nodded. "We talked on the phone. I'm Hugh Stiles. These gentlemen are kindred spirits in the matter of Dr. Reid. They would prefer to remain anonymous." Donna looked at the three men in her hallway, then stared daggers at Dan Vogle. There was an awkward silence, but Stiles stayed on task. "If Ed would join us, we can get down to business."

Without taking her eyes off Dan, Donna said, "*Ed* is not here. He left instructions for this meeting to be cancelled. Mr. Vogle evidently forgot to call you."

There was another pregnant silence while Stiles' eyes darted between Donna and Dan. "This is very awkward," was all that he could think of to say.

Braxton stepped into the gap. "Mrs. Goodwin, could I use your bathroom while you and Mr. Stiles sort this out?"

Donna's reply was frosty. "Mr. Vogle and Mr. Stiles can sort this out. I have no interest in Dr. Reid. The bathroom is this way." She left Vogle, Stiles, and Trung standing in the hall.

In the bathroom, Braxton took a radio from his briefcase and spoke into it. "Base, this is Bravo. One of our hosts is missing."

In a van nearby, Admiral Schaeffer asked, "Which host?"

"*The* host."

Schaeffer's jaw muscles tightened. "I'm coming in, Bravo. We'll proceed as planned." He turned to his driver, Pinchot. "Let's go."

Braxton stalled in the bathroom until he heard Schaeffer ring the doorbell. Then, he stepped out and joined the crowd in the hallway. Donna was already there. The admiral wore a suede jacket, dark slacks, and a hat to cover his distinctive silver hair. He smiled pleasantly and said, "Mrs. Goodwin, Mr. Vogle, I'm Admiral Schaeffer. These gentlemen are with me. I'd like to have a word with both of you, in private, if I may? It's a matter of the utmost urgency."

Reluctantly Donna led Dan and the admiral to the basement workroom. Braxton tagged along with his briefcase. Trung, Stiles, and Pinchot waited upstairs in Donna's living room. Pinchot gave the basement contingent exactly two minutes to get settled. Then he excused himself and took the stairs up to Holloway's apartment quietly and two at a time, pulling on surgical gloves as he went. The apartment was unlocked, as usual. Pinchot gave it a quick, expert search. No Holloway, but he did find Holloway's automatic, the real object of his prowl. Stiles gave Pinchot a suspicious look when he returned to the living room, but knew better than to ask questions. Trung sat quietly, watching Stiles.

In the basement, Schaeffer was saying, "I assume you know that I work for the Company." Donna glared. Dan nodded. "Good. And I know that both of you are former Company employees. So, we have common ground." He leaned forward and gave them his earnest look. "During the past few weeks, your firm has engaged in activities that have jeopardized certain Company operations—"

"Is that why your men were watching my house?" interrupted Donna.

The admiral's patronizing smile was the only indication that he had heard the question. "Specifically," he continued, "your partner Ed Holloway made inquiries about a Swiss firm called WorldCorp, the late Jack Slayton, a Mr. Dillworth, Dr. Reid, and certain of my activities in Vietnam. You served the Company well in the past," he turned to Donna, "as did your late husband and your partner, Holloway. I'm sure that it was not your intent to place our agents in danger. Therefore, the mischief-maker must be whoever hired you. I need to know that person's name, exactly what instructions you were given, and what you've uncovered so far."

He looked eagerly from Donna to Dan. Silence. Unruffled, Schaeffer said, "I appreciate your loyalty to your client, but there's more at stake here than a violation of confidentiality. I assure you that this is a matter of the utmost importance to the security of the United States. I'm prepared to compensate you for any financial losses you might incur by terminating your relationship with the client in question." Schaeffer beckoned. Braxton put the briefcase on the table and opened it, displaying neat stacks of money. "That is ten thousand dollars. It's yours, now, in return for the information I requested, and your pledge to cease your inquiries." The admiral let his eyes drift beyond his hosts to the vault door.

Donna spoke up, her voice as frosty as ever. "That's very generous of you, Admiral, but you're talking to the wrong people. We don't know the client's name. It's Holloway's case. The client contacted him, requested anonymity, and pays in cash. Holloway did the legwork and made all the contacts."

The admiral studied their faces trying to assess the truth of Donna's statement. Finally, he said, almost to himself, "Yes, of course. That's the way I would have handled it." He focused on Donna. "It's imperative that I see Holloway tonight. Where is he?"

"I don't know. Now, will you please take your people and leave. I am not involved with this. I want no part of it."

The admiral was gracious. "Of course, but would you indulge me one or two questions more?" Donna glared at him impatiently. "The vault," said Schaeffer, looking at it over Donna's shoulder, "is that where Holloway keeps his working papers?"

"The vault has nothing to do with work," snapped Donna. "I keep my fur coat and other valuables there."

"How very convenient for you. I didn't realize that this was a high crime area."

"If you will excuse me, Admiral Schaeffer . . ." Donna stood to go, but Braxton moved to block the stairs. Schaeffer raised a deliberately late restraining hand to him, and he stepped aside. It was a clear message to Donna that she was not in control. She brushed past Braxton in a huff and stomped up the steps, with him at her heels. Dan Vogle tried to follow, but the admiral caught him by the arm.

"Mr. Vogle," said Schaeffer, in his most persuasive voice, "you know that the records I want are in that vault. I mean to get them one way or another. One way is for you to simply open the vault, in return for which I will give you half the money in this attaché case. I know you can use five thousand dollars. I've seen your credit record.

"The other way is a bit more difficult for me and unpleasant for you. I have a man standing by who will come here and blow the vault open. It will take him a couple of hours, but I'm told that the explosion won't even rattle the kitchen pots. The complication is that blowing safes is a crime. I'd have to kill you and Mrs. Goodwin to cover it up. I'm prepared to do just that, if necessary." Schaeffer picked up one of the money packets and flipped through it. "Which alternative would you prefer?"

Dan Vogle went to the vault door and spun the dial while Admiral Schaeffer counted the money out on the table. The last tumbler fell into place and Dan pulled the door open.

The living room upstairs was uncomfortably quiet. Donna sat in a chair under Braxton's watchful eye. Pinchot kept an eye on Stiles, who was also ill at ease. Trung wandered silently around the room faking an interest in Donna's collection of Korean art. Suddenly, there was a loud crash and moan in the basement. Donna leaped to her feet yelling, "Dan? Dan!" and ran to the basement steps with Braxton behind her.

*   *   *

Holloway looked up from his steak to see Veronica standing at his table carrying two drinks. *Damn Lenny*, he thought.

"Hi, there. Lenny said you could use some company." Holloway said nothing. "If you don't invite me to sit down, I'll be embarrassed and you will make a liar out of Lenny. Besides, I read in *Cosmo* that I could get away with this. If it doesn't work, the sexually aggressive woman may be set back a couple of decades."

Good line, observed Holloway, with clinical detachment. He shrugged indifferently. "At this moment, I am not a fan of the sexual revolution. I liked the old days: speak when you're spoken to, come when you're called, and walk three paces behind. Sit at your own risk. I'm not feeling sociable tonight."

Veronica smiled. "Honesty *and* humor. There may be hope for you." She put down the drinks and slid into the booth, facing him.

"Is this your hobby, reclaiming drunks?" Holloway asked.

Her voice took on a sharpness. "Call it a passing interest. 'Hobby' sounds habitual. Regardless of what *Cosmo* says, I don't make a habit of carrying drinks to men at Lenny's or anywhere else."

"Sorry," said Holloway. "Why did you come over?"

"Curiosity. Lenny said you were asking about me a while back. How come you never got around to asking me about me?"

"I'm shy," said Holloway, being deliberately unconvincing.

Mischief danced in her eyes. "If you had gotten around to asking, what would you have wanted to know?"

"This is a bad day for that question, but you tell me something. How would you feel if a man liked you because you reminded him of another woman?"

"Men use that line a lot. They think it's flattering. I don't. I want a man to like me because I'm unique. No woman wants to be a carbon copy. Fashion designers have known that for centuries. Sad to say," she looked around the room, "the word hasn't made it to Lenny's." She paused. "Do I remind you of someone?"

"Yes."

"Is that why you're here?"

"I'm here to get drunk," Holloway informed her.

"Why?"

He wondered himself. "I don't want to talk about it."

"A woman giving you problems?" Veronica asked, coyly.

"No," he lied, but she seemed to know anyway and launched into a dissertation on the sorry state of male-female relationships in the District. Her retentive mind disgorged dollops of magazine psycho-babble to support her thesis, but Holloway had stopped listening. His thoughts were on Miriam.

When he focused on Veronica again, she was saying, "You do like women, don't you?" He had no idea what had led up to that question. He must have given her a hostile look. "No offense meant. It's just that you hardly ever come in with anyone, and when you do, it's with your friend Sid. People start to wonder, you know."

"I like women," he said bitterly. "Sid is a good friend. I come here alone to sit and think. Nobody bothers you here, usually." Holloway stood and dropped some bills on the table. "Would you excuse me? I've got to water the plants." Veronica watched in surprise as he moved toward the front door on legs that were none too steady.

The gin had subdued Holloway by the time the taxi deposited him at Sid Mitchell's. He went straight to bed. The plants would have to wait until morning. He slept well and awakened shortly after five with no headache, but a body that moved in low gear. After a shower and breakfast, he searched out the water can and made the rounds of the house plants. He was thankful that Sid's pet *Aralia elegantissima*, a dark mauve feathery devil, sometimes mistaken for marijuana, had survived several days of neglect. Holloway finished watering the plants and returned to the bedroom where he divided his attention between dressing and the morning television news. He paid scant attention until the announcer shifted to the local scene.

"In local news, the war for the drug trade continues. Last night, police were called to the scene of several execution-style slayings, apparently the result of competition between rival drug gangs in Arlington, Virginia, not far from the Pentagon." Holloway stopped tying his shoelace to look up at the screen. The announcer's image dissolved into a shot of ambulances and police cars with flashing lights in front of a row house. "Police were called to this house last night by a neighbor who heard suspicious noises and later saw strangers leaving in a van." Close-up of the house. Holloway's heart stopped when the camera focused on the house number. "The bodies of three men and a woman were found shot to death here." Close-up of white-coated attendants bringing out the bodies. The victim's faces were covered, but a ghoulish camera followed one of the baskets into the ambulance. Holloway, his nose almost touching the television screen, saw only the woman's salt-and-pepper hair with the ever-present pencil still lodged in it.

Holloway tried to imagine how they died, but couldn't. Schaeffer could have told him.

"Mr. Vogle," said the admiral in his most persuasive voice, "you know that the records I want are in that vault. I mean to get them one way or the other. One way is for you to open the vault for me, in return for which I will give you half the money in this attaché case. I know you can use five thousand dollars. I've seen your credit record.

"The other way is a bit more difficult for me and unpleasant for you. I have a man standing by who will come here and blow the vault open. It will take him a couple of hours, but I'm told that the explosion won't even rattle the kitchen pots. The complication is that blowing safes is a crime. I'd have to kill you and Mrs. Goodwin to cover it up. I'm prepared to do just that, if necessary." The admiral picked up one of the money packets and flipped through it. "Which alternative would you prefer?"

Reluctantly, Dan Vogle went to the vault door and spun the dial while Admiral Schaeffer counted the money out on the table. The last tumbler fell into place and Dan pulled the door open. When he turned, Schaeffer shot him in the forehead. Vogle's flailing arm sent the sideboard coffeepot crashing to the floor.

Upstairs, the living room was uncomfortably quiet. Donna sat in a chair under the watchful eye of Braxton. Pinchot kept an eye on Stiles, who was also ill at ease. Trung wondered around the room faking an interest in Donna's collection of Korean art. No one heard the shots, but the coffeepot crash brought Donna to her feet yelling, "Dan? Dan!" She ran to the basement steps with Braxton close behind. When she was half way down, he shot her in the back with a silenced revolver. The three slugs propelled Donna into a grotesque heap at the bottom of the staircase.

When he saw Braxton fire, Stiles came out of his chair in a wide-eyed panic. "Hey! Wait!" he yelled, but the waiting was over. Pinchot, now in his surgical gloves, jammed a chair cushion against Stiles' chest to muffle the sound and shot him with Holloway's automatic. Stiles fell to the carpet, his lifeless eyes staring at the ceiling.

Trung opened his case and distributed its contents: three kilos of cocaine in individually wrapped packets, a scale to weigh them, and other items that went with the wholesale end of the drug trade.

In a few minutes, the grisly business was almost finished. Schaeffer surveyed the scene as they were about to leave. The basement was a shambles. Bodies were still lying where they had fallen. The vault door was ajar, its contents stuffed into plastic trash bags to be loaded into Schaeffer's van.

"Let's wrap it up," Schaeffer ordered. "Braxton, leave your gun next to the woman's body. We don't want to carry away any incriminating evidence." Braxton hesitated, but did as he was told. When he stood up, Pinchot shot him dead with Holloway's gun.

Minutes later, the van was travelling across the 14th Street Bridge toward Washington. Pinchot said, "That was a first-rate hit, Admiral."

"We didn't get Holloway, you idiot," was Schaeffer's reply.

*   *   *

The woman who lived next door to Sid Mitchell was watching the morning news as she dressed for work. Her face was grim as the white-coated attendants brought out the bodies. She stepped into the bathroom to make a final adjustment to her hair. When she heard the anguished howl of grief, it sounded as though it had come from

Mr. Mitchell's house, but that couldn't be. Mr. Mitchell was out of town. It had probably come from someone in the crowd around the ambulance, someone close to those lowlife drug dealers. Serves them right!

"Police," continued the news anchor, "found drug paraphernalia and a wholesale quantity of cocaine on the premises. This man,"— a photograph appeared on the screen—"Edward Holloway, is being sought for questioning in connection with the slayings."

Holloway knew they were dead, but he had to check. Dan Vogle didn't answer his phone. He called his own office and a strange male voice did answer. Holloway hung up immediately. At Hugh Stiles' home, a woman who identified herself as a neighbor told him curtly that "the family" could not be disturbed just now, while someone sobbed in the background. He had saved the worst for last. Donna's phone rang several times. He could almost see some detective telling everyone to be quiet. Then another unfamiliar male voice answered. By then, Holloway had no need to ask questions. He dropped the receiver in the cradle and wept.

They had drummed it into him long ago at the course on running agents: survive first, mourn later. But survival was a matter of knowing the enemy, and Holloway didn't. Who had hit his house? Whoever it was had expected him to be there. That pointed the finger at Stiles, but he was sure that Stiles was dead. Why?

Stiles was hit because he was going to tell me something. Who would have known? The CIA? They might have had Stiles' office phone tapped when he called to make the appointment yesterday. Stiles said he wanted to talk about Dr. Reid. How did Stiles know I was interested in Reid?

The realization hit Holloway. He grabbed the phone, dialed Geneva, Switzerland and got the number from Information. It was after 2 a.m. when a sleepy Jessica Talbot rolled across her bed to pick up the receiver.

"Yes?"

"No names, okay? Do you recognize my voice?"

There was a pause while Talbot came fully awake. "Yes. I know who you are."

"Listen carefully and please do exactly as I tell you. Some hostile competitors found out about the insurance arrangement we discussed. Now, I have a health insurance problem. I have to talk to you, but not on your phone. Look in the telephone book and find the number of a public place where I can call you in thirty minutes. Don't give me the location, just the number."

Thirty minutes later, the desk clerk at Geneva's Steigenberger Hotel beckoned to Jessica Talbot. "Madam, your call has come through from the United States. You can take it in the booth."

"Our last conversation was monitored," Holloway told her. "Your office and your house may be bugged or it could be on my end. In the last twenty-four hours, some friends of mine have died, and I'm in danger. You need to take measures for your personal safety."

Talbot was calm. "Are you sure that the situation on your end is related to our previous conversation?"

"I'd bet on it, but I can't prove it."

"That's good enough for me. Thanks for the tip. It appears that things are heating up here a bit, too." Referring to Dillworth, she said, "I have a line on that missing person you came here to see. His employers have located him and are closing in with hostile intent. We're trying to get to him first. He may want to roll over on them to save his skin."

"When will you see him?"

"Anytime. I'm leaving for the Riviera this afternoon. Does that ring a bell?"

"Yes." Holloway remembered that Dillworth's second wife lived on the Riviera.

"Where can I reach you?"

"Hotel France, Rue Saint Michel in Menton, near Monte Carlo. Are you coming to Europe?"

Holloway said, "Good hunting," and hung up.

* * *

The instructor—a large, red-faced man with the nickname of "Irish" and a legend at The Farm—had said it: "When you're blown, you're blown!" Holloway could still picture him readjusting his pants over his ample belly as he spoke. "Assume," said Irish, "that everything you've ever touched and everyone you ever knew under your cover identity is blown. So, you don't go where you normally go and don't see anybody you normally see. And for God's sake, don't go back home for your suitcase or the passport stuck up behind the bathroom mirror with tape, or to say goodbye to your bastard children and screw your girlfriend one more time." Bowing to the women in the audience, he added, "Or your boyfriend, as the case may be." He lowered his head and peered over the top of his glasses. "Mind you, they'll be damned good at it if they're working for the opposition. No, no," he intoned, wagging a forefinger. "The only thing that matters is that you're blown and the only thing that can save your pitiful little ass is to make a swift, clean exit. So, always— I repeat, always—leave yourself a nice care package tucked away somewhere. Keep it in a place that you don't frequent, but one that is easy to get to, and have an escape route known only to you."

Holloway remembered that advice and, in every undercover assignment, he practiced what "Irish" had preached. There had always been little packages somewhere, though he had never been forced to use them. And, when the opportunity presented itself, Holloway, like agents all over the world, was not above rat-holing a passport that had not been called in due to some bureaucratic screw up or because operational heat overrode tidy administration. Hence, the two passports in his bank safe-deposit box. It had never occurred to him that he might have to use them to escape from the United States, which only served to prove the wisdom of the Irishman's advice. The box also contained a knife, a Smith and Wesson hammerless revolver with silencer, and some cash. Not a king's ransom, but it would get him to the Riviera. He purchased a one-way ticket to Nice at a downtown ticket office and caught a train to New York and JFK Airport.

CHAPTER 15

<u>April 1987, Menton, on the Riviera</u>

Ackerman drew back the curtain and looked down into the compound of the luxurious house below. A naked, dripping woman stood on the edge of the pool, poised for another plunge. "Is that her?"

"Yes," said the big Frenchman.

Ackerman played the binoculars over the glistening red hair on her body and licked his ugly lower lip.

The sniper, Lutz, came to the window and looked down with a professional eye as he twisted the two sections of his rifle together. "It would be an easy shot from here."

Ackerman gave him a disapproving scowl. "You don't touch her until *after* we get Dillworth.

"What's the situation?"

The Frenchman responded. "The owners of this house are on ski holiday. Madame Dillworth owns the house below. She visits her husband every day at the clinic. Every second day, they have lunch on the beach. Tomorrow is picnic day."

"Are they alone on the beach?" asked Ackerman.

"Yes, usually. They like to find an isolated spot. He fondles her in public," said the Frenchman with disgust. "Low class, but lots of money."

A fourth man trudged in with the suitcases and dropped them in the center of the living room. Like the others, he was tan, fit, and wore fashionable resort clothes.

"Tomorrow," Ackerman announced, "the three of us"—he included the Frenchman and the baggage handler—"will follow Dillworth's wife when she leaves for the clinic and hit them both while they're having lunch on the beach. Lutz, you stay here to cover the house in case anything goes wrong. If either of the Dillworths show up after we leave, kill them and get out, and be sure to call me on the radio. I don't want to drive back up here and find the police waiting for me." Lutz nodded. "Okay, let's take a look at that clinic."

* * *

The trip to the Riviera was exhausting. Holloway got little sleep on the New York-to-Nice flight. During the limousine ride along the Grand Cornish roadway to Menton he dozed, missing the breathtaking view of the sea and the coastal towns. He arrived at the Hotel France in the early afternoon and discovered that Jessica Talbot had thoughtfully reserved a room in his name. He left a note for her at the desk, went directly to bed, and did not stir until Talbot called him four hours later. They agreed to meet for dinner in half an hour. Holloway slipped into tan slacks, matching sweater, and white shirt with a brown ascot. He took one last look in the mirror. "James Bond, you ain't." He shrugged and left.

Talbot was waiting in the lobby wearing sandals and a body-hugging open-backed green dress with a mid-thigh hemline. She eyed Holloway with approval as he approached. "You cut quite a rakish figure, Mr. Holloway. Welcome to the Riviera."

He shook her hand. "Thanks for the compliment and room reservation. Forget the 'Mister.' Just 'Holloway' will do fine."

"And I'm 'Jessie'," she responded.

"Okay, Jessie, where's the restaurant? I'm starved."

She led him through streets crowded with people in every kind of apparel from the latest to the least. They ended up at a table in an outdoor restaurant on the Promenade du Soleil with a beautiful view of the sea.

"Have you located Dillworth?" asked Holloway.

"Yes. He's in a posh drug treatment clinic not far from here."

"Oh?"

"Yes. Evidently, Dillworth is an addict."

"Where is this clinic?" Holloway inquired.

"A few kilometers from here along the coast road. It's in the hills above the town of Garavan."

Holloway looked at his watch. "Can we go there tonight?"

"We can go, but we won't get in. The place is reserved for celebrities and the rich. It has security like you wouldn't believe. They lock it up tight at night. Nobody goes in or out except the staff. If you're willing to wait until tomorrow, Dillworth will come to us."

"Why would he do that?" asked Holloway.

Talbot said, "Dillworth and his wife have lunch on the beach every other day here in Menton. It must be part of the therapy. Tomorrow is their beach day. We'll drop by and join them."

Holloway was surprised at her knowledge. "You haven't been here much longer than I have. How do you know their routine?"

She smiled. "As soon as I got the tip that Dillworth was here, I sent down an investigator from my office to keep an eye on his wife. With Mrs. Dillworth going to the clinic every day and a few discreet questions, it didn't take him long to establish their pattern. He phoned me a description of the man she was lunching with, and here I am."

"Is your man still here? We might need him."

"Sorry. I sent him back to Geneva yesterday, after he briefed me. If Dillworth has a story to tell, it's going to be all mine."

"You want WorldCorp that bad?"

"I thought I made that clear in Geneva."

Tough lady, thought Holloway. He relaxed a bit. "How did you find out that Dillworth was here?"

"I have an informant in the WorldCorp security office. She overheard Ackerman and some of his staff planning to come down here and 'settle with the son-of-a-bitch once and for all.' I could kick myself for not guessing that Dillworth would hide out near his wife's place. On the other hand, it wouldn't have done me any good until now because I didn't know that the WorldCorp people were out to get him."

"Any sign of Ackerman yet?"

"No. He left Geneva by car with two men just before I did. So, it may take them a while unless they drive day and night. He could have sent an advance man like I did, though. That would give him at least three helpers on the ground."

Holloway gave the security chief's transportation arrangements some thought. "If Ackerman was in such a hurry to find Dillworth, why do you suppose he's coming by car?"

"Cars don't leave telltales like airline reservations and there are no clerks and stewardesses to remember you. I think Dillworth is in deep trouble."

Holloway nodded his agreement. "Tell me about his wife."

"Ex-wife, actually. She lives in the high rent district on Cap Martin, over there." Talbot pointed to a long finger of land jutting out into the sea a few kilometers west of Menton. "She spends her days shopping and working on her tan. Dillworth used to come down to see her every few months or so until he disappeared. In between his visits she collected young men. Mr. and Mrs. Dillworth are one horny pair."

Holloway took another sip of wine and finished his salmon. "What's your plan for tomorrow?"

"We'll follow Mrs. Dillworth when she goes to pick up her husband for lunch. They always picnic on the beach. It should be easy to approach them there."

Holloway preferred a more private location for his meeting with Dillworth, but it was Talbot's show. "Sounds fine. What time do we roll?"

"Nine, sharp."

"In that case," said Holloway, pushing his chair back, "I think I'll get back to the hotel and get some more sleep."

"Don't you want to look the town over?"

"No, thanks. I didn't come here for a vacation. I came because two of my friends are dead."

"I'm sorry. Should I ask about details?"

"No," replied Holloway.

* * *

At ten the next morning Christine Dillworth came out of her house carrying the picnic basket prepared by her housekeeper. The flouncy dress swirled around her long legs as she strode toward the garage. A wide-brimmed blue hat covered her red hair and she wore blue tinted sunglasses. Her body was lean and graceful and could have been twenty-four or forty-two. It was a body that had never known the ravages of cellulite and never wanted for a tan. Showing lots of leg, she climbed into the midnight blue Mercedes 380 SEL and blasted out of the driveway in a cloud of gravel.

When the Mercedes was almost out of sight, Jessica Talbot and Holloway fell in behind it in their rented Fiat. There was no need to stay close. They knew the route to the clinic.

Christine drove to the main road that ran along the spine of Cap Martin, followed it down to the tip and east around the coast into Menton. Traffic was moving steadily and there was plenty of it. A teenager in a red BMW convertible kept trying to pass the Fiat, but oncoming traffic held him back. Talbot followed Christine's Mercedes through Menton, moving up to a position directly behind it by the time they arrived in Garavan. Shortly before they reached the intersection where Christine was to turn off the coast road, the BMW kid saw a break in the oncoming traffic and whipped out into the left lane to take the space between the Mercedes and Talbot's Fiat. Just as the BMW whipped back into the right lane behind her, Christine slowed suddenly for her left turn, without signaling. The kid in the BMW cursed and stood on his brakes. Talbot floored the brake pedal in the Fiat, saw that she would have space to stop, then checked the rear view mirror. She saw clearly the face of the driver of the green Jaguar behind her as the car hurtled toward her trunk amid the squeal of tires. A second later, Christine made her left turn and the BMW accelerated toward the Italian border with Talbot on his tail. The Jaguar turned left and followed Christine into the hills above Garavan.

"Where the hell are we going?" Holloway asked.

"Up ahead to make a U-turn. I didn't follow Dillworth because Ackerman was in that green Jaguar behind us. I think he's been there all the way down from Cap Martin."

Before she found a turnaround, they were at the border and Talbot's rented Fiat must have been the one car the Italians decided to check that day. "Your passports please," said the guard, "and would you open the trunk?"

* * *

Christine jumped out of the Mercedes and ran up the steps of the old mansion, which showed no outward signs of being a cure house for addicts. As usual the director, a rotund, bearded Frenchman named Ducasse, was on hand to greet her and chat. This morning, Christine brushed by him with a perfunctory greeting and ran to Dillworth's room.

Randy Dillworth looked good for a sick man. The cure was almost over. He wore a yellow sleeveless sweater and white pants over hand-tooled leather cowboy boots. Christine put her fingertips over his lips when he tried to kiss her.

"Randy, someone followed me."

Dillworth got an automatic from his closet while Christine kept talking. "Two cars followed me down from Cap Martin. When I turned off the coast road, one kept going toward the border. The other one followed me right up to the gate of the clinic and drove past slowly. I'm sure the driver was looking at me."

"Did you recognize him?"

"No, but he had a cruel mouth."

"Ackerman! What about the other car?"

"It was a white Fiat with a man and a woman. I didn't get a good look at them."

Dillworth said, "Let's get out of here, baby." He shoved his pistol into the back of his waistband and led her to the director's office.

Ducasse came from behind his desk with a great display of concern when he saw the worried expressions on their faces. "What is the problem, Monsieur Dillworth?"

"Ducasse, some men followed my wife up here. I'm concerned for her safety."

Ducasse wasn't sure how to handle that one. Men always followed women on the Riviera. That was what men did, and Madame Dillworth certainly rated a side trip. However, one did not point out the obvious to a paying customer in distress. "Could the police handle the matter to Madame's satisfaction?"

"No," said Dillworth hastily. "I just want to get my wife away from here and we don't want to take the Mercedes. Can someone drive us to Menton?"

"Of course, if that is all you require. My chauffeur, Marcel, has errands in Monte Carlo today. He's leaving just now. Would you care to ride with him?"

Ducasse's black BMW 735 roared out of the clinic compound with Marcel at the wheel and the Dillworths crouched out of sight on the back seat. Several hundred meters down the road from the clinic, Ackerman observed the car through his binoculars and dismissed it. He looked at his watch. There was no need for concern. Dillworth's wife had entered the clinic only ten minutes before. He settled back to wait.

The chauffeur put the 735 through the curves like there was no tomorrow and kept an eye on the rear view mirror. By the time he approached the coast road, he was satisfied that they were not being tailed. "I think we are not being followed, monsieur."

Dillworth and his wife sat up in the back seat just as they were turning onto the coast road. At that instant Talbot and Holloway were turning into the clinic road.

"That's the Fiat!" shouted Christine.

The chauffeur had turned right onto the Menton road and saw that the left lane was clear. He geared down and floored the gas pedal. The big BMW leaped past seven cars before it swerved back into the right lane.

"The Dillworths were in that BMW!" yelled Talbot, but it was too late for her to abort her turn off the coast road. She went up the clinic road a short distance, made a quick U-turn and came back to the intersection. When she turned the Fiat right onto the coast road, there was no sign of the BMW. Talbot hit the wheel with her palm. "Damn!"

"We've got two choices," said Holloway. "Go back to the house or go to the clinic and try to find out where they're headed."

"I vote for the house," said Talbot.

* * *

When Talbot and Holloway arrived at Dillworth's Cap Martin house, it was empty. They parked the car on the road above it and waited. When fifteen minutes passed without a sign of Dillworth, they got out of the car and walked up the hill overlooking the house.

Holloway thought about Irish and his lecture on blown covers. He turned to Talbot and said, "Let's say a guy is surprised by unwanted visitors and decides to run. He can either run with what's on his back and his credit card or, before he starts out, he can pick up a change of clothes, a little travelling money, and some transportation."

"Sounds reasonable," said Talbot, "but if Dillworth is running with what's on his back, we can forget him. He could be leaving the Riviera right now by plane, boat, train, or car."

"I'll buy that," agreed Holloway. "But let's assume he had a limited amount of cash with him at the clinic and he doesn't want to leave a paper trail of credit card receipts. He could drop down to his bank in Menton and get money, but where would he go for clothes and transportation? Does he have any family or friends here who would lend him a car?"

Jessica Talbot laughed. "Take a look around you, Holloway. This is the crowd that the Dillworths run with. These people have a car for every member of the family. You ought to see some of the garages . . ." Talbot stopped in mid-sentence and looked at Holloway. "Dillworth has another garage."

"Where?"

"Near Roquebrune on the west side of the Cap. His wife owns a house over there. She leases it out. The place has two garages and Dillworth uses one of them to store his antique motorcycle collection."

"Any cars?"

"I don't know, but he might have clothes and money stashed there." She lengthened her strides toward the Fiat. "There's an apartment over the garage. Dillworth used to pick up women on the beach and take them there for the afternoon."

"Come on!" said Holloway, breaking into a run.

Lutz had noted the arrival of Talbot and Holloway at the Dillworths' Cap Martin house from his window overlooking the compound. He observed them for several minutes, then picked up his radio. "Mobile, this is Base."

Ackerman was irritated. It had been an hour since Christine Dillworth had entered the clinic and he was just about to go in himself when Lutz called. He took the radio from the seat and spoke into it. "This is Mobile."

Lutz watched Talbot and Holloway through the curtain. "Twenty minutes ago a man and a woman showed up here in a white Fiat. The man climbed the fence at the Dillworth house and rattled the doors. They're just sitting here now. Looks like a stakeout to me."

The Frenchman said, "There was a white Fiat behind Madame Dillworth all the way to Garavan this morning, but it kept going toward the border when she took the clinic turnoff."

Anger blazed in Ackerman's eyes. "Standby, Base." He drove the Jaguar down the road to the iron gate that barred the entrance to the clinic grounds. A guard came out to the car.

"We're friends of Monsieur and Madame Dillworth," said Ackerman. "They were supposed to meet us in town for lunch an hour ago, but didn't show up. We thought they might have been delayed here. May we come in and inquire?"

The guard looked them over. "Of course, monsieur."

Ackerman parked the car and the three of them followed the guard to the office of Monsieur Ducasse.

"I am afraid that Monsieur and Madame Dillworth have already left," explained Ducasse.

"Madam Dillworth's Mercedes is still in your driveway," observed Ackerman.

Ducasse's pleasant manner evaporated. "Monsieur, I have told you that they are not here. Now, I must ask you to leave."

Taking his cue, the guard stepped forward. When he did, Ackerman pulled a pistol and pointed it at the man. "Stay where you are." He turned to the Frenchman. "Check Dillworth's room." The two henchmen ran out of the office as Ducasse began to sputter. "Shut up and sit down, Monsieur Ducasse. If Dillworth is not here, we may leave quietly."

The Frenchman came in a few minutes later shoving Ducasse's secretary in front of him. "The Dillworths are gone. This one," he pushed the secretary at Ackerman, "said they left in Monsieur Ducasse's car about an hour ago."

Ackerman turned to Ducasse. "Where were they going?"

"I don't know. They asked to be taken off the clinic grounds."

"I don't believe you, Monsieur Ducasse." Ackerman took the silencer out of the pocket of his baggy pants and screwed it onto the barrel of his gun. Ducasse and the secretary went pale.

The guard knew that this would be his last chance. He shoved the secretary at Ackerman and dove for the shelter of Ducasse's desk, drawing his revolver. Ackerman sidestepped the secretary and moved toward the desk, firing as he went. He hit the guard twice in the head before the man got off a shot.

Ducasse sat there shocked, the guard's blood splattered on his trousers. The secretary was babbling hysterically. Ackerman slapped her until she lapsed into a convulsive sob. Then he turned to Ducasse.

"I don't have time to waste. If you don't tell me right now where your chauffeur took the Dillworths I will shoot this woman."

"A moment, monsieur," pleaded Ducasse.

"There are no more moments left." Ackerman's silencer spat fire. The impact of the bullet slammed the woman against the wall and she crumpled into a quiet heap on the floor. Ackerman turned the gun on Ducasse. "I'll kill you next. Where did Dillworth go?"

Ducasse was cringing in his chair, hands up in a futile attempt to deflect a bullet meant for him. He stammered, "Monsieur Dillworth asked the chauffeur to take him to Menton."

"Where in Menton?"

"I swear to you, he did not say."

"Where is your chauffeur now?" asked Ackerman.

"I sent him to Monte Carlo on an errand."

"Can you contact him?"

"I can try. He is making several stops." Hands shaking, Ducasse reached for the telephone.

"Carefully, monsieur," warned Ackerman. "We all speak fluent French." Then he took the Frenchman aside and said, "Keep an eye on him. I'm going to the car to talk to Lutz."

Ackerman called Lutz on the radio. "Base, this is Mobile. Dillworth gave us the slip. He knows we're in town."

"Then he won't be coming back here," surmised Lutz.

"What are those two people doing?" asked Ackerman.

Lutz pulled the curtain aside to check on Talbot and Holloway. "They're just walking up the hill. Wait! They're running back to the Fiat. They're leaving."

Instinct seized Ackerman. "Follow them and keep in touch by radio. Go!"

Lutz grabbed a raincoat to conceal his rifle and ran to his car. He was sliding behind the wheel as the white Fiat passed the compound headed northwest toward Roqueburne.

Ducasse looked at Ackerman and hunched his shoulders apologetically. "I have left messages for my chauffeur, Marcel, everywhere in Monte Carlo. He has not yet arrived in the city."

"What time do you expect him to return to the clinic?"

"Late, I'm afraid."

"Why late?" inquired Ackerman.

Ducasse hunched his shoulders again. "He is a young man with a nice automobile and there are many pretty girls in Monte Carlo. It is a liberty I permit."

"And one that you may regret. Where does this Marcel live?"

"In Menton."

"Give me the key to your office." Ducasse handed it over. "Write a note for your door. Say that you have gone into Menton on important business and taken your secretary with you. You expect to return late this evening." While Ducasse wrote, the gunmen put the bodies of the secretary and guard in the closet. The look on the clinic director's face indicated that he expected to join them momentarily.

* * *

Lutz lost the white Fiat with Holloway and Talbot just outside the city of Roqueburne. Having no other leads, he headed back to the Cap Martin house to face an unhappy Ackerman.

Meanwhile, Holloway and Talbot were on their way to the Roqueburne house.

"How do you happen to know about this place?" asked Holloway.

"You've got a short memory, Holloway. When you were in Geneva, I told you that I spent one of my vacations down here keeping an eye on Dillworth."

"How do you want to play this?" asked Holloway.

"We're both Treasury agents. If Dillworth cooperates, we'll take turns questioning him. You get what you need. I'll get what I need. We'll wring him out first, then move him after dark."

"Why not move now? Ackerman might know about this place."

"He doesn't. Anyway, I want Dillworth to talk now. The more they say up front, the easier it is to get them to talk later. In cases like this, witnesses sometimes have a change of heart once they're nice and safe in a federal prosecutor's office getting ready to make their deposition. Unless you have something on them personally, it dawns on them that if they don't talk, you don't have a case against anybody. I've seen careers go down the tube over things like this. It's not going to happen to me."

"Suppose he doesn't want to talk at all?" said Holloway.

"Think positively. Besides what other choices does he have?"

"He could kill us and make a run for it."

Talbot gave him a dirty look and turned the car off the road onto a trail that bordered the Dillworth property. They got out and headed toward the compound.

The Dillworth house in Roqueburne, a yellow building with a red tiled roof, was tucked away behind pine and eucalyptus trees, and surrounded by a stone fence. Talbot and Holloway worked their way around to a place in the wall out of sight of the house and climbed over. Talbot's beige linen suit became an instant casualty. She snagged her pants during the climb.

There were two garages on the property. The smaller one was close to the house. Talbot led Holloway to the second garage, which was well away from the house, separated from it by a dense stand of trees. It appeared to be a converted stable. According to Talbot, Dillworth stored his motorcycles downstairs and conducted his amorous encounters in the living quarters above. The steps to the second floor were outside on the east end of the building. When they reached the top, Holloway flattened himself against the wall to the left of the door. Jessica Talbot stood in front of the peep hole, smiled and knocked gently. Without warning, the door was yanked open and Talbot found herself looking into the barrel of Randy Dillworth's automatic.

Talbot pretended to faint. As she dropped away from the muzzle of the gun, Holloway stepped into the doorway, grabbing the automatic by the barrel and forcing the slide back so that it couldn't fire. Then he drove his knee into Dillworth's stomach and twisted the gun out of his hand. Dillworth went down and stayed there when Holloway pointed the gun at him. Holloway took the place in with a glance.

Bathroom and kitchen at the far end of the building. The room they were standing in was a combination bedroom and living room with elegant furnishings. The closet and drawers were open and there was a half-packed suitcase lying open on the floor.

"We're Treasury agents, Mr. Dillworth," said Talbot, holding her identification up. "We know you're in danger and we're here to help you. Sorry about the rough stuff." Talbot smiled and helped a puzzled Dillworth to his feet.

"What does the Treasury Department want with me?"

"Mr. Dillworth, I know that you're hiding from some business associates who mean to do you harm. I'm an investigator and I'm prepared to offer you protection in return for your testimony."

"About what?" Dillworth looked at her suspiciously.

"I'm investigating WorldCorp. I have evidence that the corporation is being used as an illegal tax shelter by U.S. citizens. I believe that your job in Geneva was to look out for their interests and keep the Swiss front men in line."

"You gotta be kidding. WorldCorp is Swiss. It has no U.S. backers."

"Why are the WorldCorp security people after you?"

"Nobody's after me. Get the hell out of here. I'm busy and I got nothing to say." Dillworth returned to his packing.

Talbot followed him across the room. "You'd better think of something, because it's going to be too late when the WorldCorp hoods catch up to you." Dillworth was apparently unmoved by that argument. Talbot persisted. "You've got two ex-wives and two daughters to think about. WorldCorp could retaliate against your family. The government could protect all of you, if you cooperate. We could put you into the witness protection program with new identities, relocation, the whole nine yards." Dillworth kept packing.

"Where's your wife?" asked Holloway, checking the closet.

"A long way from here. Were you two in the white Fiat?"

Talbot went at him again. "If you weren't afraid for your wife's safety, why did you send her away? You have children and a family to think about. The people who are after you could retaliate against them. They would be safe in the witness protection program."

Dillworth turned on both of them. "Look, I'm safe now. I have nothing to say to the Treasury Department, and I want both of you to get the hell out of here. This is private property. I could call the police and have you arrested."

Talbot retorted, "And we can arrest you now as a material witness to suspected income tax fraud."

Dillworth laughed. "In case you forgot, this is France. You got no authority here and I want you out, now!"

Holloway was at the end of his patience. Dillworth was coming from the closet with some silk neckties and a suit when Holloway hit him in the stomach with a fury that had been building since Donna's death. Dillworth doubled over in pain. Holloway drove his knee up into the Texan's face, throwing him backwards against the bed. While Dillworth sat dazed on the floor, Holloway snatched up a tie and lashed him to the bed post by the neck, viciously pulling the tie into a tight knot. Dillworth gasped and clawed at the tie, but Holloway knocked his hands away with the pistol. His anger now at a rolling boil, Holloway grabbed Dillworth's shirt front and got face-to-face with him. "I'm not with the Treasury Department, Tex. This is my authority." Holloway jammed the pistol against Dillworth's forehead and cocked it. "And I don't give a shit whether you talk or die, but you're going to do one or the other."

"You're crazy!" yelled Dillworth, keeping a wary eye on Holloway's trigger finger.

"I'm not crazy. I'm mad." Holloway's eyes were wild. "You want to know what I'm mad about?" Dillworth said nothing, his eyes glued to the gun. "Well, do you!" yelled Holloway, jamming the gun hard into Dillworth's ribs.

"I'm listening, man!" Fear showed in Dillworth's eyes.

"See, you knew the right answer all the time, didn't you?" Holloway gave him another vicious jab with the gun. "I'm mad because yesterday a guy from the CIA came to my house to tell me about Dr. Reid. My friends let him in and while he was there, somebody else dropped by and murdered everybody. What is it about Dr. Reid that causes people to die?" Holloway jabbed him again.

Dillworth winced and licked his lips. "Look, I don't know any 'Dr. Reid.' My doctor's name is—" Dillworth howled as Holloway brought the gun down hard on his kneecap.

"Maybe the Treasury Department has time to screw around with you, Tex, but I'm in a hurry. If you don't give me some straight

answers, I'm going to turn that kneecap to jelly. Understand?"
Dillworth nodded.

"Good. Now, before we start playing "Twenty Questions" again,
I'll tell you that I already know a hell of a lot about you, Jack Slayton,
and Ackerman. I pulled your Army service records. I've got Buie
Trung's immigration file and the medical records from Schaeffer's
destroyer. So, if you lie to me I'll know it and you'll be walking with
a limp for the rest of your very short life. Now, tell me about Dr.
Reid."

"Reid was the doctor on Schaeffer's destroyer. He treated us—
me, Slayton, Trung, and Ackerman—when we were evacuated from
Vietnam at the end of the war."

"That's the cover story. The truth is that none of you were on
that destroyer, were you?"

"Right."

"Why was Reid providing an alibi for you?"

"We were on a job for the CIA."

"What was the mission?"

"It had nothing to do with WorldCorp."

Holloway gave him a skeptical look. "We'll come back to that.
Tell me about Reid."

"There's not much to tell. He fixed the medical records to show
that we were in quarantine during the trip back to California. That
was the end of it."

Without warning, Holloway swung the pistol in a tight arc and
the barrel cracked across Dillworth's knee, eliciting a howl of pain.
"Wrong answer, Tex. That was not the end of it. A few months
later, Reid and his assistant in the ship's medical section were dead.
Both had large life insurance policies with Grosshandel
Versicherungen, a WorldCorp subsidiary. After their policies were
paid off, Grosshandel went out of business. You were connected
with WorldCorp. That ain't coincidence, Tex, that's planning. Why
were they killed?" Dillworth hesitated and Holloway made a
threatening move toward his kneecap.

"Wait!" yelled Dillworth, his self-assurance fading fast. "Can I
have a cigarette? They're in my coat, on the chair. Holloway looked
at the man's hands. They were nicotine-stained and shaking. He got
the cigarette pack from Dillworth's coat and tossed it on the floor
just out of reach. "No cigarette until you tell me about Reid."

Dillworth ran his tongue over his lower lip and swallowed. "I wasn't involved in the hit. Reid tried to shake us down."

"How?"

"He threatened to tell the Navy Department that he falsified the medical records to give us an alibi."

"How could he threaten you if you used him to cover a legitimate CIA mission?"

Dillworth didn't answer.

"Unless," speculated Talbot, "Reid was covering up something illegal."

Dillworth had talked himself into a corner and Holloway prodded him for an answer with the gun. He turned to Talbot for relief. "Is the offer still good for the witness protection program?"

"If you level with us," answered Talbot.

Holloway backed off and kicked the cigarette pack over to Dillworth. There was a pause while he lit up and Jessica Talbot went into the bathroom. When Talbot returned, she carefully placed her pocketbook on the bed near Dillworth's head and pulled a chair up close beside Holloway's.

Exhaling twin streams of smoke from his nostrils, Dillworth insisted, "I didn't kill anybody. What else do you want to know?"

"Tell us about WorldCorp," said Talbot.

Holloway interrupted. "Just a minute. Let's go back to this CIA mission that Reid was covering for. Did it have anything to do with those 'stolen assets' that the current Vietnamese Government is all steamed up about?" Dillworth's eyes registered surprise and he went pale. "Yes, I know about that, too," Holloway assured him, "so don't try to bullshit me." Talbot had no idea what Holloway was talking about, but he seemed to know more that she did. She let him have the lead.

Dillworth had a trapped look about him that finally dissolved into resignation. His shoulders sagged. "Our mission was to steal a Vietnamese plane."

"What was the cargo?"

Dillworth hesitated, licked his lips and said, "South Vietnam's gold reserves."

"How much?" asked Holloway.

"A hundred million dollars worth."

"Christ!" said Holloway. Talbot's mouth fell open.

"I swear, in the beginning, I thought it was a CIA operation."

"Go on," Holloway commanded, "names, dates and places. We want it from start to finish."

"You want history?"

"Do a memory dump on me, Tex. Tell us everything you know."

Dillworth scooted back against the bedpost to relieve the pressure of the tie on his neck and, reluctantly, let his mind drift back to Vietnam. "The caper started long before we stole the plane. The fact that a planeload of gold was sitting around waiting for us was history repeating itself. When Ho Chi Minh's communists took over North Vietnam in 1945, they made the mistake of not getting control of the country's gold reserves, first thing. While Ho was busy liberating the people from their capitalist oppressors, the capitalist oppressors were liberating gold from the Hanoi vaults.

"So, in the early seventies, when the North Vietnamese leadership figured that they were going to win the south, they came up with a plan to capture the gold reserves in Saigon. First, they infiltrated agents into the Central Bank where the gold was being held. Those agents kept a record of bullion shipments into and out of the South Vietnamese treasury and made regular reports to the North Vietnamese Ministry of Economics. Uncle Ho wanted to have the information necessary to trace the gold shipments after the war, in case South Vietnamese officials looted the treasury.

"When American combat troops pulled out of South Vietnam in 1973, the North Vietnamese put the second part of their plan into operation. A unit was established under the direct control of the North Vietnamese Army commander, General Giap, to plan and execute the takeover of the South Vietnamese Central Bank and secure the gold reserves when Giap gave the orders. The unit operated out of a safe house in Saigon.

"In April 1975, the North Vietnamese were on their last major offensive. Da Nang fell on April first and the Saigon government was just thirty days away from losing the war, as it turned out. The underground unit was all primed and ready to take the Central Bank, but the Saigon politicians threw in a monkey wrench at the last minute. The South Vietnamese cabinet met on April second and decided to move the gold to the Bank of International Settlements in Geneva for safekeeping." Dillworth allowed himself a wicked grin. "There was about $220 million in gold at the Central Bank. They started crating it up the same day for air shipment out of the country."

Holloway gave him a skeptical look. "You were in tactical intelligence. How do you know about the economics and politics?"

With a touch of pride, Dillworth answered, "I've read everything that has ever been written on Vietnam. The war changed my life. I wanted to understand what happened over there." Dillworth clawed the tie around his neck. "How about loosening this thing? It's strangling me."

"No chance," said Holloway. "Just keep talking."

"The South Vietnamese crated up about a hundred mil and moved it to a hangar at Tan Son Shut Airport—Hangar 11. They wanted to fly the gold out by commercial airliner, but couldn't find anyone to insure the cargo. When it looked like there was going to be a serious delay, the Vietnamese rolled a C-130 into Hangar 11 one night and loaded the hundred million on board. Their alternate plan was to fly the gold out on military aircraft if Saigon came under attack before the insurance issue was settled. When Hanoi found out about the scheme through their spies at the Central Bank, the High Command organized a raiding party to hit Hangar 11, steal the plane, and fly the gold to Hanoi. Just to keep the military people honest, Hanoi sent along a watchdog from the Economics Ministry, a Dr. Nu. Hanoi ferried the raiders to Vung Tau in a submarine, probably supplied by the Russians. The plan was for the raiders to come ashore on the beach at Vung Tau and join the stream of refugees headed into Saigon. Once they reached the city, they were to lay up at the safehouse until April twenty-eighth. On that date, the special unit would secure the Central Bank while the sub team hit Hangar 11. The hangar raid was to be coordinated with a North Vietnamese air strike on Tan Son Shut. The air strike was a diversion to cover the hangar raid."

Dillworth smiled. "Lots of people have wondered why the NVA didn't shell Saigon until April twenty-ninth, even though they were within artillery range long before that. The reason was they didn't want to spook the South Vietnamese into flying that gold out before the raiding party had a shot at it."

"How did you find out about the raid plan?"

"Me and Jack Slayton were working at the POW detention center in Vung Tau when the North Vietnamese raiding party came ashore.

One of them was captured and he spilled his guts. I was there when the South Vietnamese broke him."

"How did you get involved in stealing the gold?"

"Slayton recognized the prisoner as some big shot in the North Vietnamese Ministry of Economics. He called his CIA contact at the embassy and the guy flew down. He was there when the prisoner told us about the gold. The CIA guy planned the hijacking on the spot."

"Who was he?"

"I never knew his name. We called him 'the Embassy Man.' "

"That's weak, Tex," observed Holloway.

"Look, all of us used some phony work name in those days. Besides, I never met the guy until he came to Vung Tau for the interrogation. I met him . . . maybe five times before we hit the hangar. Never saw him afterwards. Slayton was the one who dealt with the embassy and the brass back at DAO."

"Okay. What happened after the interrogation?"

"We flew to Saigon and rounded up a team to execute the mission. Next, we located the Saigon safe house where the rest of the raiding party was holed up and took it out with a 500-pound bomb. On the twenty-eighth, we hit the gold storage hangar at Ton Son Nhut Airport. Everything worked like a Swiss watch. The NVA air strike came at 1800 hours with our diversion and we blew the control tower to boot. The South Vietnamese Air Force scrambled fighters to deal with the air strike and we slipped away in the confusion."

"When did you find out that it wasn't a CIA operation?"

"Right after the raid. The plane was out over the South China Sea. They gave me two choices: go in with them or swim home." Dillworth took a puff and looked at the ceiling.

"Where did you take the gold?" Talbot asked.

"Taiwan. Ackerman had a Chinese connection there. He met us at an isolated airfield with a chartered civilian plane. The connection got the C-130 and a million in gold on the spot. We loaded the rest of the gold aboard the charter and flew to Zurich."

"Who else was in on the raid besides you, Slayton, Ackerman, and the Embassy Man?"

"Buie Trung and a couple of hired guns named Saxby and Walker. Roper was our pilot and a fellow named Yarborough was the crewchief. They were both Air Force." Holloway wrote the names in a small notebook. "All of us hit Hangar 11 and left on the plane."

"What ever happened to the old gang?"

"Everybody survived the raid except Saxby. He was killed by a Vietnamese guard. We buried him at sea en route to Taiwan, along with his friend Walker."

"What happened to Walker?"

"He got greedy. Yarborough died a year later in an air crash."

Holloway made notes while Talbot continued the questioning. She asked, "What happened after you got to Zurich?"

"The Embassy Man stayed in Switzerland to handle the business arrangements and the rest of us flew back to California and laid low until Schaeffer's ship docked in San Diego. Then, we made contact with the military authorities and said we'd just gotten off his boat. Nobody had a reason to suspect that we hadn't. It was a cakewalk."

"Not quite. Reid tried to shake you down," Holloway reminded him. "How did he find out about the raid?"

"Reid never knew about it. Schaeffer created the problem himself. The Admiral is one of those people who thinks he can either buy or burn anybody. He's kinda light in the finesse department, if you know what I mean. After Reid cooked the books, Schaeffer gave him a cash 'bonus' and had him sign a receipt and some phony form about not divulging national security information. Schaeffer figured that the cash would compromise Reid and keep him quiet if he had any second thoughts. A few months later, Reid got out of the Navy, looked Schaeffer up, and asked for a 'loan' to set up his civilian practice—and help him forget about the phony medical records. Schaeffer figured right off that Reid was going to be a long-term problem. He told Reid that he would arrange for him to get the loan from a third party. We took out a big life insurance policy on him with Grosshandel Versicherungen, and let Reid borrow against it."

"Then you killed him?"

"He died."

"And his mother got a big insurance payment."

"I hear, the bigger the insurance payoff, the less fuss families make about how their loved ones happen to pass on." There might have been a smirk playing beneath Dillworth's poker face.

"And Reid's assistant in the medical section got the same treatment. Why? Was he another loose end?" asked Holloway.

"You said it, I didn't."

"So, after the claims were paid on Reid and his assistant, Grosshandel went out of business. Anyone interested in tracing those life insurance payments would hit a brick wall."

"Some might see it that way," drawled Dillworth. "I say Grosshandel went out of business because our actuaries were lousy at predicting the health risk to our clients. Consequently, the company suffered serious financial losses."

Holloway turned the Reid episode over in his mind, along with the memories of Donna, Dan, and Hugh Stiles. "So," he said, almost to himself, "the person in Washington with a CIA connection and the most to lose if the Reid story got out was Admiral Schaeffer."

"Yep," was all that Dillworth would say.

Holloway's lips compressed into a thin, angry line as he drew a circle around Schaeffer's name. He had gotten what he wanted. Now, he forced himself to concentrate on what the President wanted. Carefully, his pencil moved down the page, making a check mark in front of each name. "Counting Schaeffer and Jack Slayton, you started with nine men and ended up with six?"

Dillworth shook his head. "We started with ten and finished with seven."

The number "seven" froze Holloway. His stare was so intense that it made Dillworth uneasy. Holloway's question came out in a raspy voice. "Who was the seventh man?"

"Jules Vaterman. He was a Treasury Department advisor to the South Vietnamese Government and the Embassy Man's pipeline for information on Saigon's gold reserves."

Jessica Talbot and Holloway exchanged glances again.

With a trembling hand Holloway counted down the list once more. Seven. Six names and the Embassy Man. His thoughts raced back to the warning in Jack Slayton's unfinished letter. "Beware of The Seven . . ." This was the first solid "seven" he had run across, but there were other questions. Who is the Embassy Man? Had he and Slayton been plotting against the President? Why? What had they been planning? Holloway's guts churned with excitement. He forced himself to concentrate on Talbot, who had taken up Dillworth's interrogation.

"Did Schaeffer arrange an alibi for Jules Vaterman?" she was asking.

"No. Vaterman, the Embassy Man, and our pilot and crewchief had other arrangements. I don't know how they covered themselves."

"So, the seven of you used the proceeds from the sale of some of the gold to establish WorldCorp?"

"Yeah. Well, what we did was buy five Swiss businessmen to front as a board of directors and they set it up. They—"

"But," interrupted Talbot, "the real board of the directors consisted of the seven survivors of the raid: you, the Embassy Man, Slayton, Trung, Roper, Schaeffer, and Jules Vaterman." She sounded as though she already had Dillworth on the witness stand.

"That's right."

"How did you get money out of WorldCorp?" asked Talbot.

"Me, Ackerman, Trung, and Yarborough went to work for WorldCorp as consultants. The rest were paid dividends on phony investments, but," recalled Dillworth, with a smile, "nobody wanted a life insurance loan, after what happened to Reid."

Talbot wanted to know how corporate financial decisions were made. "At first, we gave the front men a pile of money and told them to make a profit. Later, Vaterman planned our financial strategy. He was the only one of us who had any experience with big business and, let me tell you, that ol' boy had the Midas touch. Everything he looked at turned to money."

Holloway knew that Talbot wanted to follow the money trail, but he was more interested in the people. "What happened to everybody after WorldCorp was up and running?"

"Ackerman went back to the Far East and started a business. Trung did the same thing in the States. Slayton got out of the Army and, after a while, went to work at the Pentagon as a civilian. Schaeffer was there, too, on the Navy Staff. The Air Force sent Roper to Idaho for a year." Dillworth chuckled at the thought. "Me and Yarborough had the best deal. We got to stay in Geneva and make sure the front men didn't rob us blind."

"What about the Embassy Man?" asked Holloway.

"I never saw him after we got the gold to Zurich, but he kept his hand in. Vaterman always had his proxy at the committee meetings."

"What committee meetings?"

"The Seven Committee. That was the name that Vaterman came up with for us, 'the lucky seven from Hangar 11.' " said Dillworth, smiling.

Beware of the Seven Committee!, thought Holloway. That was what Slayton had been trying to tell the President in his unfinished letter.

Once more, Talbot began pumping Dillworth about the money. Did the Committee make decisions about the corporation's finance? How? How often did they meet? Where? Any reason for alternating the meetings between Geneva and Washington? And always the questions returned to Vaterman's role in the direction of WorldCorp.

Holloway's attention was focused elsewhere. Reason told him that the key to Slayton's warning would not be found by following the money trail because his decision to split with the Committee couldn't have been over money. There was too much of it to argue about. The price of gold had skyrocketed since the Vietnam War and, from what Dillworth was telling Talbot, WorldCorp had gold holdings alone worth four hundred million dollars. Anyway, if Slayton had wanted to spend his share on a lavish lifestyle, he wouldn't have stayed in government service. There had to be another reason why he split with The Seven and tried to warn the President about them.

Holloway watched Jessica Talbot work, firing question after detailed question at Dillworth. She never took a note. Holloway guessed that she had a phenomenal memory. Finally, her interrogation hit a lull, and she said to Holloway, "I've got to go to the bathroom. How about keeping it on 'hold' until I get back." She took her purse from the bed and left.

"Some woman," Dillworth observed as he watched Talbot leave. "She don't miss a thing. I'm glad she's gonna be on my side in court." He shifted uncomfortably. "Mind if I stand up and stretch?"

"Go ahead, but I'll put a bullet in that kneecap if you try to run."

Dillworth freed his neck from the bedpost and stood up.

Holloway moved away from the Texan and positioned himself to block the door. "Why do your old friends want to kill you?"

Dillworth lit a cigarette. "I broke the only rule we had: no dope. You could buy the stuff on any street corner in Vietnam, but I never fooled with it. Then, one weekend about a year ago, I was in New York on business and a fella introduced me to this long-stemmed American beauty, name of Rusty. Pretty thing, and built like an Arapaho pony. Hot damn!" he said at the memory of her. "Me and Rusty spent the weekend together. She turned out to be a coke head, but I didn't find out 'til Saturday night. By then, I was in love and as drunk as a skunk. I let her turn me on." He inhaled loudly through his nose. "I had a few tough months. Then, I went for the cure.

"Around Thanksgiving I was at a party in Washington and fell off the wagon. Schaeffer must have had somebody keeping an eye on me. He's death on drugs and threw everything on the table at the next Committee meeting. Somehow, he found out about my cure, too. There was a big blowup and they started asking each other what to do about me like I wasn't there. I'd be damned if I was gonna end up with one of them Grosshandel insurance policies. When we broke for lunch, I just kept on going. I've been laying low at the cure clinic ever since. I reckon they brought in Ackerman to take my place and gave him the contract on me."

"What were you planning to do, Tex, just walk away from all that money?"

"All the money a man needs is enough," said Dillworth, easing his lanky frame into Talbot's chair. "I put a little aside over the years; got myself some property here and there. I'll make it."

"If Ackerman doesn't catch up to you."

"I don't have to worry about it now that I've got you and the little lady to protect me." He smirked.

"Was dope the only reason they wanted you out of the way?"

"Well, ah, no." Dillworth looked away. "They were gettin' into some things that were a little out of my league."

At that moment, Talbot returned to the room and appeared disturbed to see Dillworth sitting in a chair.

"Sit on the bed, Tex." Holloway, waved the gun in that general direction. Dillworth stretched out on the bed and folded his arms comfortably behind his head.

Talbot carefully laid her purse on the night stand next to him and picked through it awkwardly for a cigarette. "Okay," she said, crossing her legs under Dillworth's watchful eye, "you were telling us about how the money was managed."

Holloway interrupted. "Before we get back to the money, let's talk about Slayton. There came a time when he had a falling out with the Committee. What happened?"

Talbot was irritated. "Holloway, is this necessary?"

"It's the reason I came here," he said, and none too gently. Turning back to Dillworth, he asked, "Why did he fall out with the Committee?"

"That's a long story," said Dillworth, hoping to avoid the topic.

"You got nothing but time to tell it."

Dillworth shrugged. "It was about two years after we set up WorldCorp. We were going along happy as a pig in slop and making more money than you would believe, when the Washington crowd came in with this brainstorm."

"Who were the 'Washington crowd'?"

"Schaeffer, Slayton—and Vaterman, with the Embassy Man's proxy, as usual. They thought we ought to do something patriotic with some of the money. At that time, the CIA's covert action capability was gutted and since most of us knew something about intelligence, the Washington crowd voted to work in that area. I thought we were asking for trouble and Trung didn't care one way or the other."

Talbot was all ears now, the quest for the money and Vaterman's hide having been temporarily moved to the back burner.

"What operations were you involved in?" asked Holloway.

"Just logistical support. Somebody in Washington would need something and we made sure that it was delivered."

"How did you get your missions?"

"Mostly from Slayton, in the beginning. He had a lot of contacts in the intelligence community. He would talk to some spook over lunch or at a cocktail party and find out that a plane was needed here or some money was needed there. Slayton would pass it to me in Geneva. I'd make the arrangements and pass them to Slayton. He would contact the spook through a cutout and tell him who to contact for the plane or that the money was deposited in a certain account. Money transfers were clean and easy. WorldCorp owned a couple of private banks in Geneva and Zurich."

"Did these missions come in regularly?"

Dillworth forced his lips into a thoughtful pucker. "Yeah, pretty regular. At least twice a month; sometimes once a week."

"Do you know for a fact how Slayton got his missions, or are you telling me what he told you?"

"All I know is what he told us."

Holloway got up and walked around the bed. "You know, Tex, I'm having a hard time visualizing Slayton regularly meeting spooks to discuss the details of covert operations over lunch at the Mayflower or at Georgetown cocktail parties. It's bad security and it wouldn't take long for word to leak that Slayton was the fixer when you needed undercover logistics. That would not only end his usefulness, it might get him into big trouble. From what I know of Slayton, he wouldn't have risked that kind of visibility. It would make more sense if he got these missions from one person, a person Slayton could trust with the knowledge of his WorldCorp connection. Do you agree?"

"Could be."

"Who was feeding him?"

"I don't know."

"Who do you *think* it was?"

Dillworth smiled. "Either Schaeffer or the Embassy Man?"

"That's my guess, too," admitted Holloway. "And you have no idea who the Embassy Man is?"

Dillworth shook his head and yawned. He was tiring.

"Okay," said Holloway, "Let's get to the part where Slayton split with the Committee."

Dillworth thought about it for a few moments and his mood turned serious. He swung his legs over the side of the bed and sat up, forearms resting on his thighs. "We'd been supporting these covert requirements for about a year. Meantime, Ackerman and Trung were hobnobbing with a lot of business people and politicians in the Far East, and the Pentagon had sent Roper to the Air Attaché's Office in Egypt, his last tour before retirement." Offhandedly, Dillworth added, "Roper had some kind of degree in Middle East Studies. Anyway, the Washington crowd came up with another brilliant idea. They wanted to start running some private spy networks using the contacts that Roper, Ackerman, and Trung had developed. I was against it, but the rest of the Committee voted us into the spy business."

Talbot was puzzled. "How did you recruit people?"

"We used the false flag approach. Told them they were working for the CIA, the Mossad, even the KGB." Dillworth laughed. "We used whatever worked and paid top dollar."

"What about training?"

"In the late seventies, a lot of good people were booted out of the CIA. We didn't have any trouble finding trainers. They were glad to be working again and didn't ask questions."

Holloway reminded him, "You were telling us why Slayton split with the Committee."

"Yeah. Well, Roper caused the first problem. He retired from the Air Force, took a teaching job in Beirut and ran his Middle East network from there. His product was acceptable. We fed it directly to Schaeffer, who had moved over to the CIA. I was almost convinced that the spy networks had been a good idea until the Hezbollah started kidnapping westerners in Beirut. As people disappeared, some of us started to worry about Roper. What would happen if they snatched him and he talked about WorldCorp? Roper was a good man and all that, but there are ways to break anybody. Slayton wanted Roper out and I agreed with him. Roper wanted to stay. His network was doing okay and he had a woman. We put it to a vote and Roper stayed."

"How did the Embassy Man vote?" asked Holloway.

"For Roper. Vaterman had his proxy."

"And Slayton?"

"He lost confidence in the Committee. He said they were courtin' disaster. That was the beginning of the end. The Washington crowd started to give him a little distance. Pretty soon, Schaeffer was bypassing Slayton and giving the covert requirements directly to me."

Holloway prodded him. "When did the big split come?"

"When Hezbollah kidnapped Roper. He disappeared on his way to the university on March 16, 1984. As far as we know, there were no witnesses, but Roper sent us a pre-planned signal. He knew Beirut was dangerous and cooked up a little scheme to warn us if he was taken. He put a million dollars in an account at our Geneva bank. If he was captured, his plan was to give the kidnappers the account number and a code word. With those, they could transfer the money, by phone, to any branch of Credit Suisse in Switzerland. Instructions went along with the money notifying the bank that anybody who showed up with the code word and account number could withdraw a hundred thousand dollars, no questions asked. Along with the money, the kidnappers would get a letter telling them that the rest of the money would be released when Roper was delivered alive to our Geneva bank and his identity verified by handprint.

"Sure as shootin', two weeks later, we got a call to transfer the ransom money to Zurich. That was the first time we knew for sure that Roper had been snatched. I called Slayton in Washington to break the bad news. By then, I had the feeling that he was the only one back there with his head screwed on straight. He was pissed. I've heard some cussin' in my time, but on that particular occasion, the man's command of anatomy and descriptive adjectives was awesome."

Holloway nodded. That tracked time-wise with Miriam's description of Jack Slayton's anger after he had received the overseas call that started his downhill slide into Iran-Contra and a heart attack.

"Did Slayton came to Geneva to see you a few days later?"

Dillworth squinted at Holloway. "You're damned well informed. Yeah, he came over so that we could work out a plan for gettin' Roper back without interference from the Committee."

And Sheila Hamilton saw the two of you together in the WorldCorp building and was murdered for her trouble, thought Holloway.

"Long story short," continued Dillworth, "a fella showed up at Credit Suisse in Zurich to collect the hundred thou'. We traced him to the family of one of Roper's students in Beirut. Best we could tell, the kid turned Roper in to Hezbollah. Maybe Roper gave him a bad grade or somethin'," laughed Dillworth. "More likely, Roper tried to recruit the kid for his network and it backfired. We never did get the real story or find out where they were holding Roper.

"We were still hoping that the nine hundred thousand in Zurich would be attractive enough for the kidnappers to release Roper, but they didn't bite and Slayton figured we'd better back off. There was nothing to link Roper or his ransom money to us. We didn't know what story he was giving Hezbollah. So, making a fuss over Roper would only raise questions about him and WorldCorp. What we needed was an international effort to get *all* of the hostages released. That way, Roper and WorldCorp wouldn't be alone in the spotlight." Dillworth wearily ran a hand through his hair. "Actually, that was when The Seven Committee set the Iran-Contra scandal in motion."

CHAPTER 16

<u>Cap Martin on the Riviera</u>

It was dark. Ackerman looked at his watch and pushed the telephone across the table to Ducasse. "Well, Monsieur Le Directeur, time to summon your chauffeur. He should be home by now."

Ducasse dialed. "Marcel? Doctor Ducasse. Marcel, I need to see you immediately. Write down this address and bring the car here." Ducasse gave him the address.

"Excellent, Monsieur," said Ackerman.

Marcel, a handsome lad in his twenties, arrived half an hour later and was ushered into the living room to find Ducasse tied to a straight-backed chair and chaperoned by two muscle men and Lutz. Marcel turned back toward the door and found himself looking into the barrel of Ackerman's gun. Ackerman shoved the young man into a chair. "Marcel, the hour is late, there is work to do and we are all tired. So let's not waste my time. Tell me where you took Monsieur and Madame Dillworth today."

Marcel looked at Ducasse, who vigorously nodded his consent.

"To the railroad station. Madame took the train."

"Where to?"

"I don't know, Monsieur. I waited in the car while they went in. Monsieur Dillworth returned without her."

Ackerman snorted his exasperation. "Where did you take Monsieur Dillworth?"

"To the bank. I left him there and went on to Monte Carlo."

"Where was Monsieur Dillworth going after he left the bank?"

"I don't know."

"Marcel, you are a major disappointment." Ackerman walked to the window and looked down at the dark outline of the Dillworth house. Suddenly he banged his fist on the windowsill in anger. "Take Monsieur Ducasse and Marcel upstairs and dispose of them."

Before anyone could respond to the order, Ackerman peered into the darkness again. "Wait! There's a light on in Dillworth's house. Lutz, come with me. You may earn your money yet."

The woman didn't hear them enter the house. She screamed and dropped the pitcher of juice when she turned and saw them standing in the kitchen.

"Sorry to frighten you," apologized Ackerman in his best French. "We are friends of Monsieur Dillworth from Geneva."

The woman squinted at them. "How did you get in here?"

"Monsieur Dillworth gave us a key," he lied. "Who are you?"

"I am Madame's housekeeper. I live here."

"We had arranged to meet Monsieur Dillworth here, but we understand he and Madame are away. They may have gone to Roqueburne. Is there a particular place they might visit?"

"Madame has a house in Roqueburne. She keeps a small apartment above the garage. But I can't imagine why—"

"Ah, you see, Lutz," explained Ackerman, "we came to the wrong house." He turned to the housekeeper. "Would you be good enough to give us directions to the Roqueburne house?"

It was the last thing she ever did.

* * *

A fresh cigarette dangled from Dillworth's fingers as he told Talbot and Holloway how The Seven Committee set in motion the events that resulted in the Iran-Contra scandal. "Conditions were ripe for an international effort to free all the hostages. Slayton knew that the President wanted them out. Iran had leverage with Hezbollah and needed U.S. weapons to keep the war going with Iraq. It could have been the perfect marriage except that the U.S. and Iran weren't on speaking terms. It was a standoff and every day Roper spent in captivity moved WorldCorp closer to exposure. We looked for a middle ground and found Israel. The Israelis had the missiles that

Iran needed and could sell them without the U.S. getting involved. Besides, they were not particularly happy to see their old enemy, Iraq, whip up on Iran. Slayton came up with a plan to generate interest in an arms-for-hostages swap that allowed both sides to save face and get around the law."

"That was Jack Slayton's idea?" asked Talbot, wide-eyed.

"Well I helped a little, too." Dillworth allowed himself a modest smile. "We mapped it out in Geneva and Slayton took it back to Washington and presented it to the rest of the Committee. They bought it. Hell," he snorted, "they didn't have much choice—and they were happy to have us pull their bacon out of the fire."

"Tell us about the plan," said Holloway, steadily making notes.

"Vaterman handled the Iran end. He had brokered some oil deals there in the early seventies and still had a lot of contacts. He told an Iranian diplomat in Geneva that the U.S. would make weapons available to Iran through Israel in return for release of the hostages. The negotiations had to be handled through third parties and kept hush-hush to avoid political flak on both sides. Iran agreed and tapped Ghorbanifar to make the approach to Israel.

"Meantime, Slayton went back to the National Security Council and circulated the story that there were moderates in the Khomeini regime who ought to be wooed so the U.S. and Iran could have normal relations after Khomeini passed on. That little rumor started a reassessment of U.S. policy toward Iran. According to Slayton, the Director General of the Israeli Foreign Ministry showed up at the White House right on cue and confirmed that Iranian moderates wanted political contacts with the U.S. and were willing to trade hostages for missiles as a show of good faith. The Israelis were willing to sell the missiles to Iran as long as the U.S. replaced them. A deal was cut and all we had to do was sit back and wait for Israel to deliver the missiles and Hezbollah to release the hostages.

"Well, that's where it started to go bad. Iran got five hundred missiles and only one hostage came out: Ben Wier. It turned out that the Iranians didn't have the clout with Hezbollah that we thought. At the same time, the situation started to get nasty in the Middle East. The Israelis bombed PLO headquarters, the PLO hijacked the Achille Lauro cruise ship, and we got word from Schaeffer that Hezbollah had killed a hostage, the CIA chief of station in Beirut.

Things didn't look good for Roper, but Slayton told us to hold on. Another missile delivery was scheduled for November. Iran got the missiles, but no hostages were released. Slayton called an emergency meeting for New Year's Day 1986. It was more bad news."

According to Dillworth, the Committee met in Schaeffer's downtown Washington office. The admiral, in mufti, sat at the head of the table, with Jack Slayton at his right. The two men were not happy with each other.

Slayton announced, "Roper is being tortured."

"Mistreated," said the admiral.

"He's getting his ass kicked! Call it whatever you like!"

"How do you know?" asked Ackerman.

"We know," the admiral assured them.

Trung, who rarely talked at these meetings, spoke up. "Where are the kidnappers holding him?"

"They move him constantly," replied Schaeffer. "No chance for a rescue, if that's what you were thinking."

Trung made a sour mouth and shook his head solemnly.

The admiral looked down his nose at Slayton. "Jack is afraid that Roper might confess our sins to his captors." There were murmurs of concern around the table.

"Jack can speak for himself," declared Slayton.

"Then, tell them what you propose to do to our comrade in arms." Schaeffer's tone was mocking.

Slayton looked around the table, ignoring Schaeffer. There were bags under his eyes. He looked worn out. "I don't know about the rest of you, but I haven't had a decent night's sleep since Roper was kidnapped. Things are getting worse in the Middle East. We've got to face the fact that Roper isn't going to get out. None of them are."

"You don't know that!" snapped Schaeffer.

"I know one thing: The Iran initiative is going to blow up in everybody's face. The Iranians are paying through the nose and they can't get the stuff they want. That last missile delivery was a clown act. The shipment showed up in Iran with the Star of David painted on the packing crates, for God's sake! And they were the wrong damned missiles!"

"They will fix it next time," Schaeffer assured the group.

Slayton pounded the table. "There may not be a next time. Ollie North is taking over hostage negotiations for the National Security Council and—"

"Who the hell is Ollie North?" asked Ackerman, his knowledge of Washington personalities being inversely proportional to the square of the distance to the Taipei massage parlor that served as his headquarters.

Schaeffer glided in again. "He's a counter-terrorism policy specialist at the White House."

Slayton elaborated. "He's a no-nonsense Marine and it's going to take him about five hot minutes to cut through all the bullshit and get to the bottom line: The Iranians can't deliver the hostages. That's what he'll tell the President and that will be the end of the negotiations. The hostages are going to rot. We've got to do something about Roper now!" He slammed the table with his palm.

"What do you suggest?" asked Trung.

Slayton took a deep breath. "We've got to take him out. We've got to hit him, for his own good and for ours."

The group got quiet.

Trung asked, "Can it be done without our involvement?"

"Yes. Randy has a contact. We just deposit the money."

Ackerman asked, "How do we know the contact can deliver?"

"We don't," Slayton said gravely. "We're just out of options."

Ackerman turned to the admiral. "What do you say, Schaeffer?"

"I say it's a bad precedent to start hitting members of the Committee." There were murmurs of agreement. "And what Jack neglected to tell you, because he doesn't know yet," Schaeffer gave Slayton a smug glance, "is that the President will sign a finding in the next few days officially authorizing agents of the U.S. Government to conduct secret negotiations for the release of the hostages. That will strengthen Colonel North's hand considerably in dealing with the Iranians and fixing some of the glitches that have occurred. North is a good man. If anybody can get the hostages out, he can."

Heads turned to Slayton for a rebuttal.

"That finding," declared Slayton, "isn't going to make a damn bit of difference. I'll say it again: The Iranians can't deliver. You can fix all the glitches and deliver all the missiles you want. And another thing, North is going to make a lot of people unhappy. He wants to dump the Israeli and Iranian middlemen and deal directly with the Iranian Government. The middlemen are making a fortune off every missile shipment. If North cans them, they're going to be mad. They might blow the whistle on the negotiations just to get even, and we'll be right back where we started. We have got to do something about Roper!"

"Maybe," said Jules Vaterman, speaking for the first time, "we need to do something about Colonel North to maintain his interest in continuing the hostage negotiations."

"He won't take a bribe, Jules. Forget that," advised Slayton.

"I wasn't thinking of a bribe per se. I understand that North's favorite charity is the Contras, the rebel anticommunist movement in Nicaragua. He's been soliciting funds from various quarters to keep war materiel flowing to them, in spite of the congressional ban on lethal aid. Isn't that's one of his principal duties at the White House?"

"That's right," said Slayton.

"Well then, suppose we passed the word to the middlemen that Colonel North might feel more kindly disposed toward them and the negotiations if they volunteered some of their profits for the Contra cause? In fact, one of them might suggest such an arrangement to the colonel. That should keep all the players in place and happy and the negotiations on track long enough for Colonel North to work out the glitches. It would also give us time to consider the drastic step of putting poor Roper out of his misery. On a personal note, I have an aversion to starting off the year by condemning one of our own to death. The arrival of a new year has always been, for me, a beacon of hope rather than a harbinger of despair."

Schaeffer leaned toward Vaterman. "Well spoken, Jules."

Disgusted, Slayton sank back in his chair. They were being stroked out of taking action once more by the silver-tongued devil.

"How will North get the word?" Ackerman asked.

"I'll handle it through my Iranian friend in Geneva," said Vaterman. "He will see to it that the suggestion is passed through Tehran to Ghorbanifar. I'm sure Ghorbanifar will be delighted to make the suggestion to Colonel North, since he stands to make a great deal of money—or lose it."

Schaeffer piped up again. "We can do better than that. Ghorbanifar is here in Washington right now."

"How fortuitous," said Vaterman." Vaterman and Schaeffer exchanged knowing glances.

Schaeffer moved to close the meeting. "Subject to an objection by a majority, we will postpone any consideration of Roper's fate until Colonel North has had his chance to negotiate for the hostages."

Slayton was the only one who spoke. "You're making a mistake just like you did before, when you let Roper stay in Beirut."

"Thank you, Jack," Schaeffer said briskly. "Any other business?"

"One more thing," said Vaterman. "You all remember that our bank made a little money on those first arms transfers to Iran." He looked down the table. "Randy, when you get back to Geneva, sit down with your people and be sure those accounts are scrubbed along with all related paperwork. On the odd chance that Jack is right and this thing does blow, rest assured that there will be an investigation. People may start pointing fingers and we want our skirts to be clean. It might also be wise not to handle anymore business from the people involved in the Iran transactions. Refer them to another institution."

Dillworth ground out the remnants of his cigarette and continued his story to Talbot and Holloway. "None of this satisfied Slayton. He spent the night in my hotel room talking about the good old Army days, but I could tell he had something else on his mind. Gradually, he got around to asking me about the arrangements for the hit on Roper. Who was my contact in Beirut? How much would it take? What were the payment arrangements? I went back to Geneva the next day and forgot about it. A week later, Slayton called and said he needed five million put into an account for a covert mission. The money was withdrawn the same day I deposited it. Two months later, I got a package by special messenger with a note telling me to verify the contents using our handprint file. They . . ." Dillworth shook his head. "They sent me Roper's hands. Without Committee approval, Slayton had taken out a contract on Roper. The poor guy was poisoned by one of his guards. We never told Schaeffer and the others."

CHAPTER 17

Dillworth stretched out on the bed again and continued his story. "The last meeting of The Seven Committee that Jack Slayton and I attended was held on November 15, 1986, in Geneva. They were tired from travelling and in an ugly mood. It would have been easier to meet in Washington, but nobody wanted to be seen with Slayton. The Iran-Contra scandal was breaking and it was common knowledge there that he was on Ollie North's Contra supply staff. There was another reason, too. Schaeffer and Vaterman didn't want to take any chances that what they were hatching would be overheard in Washington."

The Committee met in a secure conference room on the fourteenth floor of the WorldCorp building. The Washington crowd—Schaeffer, Vaterman, and Trung—sat together. Slayton had isolated himself from the group and was showing signs of extreme fatigue.

Schaeffer called the meeting to order. "Gentlemen, could we get under way? By now, all of you know that the secret hostage negotiations with Iran have been exposed by the Lebanese newspaper, *Al-Shiraa*, and that the details of the Contra arms supply operation are also leaking—as Jack predicted. I'm afraid that this is the end of the game. Jack, we should have listened to you."

Slayton conducted a bored examination of the ceiling.

"Let there be no doubt," Schaeffer continued, "that Congress will investigate both of these operations thoroughly. Forces are already marshalling on The Hill. I'm sure a special prosecutor will be appointed in the near future and the White House is considering some sort of fact-finding panel. We must develop a response, in the eventuality that Iran-Contra money is traced to our bank." He looked down the table at Slayton. "And, of course, we must help Jack plan for his future. I fear his days at the White House are numbered."

Slayton gave no indication that he had heard the admiral.

Schaeffer bristled. He was not used to being ignored. "With regard to the financial arrangements, I understand some people in Washington are already compiling a list of the banks involved in the Iran arms transactions. Let's assume that ours is on that list. Feelers have gone out to the Swiss seeking their cooperation in tracing the Iran money. I hope," said Schaeffer, fixing his eyes on Dillworth, "that our people have sanitized the accounts associated with those missile deliveries."

Dillworth shifted uneasily in his chair. "'Fraid not. We had a husband-and-wife team of accountants working on that problem. When news of the hostage negotiations broke here, they cleaned out one of the accounts and left the country. I reckon they figured we couldn't raise a fuss about it, under the circumstances. The paperwork's a mess." The din that went up was too loud for them to hear Dillworth add, "Our chief accountant is personally trying to straighten things out." It wouldn't have mattered. They were irritated by the events that had prompted the meeting and Dillworth was a convenient scapegoat. Slayton remained oblivious while the others vented their frustration.

Ackerman was Dillworth's sharpest critic. "You heard Schaeffer. The Swiss are going to cooperate. Those investigators could walk in here next week and take this place apart looking for missile money. Who knows what else they might find?"

The normal order of their meetings dissolved into a chorus of angry grumbling until Vaterman's voice cut through the din, crisp and clear. "They won't be looking for the money."

Ackerman squinted at him. "What did you say?"

"I said, 'They won't be looking for the money.' "

"What the hell will they be looking for?"

"The President."

"What are you talking about, Jules?"

Vaterman's legs were cramping. He got up and strolled around the room. "The congressional investigators, if they come, won't give a hoot about the money. A few million, that's peanuts. What they will want to know is if the money trail leads to the White House. They want the President. After all, this Iran-Contra thing is essentially a power struggle between the President and Congress. The investigators will be out to get the President, to weaken him. If we are investigated, the real question for us may come down to, 'Do we give them the President or ourselves?'"

Slayton snapped out of his trance and focused on Vaterman. "What are you suggesting, Jules?"

Vaterman stopped in front of the window and hooked his thumbs into his vest pockets. "The investigators will come with limited time and a preconception of involvement by the President. If they find evidence here to reenforce that preconception, chances are they will go away and not pry further into WorldCorp operations. There are things that could be done, only if necessary," he paused to emphasize the point, "to create the impression of culpability in the White House. We could let them find certain evidence. . . ."

"You mean frame the President?"

"In a word, yes."

"No!" yelled Slayton, jumping to his feet. "No, no, no!" He pounded the table. "You're crazy. I don't want to hear another word about this. If the bank gets into trouble, let one of our Swiss front men take the fall. That's what they get paid for. And if I ever see anything that faintly resembles a frame, I'll go to the Justice Department and blow the whistle on all you stupid bastards!"

There was dead silence as the impact of Slayton's threat sank into the collective consciousness of the Committee.

Trung cleared his throat. "Jack is right. There must be some other way to handle this, but without the Swiss. If we want them to take the heat, we will have to tell them too much."

"I agree with Jack and Trung," said Schaeffer. "There's no need for extreme measures. We have options." He gave his colleagues a reassuring smile. "This so-called scandal has two parts: Iran and Contra. On the Iran side, the President tried to free hostages and it didn't work out. Does the American public give a damn if the Iranians got screwed out of a lot of money in the process and some businessmen made a few dollars on the deal? Hell, no. Can Congress put together enough votes to impeach the President for shipping missiles to Iran? No, again. The President will get an 'A' for effort and life will go on. The whole thing is a dead letter.

"The Contra issue has a little different spin on it. Public opinion is divided and Congress passed a law expressly forbidding lethal aid to the Contras. The White House violated that law. This is a serious matter to the public and a constitutional confrontation. If Congress is going to nail the President on anything, it has to be the Contra issue. We didn't handle any Contra money. So what we have to do is keep the investigation focused on the Contra operation."

"By the time Congress gets its ass in gear," said Slayton, "there won't be anything left to focus on."

"What are you talking about?" asked Ackerman.

"The White House is shredding every piece of paper it has on the hostage and Contra operations."

"Jack is correct," confirmed Schaeffer. "Jack is also the solution to that problem." Slayton gave Schaeffer a quizzical look. "You still have access to Colonel North's office, don't you?"

Slayton cautiously replied, "Yes."

"Then you will have to make sure that all the evidence concerning the Contra arms operation is not destroyed before North's files are seized by the investigators."

"How am I supposed to do that?"

Schaeffer opened his briefcase and took out several photocopies. "You will remember at our January meeting Jules suggested that the middlemen might donate some of their profits to buy arms for the Contras? Well, in February, Mr. Ghorbanifar made the suggestion and Colonel North accepted. In fact, I have copies of a memo that North wrote to his boss on the subject." Schaeffer passed a stack down the table to Slayton and gave copies to the others. "Now, if those memos were slipped into Colonel North's files *after* he sanitized them for the investigators, it would provide a nice diversion away from the Iran end of the scandal—and away from us."

Slayton read through the memo, shaking his head.

"And," said Schaeffer, "I have a floppy disc that I want Jack to feed into the PROF System when he gets back to the White House."

"What's the PROF system?" Dillworth inquired.

Slayton gave them a sullen explanation. "It's the Professional Office System, a computerized interoffice mail system for the National Security Council." He turned to Schaeffer. "What's on the floppy?"

"Insurance," replied Schaeffer, with a sly smile. "The disc contains Contra arms supply documents that Colonel North sent over the PROF System and later deleted from the computer's memory. I want you to feed them back into the system so that they can be discovered when the investigators come calling."

"How the hell did you get that?" asked Slayton.

Schaeffer gave him a slight smile. "I'm a spy, Jack. I get paid to steal secrets."

Slayton collected the floppy and the memos. "Is my name in any of this stuff?"

Schaeffer gave him a pained look. "Of course not."

"Poor Ollie North is in a world of hurt." Slayton shook his head in genuine compassion for the man. He got up and walked to the door. "Ever met a man you didn't screw, Schaeffer?"

Schaeffer's jaw tightened. "Be careful, Jack!"

Slayton left and headed for the airport. There was no point in staying to discuss his future in Washington. He didn't have one.

Dillworth took a break from his story-telling to light another cigarette while Holloway and Talbot considered the former security chief had revealed.

Jessica Talbot asked, "Do you know what happened to the memo that Schaeffer gave Slayton?"

Dillworth said, "I read in the papers that somebody from the Justice Department found a copy in North's files about a week after our meeting." He laughed. "I guess Jack sandbagged North after all. I wasn't sure he'd do it when he left Geneva."

"In case you haven't heard," said Holloway, "they also pulled a lot of documents out of the PROF System that North claims he deleted."

Dillworth chuckled and shook his head.

"This meeting you just described," Holloway continued, "was it the same one where Schaeffer exposed your drug addiction?"

"Yeah—and threatened to kill me."

"And you just got up walked away from WorldCorp?"

"What the hell was I supposed to do, beg for forgiveness and promise not to do it anymore? These boys had just finished talking over a plan to frame the President of the United States. You think they were going to cut me any slack?" Dillworth thought the situation over and added, "To tell you the truth, I was glad to leave. I thought Schaeffer and Vaterman had gone over the edge. I don't mind travelling in fast company, but treason is out of my league."

"You always were bush league, Randy—you and Jack." It was Ackerman who had spoken. He stood just inside the bedroom door. His two gunmen slipped in and stationed themselves on his flanks. Lutz was absent. Ackerman greeted Holloway. "We meet again." Turning to Talbot he asked, "Who are you?"

"I'm Mr. Dillworth's private nurse."

"Really?" Ackerman flashed an evil smile and started to walk past her toward Dillworth. Suddenly, he turned and slapped Talbot. "You lying bitch." The blow stunned Talbot and she fell backwards against the wall. Ackerman stayed with her and slapped her again. Holloway made a move to help her, but one of the gunman waved him off with a Baretta. Ackerman slapped Talbot twice more and she sank to the floor dazed, blood gushing from her nose. Ackerman stood over her until she ceased resistance. Looking down at Talbot he asked Dillworth, "Who is she, really?"

"How do I know? She came with him." Dillworth nodded toward Holloway. Talbot was pushing herself up the wall to a standing position.

"We'll find out soon enough, not that it matters." Ackerman turned away from Talbot and was taking a step in Dillworth's direction when Jessica Talbot uncoiled with an ear-splitting yell and drove the toe of her shoe deep into his kidney. Ackerman howled and staggered forward. The Frenchman with the Baretta was slow. He couldn't decide who to shoot first, Holloway or Talbot. By the time he decided on Talbot, it was too late. She was bringing her .38 to bear on him. "Drop it!" He didn't. Instead, he tried to drop into a shooting crouch. Two slugs from Talbot's gun took him out of action.

Holloway grabbed the stunned Ackerman and shoved him at the second gunman. Both of them fell to the floor, the gunman firing wildly as he went down. Dillworth yelled as one of the slugs threw him backwards over the bed. Holloway pulled the gun he had taken from Dillworth, while Ackerman and the gunman tried to disentangle themselves.

Talbot was yelling, "Hands up! Hands up!" But nobody was listening. Ackerman and the second gunman rolled away from each other and came up shooting. Holloway dropped the gunman with a single shot. Ackerman was screaming obscenities and firing at Talbot. She held her gun in both hands and fired three bullets into his chest. While Holloway looked on in amazement, Talbot checked each of the bodies and collected the guns.

"Where did you learn to shoot like that?" asked Holloway.

"In the Army. I had a reserve commission in the Military Police Corps before I went to law school." Talbot reloaded her gun and slipped it into the holster clipped to the belt under her jacket.

"How do you happen to be packing?" asked Holloway.

"When you called all the way from the States to tell me that I might be in danger, I figured I had better take some precautions. Mother Talbot didn't raise any idiots."

Dillworth was crawling across the bed with blood on his shirt. They helped him to stretch out, and examined his wound. Talbot gave her assessment. "Looks like the bullet skidded along your ribs and kept going. I'll make a field dressing and we can get out of here."

"Damn good idea," said Dillworth through clenched teeth.

He sat on the toilet seat while they bandaged his wound. Holloway asked a final question. "Did Vaterman ever say how they were planning to frame the President?"

"No. They played that one close to the chest."

While Holloway was in the bathroom with Dillworth, Talbot went into the bedroom and got her pocketbook from the nightstand. She reached inside, turned off the miniature tape recorder, and smiled. It had run out of tape long ago, but what she had collected was two solid hours of Randy Dillworth's Greatest Hits. She imagined herself in Jules Vaterman's job at the Treasury Department.

Minutes later the three of them stepped out into the chilly night air, Talbot and Holloway on either side of Dillworth, helping him. They negotiated the steps and walked to the edge of the compound as fast as Dillworth's wound would permit. Talbot climbed the wall to bring the car up. While the two men stood there waiting, a red spot appeared on the back of Dillworth's head. A second later, the spot was replaced by a small, round hole. Dillworth screamed as his head exploded.

Off in the darkness, Lutz separated and packed the sections of his rifle. Then, he quietly slipped away. There was no need to concern himself with Ackerman. Lutz collected his fees in advance.

* * *

Talbot drove Holloway to the station in time to catch the last train out of Menton. Standing on the platform, Holloway asked, "What will you do about WorldCorp, now that Dillworth is dead?"

"Go back to Geneva and resubmit my WorldCorp file to the Treasury Department. Of course, I can't go through Vaterman. I'll carry it directly to the Secretary of the Treasury. When he hears what Dillworth told us, there won't be any trouble getting cooperation from the Secretary, the Justice Department, and the Swiss Government for a WorldCorp investigation." As an afterthought she mused, "Boy, this will blow the Iran-Contra case wide open."

Holloway responded with a remote, "Yeah." There were other things he was planning to blow open.

The next morning Jessica Talbot drove her rental car to the airport at Nice and went directly to the Swissair reservations counter. "I'd like to exchange this ticket to Geneva for a flight to Washington, D.C."

The clerk consulted her computer. "There is an evening flight direct from Nice to Dulles Airport in Washington. You will arrive at nine o'clock tomorrow morning."

"That will be fine," said Talbot.

CHAPTER 18

<u>May 1987, Washington. D.C.</u>

Jessica Talbot landed at Dulles International Airport and checked into a nearby hotel long enough to freshen up and change clothes. The flight from Nice had been long, but her energy was high and she knew that she could not sleep until she talked to Jules Vaterman. After calling to be sure that he was in, Talbot drove her rented car directly to Vaterman's office at Treasury Department headquarters, across from the White House.

As Talbot expected, Vaterman found an immediate vacancy on his calendar. He crossed his cavernous office to greet her, arms outstretched. "Jessie, this is an unexpected pleasure." He gave her the two-handed grip and crocodile smile to assure her that it was true.

"How are you, Jules?"

"I'm well, thank you," said Vaterman, noting her jaunty confidence. "Sit down," he said. A little less enamel was showing in his smile. "I didn't expect you for two weeks."

"Something came up. I decided to put myself on leave earlier than we had planned."

"Well, good for you. You've earned a rest." He looked her over. "I was going to discuss this later, but we might as well get to it now. You're due to come home from Geneva in a few months. It's time we found you a job back here. I was thinking of something in the general counsel's office. A little more emphasis on your legal background might be in order at this juncture." His satisfied smile said it was already a done deal.

"Frankly, Jules, I had something a little higher up the ladder in mind. There are rumors that the general counsel might be moving on. I'd like to be considered for his job, if he leaves. If he stays, here are a few others that would interest me." She took a file card out of her briefcase. "Here's my wish list."

Vaterman held the card gingerly between his thumb and forefinger, his eyebrows arching as he read. He carefully put the card aside and brought his fingertips together with papal solemnity. "Yes, well, I'm sure you realize that those positions would, in the normal course of things, go to someone more senior than yourself. And while you have done excellent work in Geneva, I would suggest that you lower your sights a bit." He made offering motions with his hands. "Get some broadening experiences before you move into a policy-making position."

"Before you give your final word, Jules, I think you should know that I had a long chat with Randy Dillworth yesterday. He had lots to say about the operation of WorldCorp and The Seven Committee."

Vaterman's look was stone cold. "I doubt that Dillworth will be of much use to you in his present condition."

"I have his comments on tape." Talbot withdrew a miniature cassette from her briefcase and placed it on top of the file card. "Your copy." Vaterman sank back into his captain's chair as though the air had been let out of him, his eyes fixed on the tape. "I'm sure this is a disappointment, but you can relax," Talbot assured him. "I don't want a Swiss bank account or a seat on the board at WorldCorp. Whatever you have done or plan to do with WorldCorp is no concern of mine. Although, I do think that this spy business is lunacy."

"What do you want?" asked a weary Vaterman.

"You know that I've always been more interested in campaign finance than corporate finance. I want to spend a year in a policy job here at Treasury, while I reestablish my Washington contacts. After that, I plan to go back home and run for Congress. You have lots of money and influence in the Party. When I start my campaign for public office, I want your political clout behind me and your unlimited financial resources at my disposal for as long as it takes. When I'm elected, I will consider us even. Is that a deal you can live with?"

It was a far better deal than Vaterman had expected. Jessica Talbot would do well in politics. She had mastered the compromise. "Done," said Vaterman.

They rose and went to the door. Before he opened it, Vaterman said, "I presume that you were the woman in the white Fiat."

"Yes."

"And the man?"

"Ed Holloway."

"Of course," said Vaterman. "I should have guessed it would be him. Does he have a copy of the tape?"

"No. He doesn't know that it exists, but he heard everything directly from Dillworth and he's not happy. He thinks your group was responsible for killing his friends."

"Do you know what his plans are?"

"No, but, I'd bet he's coming after all of you."

"Umm. Mr. Holloway will have to be dealt with."

"I don't want to know anything about that, Jules."

As Jessica Talbot departed, the secretary ushered an Oriental man into Vaterman's office. He was a representative of the Socialist Republic of Vietnam.

"Le Kim," said, Vaterman, turning on his megawatt smile. "Thank you for coming. Please sit down." Le Kim took the chair near Vaterman's desk. This was a crash meeting and a desperate move for Vaterman. The Iran-Contra investigators had their bloodhounds hard on the money trail and Vaterman wanted to eliminate the Vietnamese wild card before it caused The Seven anymore trouble.

"You understand," said Vaterman, "that what we say here is strictly confidential and unofficial. I am not speaking for my government. In this instance, I represent private parties who have an interest in Vietnam."

"I understand completely."

"Good. Then let's get down to business. There are wealthy American patriots who want to see the POW/MIA repatriation issue resolved, followed by the establishment of normal diplomatic and commercial relations between our two countries. They are confident that this will happen in the near future and they understand the needs of your country as it converts to a peacetime economy. As a gesture of their confidence, they are willing to assist you in the development of your tourist industry. Not moving in to take it over, mind you, but establish it, train your people in foreign schools and at home and, in time, turn over all or part of the operation to your government or to private industry, as you see fit. These people believe that tourism is your best and most immediate source of foreign exchange, with the least investment. I'm sure you realize that Americans would flock to your country by the thousands. Furthermore, this private assistance is in addition to any U.S. foreign aid that might come your way after relations between our two countries are normalized."

"What, specifically, do these private investors require in return?" Le Kim asked.

"First, they feel that they cannot make a commitment until your country terminates the occupation of Cambodia. It contributes to unrest in the area and prevents my government from extending recognition—and foreign aid—to yours. We also know from our intelligence reports that the war is draining your economy of capital it needs for development."

Le Kim smiled. "Your intelligence on the viability of the Vietnamese economy has been less than adequate in the past."

Vaterman smiled, too. "I can't argue with that, but the past is past. This conversation is about the future. I believe it is accurate to say that Vietnam's future is better served when its treasure is spent on Vietnamese soil rather than in Cambodia. Now, just between us, is there any movement on that front in your government?"

"Just between us, yes. There is a struggle going on between those who would stay in Cambodia until it is stabilized and those who counsel us to cut our losses and leave immediately. The occupation cannot last much longer than a year; two, at most."

"That is good news. Well, then, I have been authorized to tell you that on the day your forces withdraw from Cambodia, certain private sources are prepared to extend to your government a line of credit for economic development in this amount." The platinum tip of Vaterman's Mont Blanc pen glided across the note paper. Vaterman gave the paper to Le Kim. "These funds are to be used exclusively to develop your tourist industry, with the government—or private parties, as you wish—having a controlling share."

Le Kim's eyebrows went up in surprise.

"You will, of course, want to consult with your colleagues in Hanoi, but, based on that figure, I'm sure we can agree to pursue further discussions."

Le Kim folded the paper carefully and put it into his pocket. "Your offer will generate a great deal of discussion. Be warned that much of it will be ideological. Many of my colleagues will see this as a betrayal of the principles of the revolution."

"Of course. I understand that. But if this century has revealed a single undisputable truth, it is that communist revolutions produce temporary euphoria and permanent hunger. Men who would rule successfully understand that empty bellies are a poor foundation for the state. That's why they employ people like you and me."

"Jules, you talk more like a politician than a finance minister."

"A finance minister must have tools other than the abacus. Speaking of numbers, there is the matter of the MIA numbers. For my offer to be good, there are two other conditions."

"And they are?"

"There must be continuing progress on the MIA issue. There can be no foot-dragging, with the delivery of remains contingent upon public or private aid from sources in the United States. If there is even a whisper of such an arrangement, the deal I quoted is off. The people I represent cannot afford to have their friendly efforts to revitalize your economy viewed as the product of blackmail."

"And for your part," countered Le Kim, "you must stop the rumors that my government is holding remains of your MIA soldiers and airman in cold storage in a Hanoi warehouse. That is simply not true."

Vaterman took a deep breath. "That claim comes from the Defense Department. I have no control over what they say. You could eliminate the rumors by inviting an American inspection team to look at the warehouse in question."

"You ask a great deal and offer little in return."

"You have my offer in your pocket."

"Is there another shoe to fall?"

"Yes. One more. We want your intelligence service to give up the search for these 'assets' that were allegedly stolen from you at the end of the war. Call off Colonel Can and his 'researchers.'"

Le Kim studied Vaterman for a moment. "What a coincidence that you should mention Can. He seems to have disappeared."

"Oh, really? Perhaps he found the Golden Fleece and decided to keep it. More likely, he defected after being exposed to the advantages of capitalism." Vaterman gave Le Kim a friendly smile.

"Whatever Colonel Can's fate, I cannot promise you that the search for the legitimate property of the Socialist Republic of Vietnam will be discontinued. That would require a decision at the highest level of my government."

"In that case, I hope you will present that request when you discuss my offer of private investment because they are linked."

"You drive a hard bargain, Jules Vaterman."

"Console yourself with the fact that five years from now, when your tourist industry is flourishing, you will have the pleasure of showing Americans the battlefields on which you defeated them and making them pay in dollars for the experience. Is that not sweet revenge?"

Le Kim smiled. "You are a very good salesman."

CHAPTER 19

<u>May 1987, Washington. D.C.</u>

Holloway returned to the States through JFK Airport. He came in via Genoa-Milan-Frankfurt connections, taking the roundabout route in view of his fugitive status with the U.S.—and, by now, the French—police. This time, he slept during the transoceanic flight, but had bad dreams about Admiral Schaeffer. Holloway could see him shooting Donna. He woke up wet and angry, and made yet another vow to kill Schaeffer. When he went back to sleep, there was Jack Slayton and behind him, just out of focus, the Embassy Man, whispering into Slayton's ear and pulling the strings. Holloway's eyes popped open. He knew he had to see Slayton's records again. He wanted to verify what he suspected but could not bring himself to believe. From then on there was no sleeping and he prowled the cabin or squirmed listlessly in his seat until the seatbelt sign went on for the JFK approach. All the way he prayed that Jack Slayton's records were still in Donna's basement.

Holloway breezed through customs using his second passport and found an out-of-the-way telephone from which he called Sid Mitchell at the White House.

"Where are you?" asked Mitchell. "Are you okay?"

"I'm still moving, if that's what you mean. How about dinner at your place this evening, early?"

"Fine." Hesitation. "You want me to have a lawyer there?"

"No. Have you been to my house?"

Mitchell's voice came back at him filled with anguish, "God, yes."

"Had the vault been tampered with?" asked Holloway.

"It was open and stripped clean."

"What about the computer? I had personnel records on the hard drive. You know the ones." Holloway was referring to the files Mitchell had given him on Dillworth, Slayton, Ackerman, and Trung.

"The police checked your computer. Whoever did the deed knew about the records. They used a special program to wipe out the computer's memory. The records and the operating program were destroyed. All of the memory cells were filled with zeros or ones. Who else knew that you had those records besides Donna and Dan?"

Heat rose in Holloway's chest, burning his breath away and numbing his mind. Who, indeed? No one else could have known but Miriam Slayton!

"Ed, are you there?"

"Yeah, Sid. I'll call you back." Holloway hung up the phone and refused to let his mind deal with it until he could sit calmly and focus. He found the men's room and washed his face in cold water. Then, he went into one of the stalls, dropped the toilet seat and sat there, his anger boiling. Miriam had used him. One of The Seven had killed his friends—and with Miriam's help. He was sure of that. Her quick departure from his apartment just before Donna and Dan were murdered was just too much of a coincidence.

Miriam! You bitch! You black widow bitch! He rammed his fist into the stall door. *I will find you! But how? You could be anywhere, except Kansas. That would be too easy.*

Kansas! Holloway had an inspiration. He turned his suitcase on its side and emptied out the contents of his wallet. Carefully, he worked through a wad of charge card receipts until he found the one he wanted. It was for the night that he and Miriam had stayed at the hotel in Baltimore, the night before Holloway had visited Dr. Hong. Miriam had called her aunt long distance, from the room, to get Denise French's blood type. Stapled to the receipt was the actual hotel bill and on it Holloway found the telephone number for Miriam's aunt in Kansas. He went back to the telephone. It took him one minute to cook up the story that he was a Washington real estate dealer with a house for Miriam and five minutes on the phone to sell the story to

Miriam's elderly aunt. He came away with two local numbers where Miriam could be contacted, numbers that Miriam had phoned to her aunt after she moved out of Holloway's apartment.

Holloway called Sid Mitchell again. "It's Ed. I need names and addresses for a couple of phone numbers." He read them. "There's one other thing, Sid. Check the White House personnel files and tell me who sponsored Jack Slayton for his job on the National Security Council staff."

"Okay. I'll take care of it." Mitchell's voice went low. "Have you got an alibi?"

"I was at Lenny's for most of that evening. I think I spent the time insulting Veronica."

"Any idea who hit your place?"

"Maybe I'll know when you give me some names for those telephone numbers. See you this evening." Holloway hung up and caught his connecting flight for Washington.

When Holloway arrived in the Washington, his first stop was the bank. He returned the passports to his safe deposit box and took out the .38 and the silencer. He left the bank wondering if he could kill Miriam, and wondering if he could not.

* * *

They sat at the kitchen table drinking beer and eating Chinese take-out. Mitchell wiped his hands and took a paper from his shirt pocket. "Both of the phone numbers you gave me are unlisted. The Maryland number belongs to Admiral Schaeffer of the CIA. He has a Baltimore hideaway. His official residence is at Fort McNair. The Virginia number is the country residence of one Jules Vaterman, an old money millionaire with lots of political clout. He's presently serving four to eight at the Treasury Department: *noblesse oblige*. Did these people have anything to do with killing Donna and Dan?"

"Yes, and with Miriam's help," Holloway added bitterly.

"Miriam?"

"It had to be her. The same day that Miriam left me, she called her aunt in Kansas and left those phone numbers as the places where she could be contacted. The next day, CIA hoods hit my place and killed Donna and Dan. It had to be Schaeffer."

"Why would Miriam Slayton sell you to Schaeffer?"

Wearily, Holloway said, "I'm not exactly sure, but somehow it's tied in with WorldCorp. By the way, I caught up with Randy Dillworth yesterday on the Riviera. He told me about WorldCorp, The Seven, the CIA connection, everything. I'm too tired to go over the story, but it's here, if you want to read it." Holloway took a box of writing paper out of his suitcase and gave it to Mitchell. Every sheet was covered with Holloway's scrawl. "It's Dillworth's last testament. One of Ackerman's hoods killed him last night." Holloway picked up his suitcase. "Can you harbor a fugitive for a few more hours? I'm tired." Without waiting for a reply, Holloway went upstairs to Mitchell's guest room. He set the alarm for two hours and barely got his shoes off before falling into a deep sleep.

Mitchell had finished reading the WorldCorp story and was nursing a fresh beer when the guest room alarm went off. Holloway came down, dressed in dark slacks and a black summer jacket over a lightweight turtleneck, also black. He took a soft drink from the refrigerator and straddled a chair across the table from Mitchell.

"You're dressed for second-story work," observed Mitchell.

"Yeah. I'm going to find Miriam." Holloway was looking past Mitchell into some vision only he could see.

"It's bad tactics to go after her first. You'll warn the others."

Holloway's eyes blazed. "I want her first!"

Mitchell let him calm down. "Do you want any help?"

"No. Have you got a Virginia map? I'm going to check Vaterman's place first."

Mitchell got a map from the counter and spread it out on the table. He had already circled Vaterman's estate in red ink.

Holloway studied the location and put the map into his pocket.

"What about this?" Mitchell pointed to the box of papers containing Dillworth's story.

"If I don't surface in a week, send it to the Iran-Contra investigating committee."

"Ed, who do you think the Embassy Man is?"

"You checked the White House personnel files, Sid. Who sponsored Slayton for his job on the National Security Council? Who was his godfather?"

They both knew.

"Jesus! I can't believe that," said Mitchell

"Believe it," Holloway assured him.

* * *

The entrance to Jules Vaterman's estate in the Virginia hinterlands was down a seldom-used road flanked on either side by steep, wooded embankments. The property had no fence. There was only one road in. Anyone entering by that route would be easy to spot from the house. Holloway didn't see a guard as he drove by the entry road. He continued down the main road for half a mile until he found a break in the embankment large enough to hide the car. He parked there, climbed the embankment and backtracked through the woods until he was opposite the entry road to Vaterman's estate. There was no sign of life. The entry road wound gently uphill for three hundred meters, and terminated at a large, two-story house, the main residence. Fifty meters to the left, Holloway could see a smaller stone cottage. The sky was gray. At most, there would be another forty-five minutes of daylight. He hunkered down against a tree to watch and wait.

Twenty minutes later, his patience was rewarded. The man in the woods near the entrance stood up to stretch. It was Buie Trung. When he raised his arms, his short jacket rode up and Holloway could see the pistol holster attached to his belt. In another few minutes Trung's relief man, Pinchot, ambled down to the guard post. The two men had a quick conversation, laughed, and Trung headed in the direction of the big house. Pinchot settled into Trung's vacated chair.

An hour after darkness engulfed the estate, Holloway made his way through the woods to a point a hundred meters up the road from the guard post, crossed, and climbed the embankment to a stand of trees on Vaterman's property. Cutting a wide path around the guard post, he came out of the trees a hundred meters from the big house. Lights burned on the first floor and in the cottage. Holloway was trying to decide which building to check first when the door to the big house opened and a man came out. Holloway stepped back into the trees. The man walked over to the cottage and stood for a few seconds, peering into an open window. Then he came down the road on his way to the guard post. As he passed, Holloway identified him as Trung. A few minutes later, Pinchot walked by and paused at the cottage window, before going to the big house. Holloway looked at the luminous dial of his watch. The guards were on two-hour shifts.

Holloway dashed across the clearing and circled the big house to see if there were more guards. The lights were out on the second floor. Through the first floor windows, he saw Pinchot eating and watching television. He was alone—no more guards, no Vaterman, no Miriam. Holloway went to the cottage.

He looked into the open window where Trung had lingered and saw the reason. Miriam Slayton was lounging on the couch in a sarong-like gown cut to the thigh, Pavarotti was on the turntable and a half-empty decanter of something stood next to her on the floor. She was alone. Holloway leaned into the window and said, "Hello, Miriam." It was the kind of hard "hello" used when you catch someone doing something they shouldn't.

Miriam jumped up, startled. "Holloway! God, you scared me."

"Can I come in?" he asked.

Miriam opened the door and experienced an awkward moment after Holloway entered. She hesitated, then kissed him while he stood there, passively. The odor of Scotch was on her breath. Miriam stepped back and looked at him. "Well, absence evidently does not make all hearts grow fonder." She raised her chin and went back to the couch. "How did you find me?" The question sounded like she didn't much care about the answer.

Holloway's voice betrayed his smoldering anger. "I looked real hard." He surveyed the place quickly. There were three rooms: a bedroom to his left, the living room, where they were, and a kitchen to his right. "What are you doing here, Miriam?"

"The owner is an old friend of mine. I ran into him after I left you and he offered me this cottage for as long as I want to stay."

"How nice." There was a fireplace on the far wall of the cottage and a window next to it. Holloway went over and looked out into the night. Nobody was looking back at him.

"Here of your own free will?" he asked.

"Of course!"

He checked the kitchen, returned, and stood in front of her. "There are a couple of armed guards patrolling the grounds. They look into your window when they change shifts. Do they just like your legs or are they making sure you don't leave?"

That information seemed to come as a surprise to Miriam. She got up and walked to the table for her cigarettes. "They're my bodyguards."

Holloway sneered, "I can believe that. They don't want you to get away from here and talk about WorldCorp."

"I don't know what you're talking about." Miriam looked away and put a match to her cigarette. Her hands trembled slightly.

"Let's get rid of the light. I don't want to be surprised by your keepers." He turned off the lamp and led her to the bedroom. Moonlight was the only illumination there. Miriam put out her cigarette and fell onto the bed. She was smiling at him.

"I had a long talk with Randy Dillworth," he told her. "I know all about The Seven Committee, Vaterman, Schaeffer, and your husband. Dillworth told me about everybody except you."

Miriam's nostrils flared in anger "I still don't know what you're talking about. And as for that degenerate, Dillworth, he would say anything about anybody for a whiff of cocaine." She got up and came close to Holloway assuming a defiant stance, head back and slightly to one side, arms akimbo, feet spread wide enough apart so that the sarong slits exposed her thighs. "Did you bring me in here to talk or make love?" It was a strange feeling for him, wanting to make love to a woman and kill her at the same time.

"I brought you in here to find out why my friends are dead."

"Oh, for Christ's sake!" Miriam hissed. She tossed her head and turned away.

"When the investigators followed the Iran-Contra money to Switzerland, the WorldCorp gang got nervous. They came up with a plan to frame the President as a way of taking the heat off of themselves."

"You are insane!" cried Miriam.

"Your husband wouldn't go along with that and they decided to get rid of him. Meantime, he tried to warn the President. There's poor Jack Slayton, his career in a shambles, no friends, all those nasty little secrets running around inside his head, and a belly full of guilt. He has nowhere to turn, no one to talk to . . . except you, Miriam. Sometime before Slayton died, he told you about WorldCorp and The Seven Committee. Did he say, 'If something happens to me, call the President'?"

Miriam said nothing.

"He told you everything, didn't he?" Holloway grabbed Miriam by the shoulders and spun her around. "Didn't he!"

Miriam could contain her feelings no longer. Her face contorted into a mask of anger and disgust. "Yes! He told me!" she hissed, twisting herself free of Holloway's grip. "First, he unburdened himself to me in a letter, which I have carefully hidden away." She uttered a derisive laugh. "I thought he was making it all up. Then, he flew out to Kansas three days before he died. He came sniveling to me, spewing out his tale of woe and his," she spat the words, "personal devotion to the President. This was the same President who had kicked him out at the first hint of scandal and left him to—what was the phrase—'twist slowly, slowly in the wind,' while the media hounded us like wild dogs!"

For a moment, Miriam was so overcome by the memory of those days that she could not speak. Slowly, she calmed herself and spoke with a quiet bitterness that had been building in her for months. "Keeping the Iran-Contra investigation away from WorldCorp was the ultimate challenge for a billion-dollar empire and instead of facing up to it, Jack folded. After all of the lying, spying, and killing, he suddenly dredged up a moral scruple. He certainly cared more about the President than the President cared about him."

"So," said Holloway, "after your husband died, instead of telling the President about the plot, you contacted The Seven and tried to blackmail them."

Miriam lifted her chin to a defiant angle. "Yes!" she hissed. "Those bastards owed me." She turned on him wide-eyed, anger blazing. "I lived a lie, Holloway! For twenty years, I lived a lie! Do you have any idea what it was like for me to make that discovery after my best years were wasted? Do you!" Her body shook with rage.

"I could have had my own career. I could have had anything I wanted. All that money, and Jack never told me. That son-of-a bitch never told me!" she screamed. "While I worried about mortgage payments and educating the kids, he made millions from WorldCorp!"

"And you intend to make up for that by blackmailing The Seven?"

"Yes!" As she dried her eyes, anger again replacing self-pity.

"What did you ask for?"

"One-seventh of the net worth of WorldCorp—Jack's share, in cash."

"Did Vaterman and the others agree?"

"They're trying to bargain me down," she said contemptuously. "But they'll come around or rot in prison."

"You knew about WorldCorp and The Seven before I came to see you in Kansas?"

"Yes, I knew." She spoke defiantly, but would not look at him.

"And you had approached them with your demands, but they were stalling you, just like they're stalling now?"

"Yes." She still refused to look at him.

"Then you were using me from the first night we slept together."

She looked up at him. "No!"

"Yes, Miriam. You used me," he said bitterly. "They were stalling with the payoff. You needed some pressure to get them off dead center. So, you told me about Sheila Hamilton, knowing that she would send me on to WorldCorp. Once I started poking around in Geneva asking questions about your husband and Randy Dillworth, you knew that would shake them up. My presence was supposed to convince The Seven that you were serious about your threat to expose them if they didn't give you what you wanted."

"Holloway, listen—" pleaded Miriam.

Holloway's own anger was rising. He was in no mood to listen. "Your plan developed a little kink. Before I could trace your husband to WorldCorp and make the connection between him and Dillworth, Colonel Can, the Vietnamese, got involved. Can suspected that your husband was involved in the gold theft and was following him. When Slayton died and Dillworth disappeared, Can was out of leads. So, he went out to Kansas to torture the names of the other partners out of you, but killed your cousin, Denise, by mistake.

"You thought The Seven had sent him to kill you instead of buying you off. You panicked and came running to me for protection. When I returned from Geneva and told you that Denise's killer was working for Vietnamese intelligence, you figured that The Seven were not trying to kill you. You didn't need my protection anymore. So, you left me and renewed your blackmail ultimatum with Schaeffer and

Vaterman. And here you are, right back where you were when I met you, stalled while you negotiate your payoff." Holloway looked her up and down, the bitterness churning inside him. "You used me from Day One."

Miriam looked away. Quietly she said, "That's not all there was to it. That's not the way I wanted it to be. I was attracted to you. I hadn't made love in months, I— "

"You even used me in bed."

"Yes. That's true, but it was more than that Holloway. I like you. I thought we could be partners. You know your way around these people. I wanted you to be my partner," she pleaded. She came to him, but he moved away.

"Is that what all the 'moral ambiguity' talk was about?" he asked. "Were you interviewing me to find out if I was crooked enough to help you blackmail The Seven?"

In a voice that was barely audible, Miriam said, "Yes." She turned away and walked to the window. Holloway looked at the moonlit curves of her shoulders with a combination of contempt and lust that made him uneasy.

"We could still be partners," she said, turning to face him. "You like me. I like you. Money is not a problem." She walked toward him slowly. "We could spend the rest of our lives doing whatever we want, together." She was standing against him now and he could feel her breath on his cheek. A fireball ignited in his chest and radiated up and down, until his throat was parched and his loins were on fire.

Miriam laid the flat of her hand against his chest. "I made some mistakes with you, Holloway. But it wasn't because of you. I was just angry at Jack. I wanted revenge any way I could get it. I would have used anyone. I'm sorry." She kissed him. "I can see things more clearly now. I'm no good at negotiating with these people. I don't know the tricks. I need you. Be my partner. Please."

He pushed her away. "I'm afraid to be your partner, Miriam."

"Afraid? Of what?" she asked.

"That you might sell me out to Schaeffer again."

"What are you talking about?"

Holloway laid it out for her. "When you found out that The Seven didn't send the Vietnamese to kill you, you went to Schaeffer and told him that I had connected him to your husband and the others.

That's why he hit my place and killed Donna and Dan. You know they're dead, don't you?"

"Yes, but I didn't tell Schaeffer anything about you."

"You didn't? Am I supposed to believe that you just popped up on Schaeffer's doorstep after hiding at my place for two weeks and he welcomed you with open arms and no questions asked? What did you say? 'Hi. I've been shacking up with this guy whose been asking all those questions about you, but trust me.' I don't buy that, Miriam, and neither would Schaeffer. He would have been suspicious and besides you knew his men were watching the house. They might have seen you and reported it to Schaeffer."

Miriam stared at him in silence.

"You had to give Schaeffer something to prove your good faith. You told him that I had records on Trung, Dillworth, Ackerman, and your husband, that I had traced all four to his destroyer. When you told him that, you might as well have killed Donna and Dan yourself."

"No!" cried Miriam in anguish.

"Yes! You would have killed me, too, but when Schaeffer's hit men came calling, I was out getting drunk because you left me."

"Holloway, I swear I didn't tell him about the records. I swear!"

"It couldn't have been anyone else but you. The people who killed Donna and Dan wiped out my computer's memory. It takes a special computer program to do that. Schaeffer's hoods had one the night they came to my house. They knew in advance that we had incriminating information in the computer. You and I are the only ones left alive who could have told them."

Miriam began to cry and deny. "I didn't want that to happen!" she repeated between sobs.

"It happened," he reminded her, and he was ashamed of the fact that he was enjoying her pain. Holloway went to the living room and looked up the hill at the windows in the big house. He could see the television glowing and the shadow of Pinchot's head against the back wall. It would be a good hour before the guard changed again. There was enough time to get the rest of the information out of Miriam, if he had the discipline not to kill her first. He locked the doors and windows against surprise visitors.

Returning to the bedroom, he took a cigarette from the pack on the nightstand, lighted it, and handed it to Miriam. She accepted the smoke without looking at him. It glowed bright red against the blackness of the room. Holloway pulled a chair up to the bed where Miriam was seated and spoke in a soothing voice. "If we're going to trust each other," he said "we've got to admit how really rotten we are. I'll lay my cards on the table. I won't miss Dan and Donna. Dan was never that close to me and Donna was always trying to get too close. Her attention was getting on my nerves. There's no love lost on those two, as far as I'm concerned. I just don't want you to think that I'm stupid enough to believe that you didn't know Schaeffer would kill everybody in my house. You knew that, didn't you?'

Her "yes" was slow in coming.

"You knew he was going to kill me, too."

"For God's sake, Holloway, do you want me to write it in blood!"

In his head, a voice screamed, *Yes, I want it in blood!* "No need for that," he said, soothingly. "I just want you to acknowledge your responsibility for what happened to Donna and Dan. We have to admit that we would do just about anything, for the kind of money we're talking about. Once you get past framing the President and a few murders, you've got nothing to lose but the money." He chuckled softly in the darkness. "Now, were you serious about me being your partner?"

Miriam hesitated, but said, "Yes."

"Then, listen to me. You have to face up to the fact that you are a prisoner here, not a guest. The Vietnamese guard outside is Buie Trung, one of the founding fathers of WorldCorp. Trung's presence here means that these people are serious about keeping you on ice until they figure out how to handle you, and I don't think their plan includes giving you a one-seventh share of WorldCorp. They will stall you while they try to find out where you hid your husband's letter outlining the history of The Seven Committee. They're probably searching all the likely places right now. When they find it, they'll kill you. Believe me."

"They won't find it."

Holloway laughed. "You hid it someplace in Kansas, right?" Miriam gasped. "That's logical because you were at home until you moved in with me. You're smart enough not to be walking around with the document, and Washington is not a secure place for you. So, it has to be in Kansas. I would guess it's hidden on your property, maybe even in your house or car. They'll search those places first."

Miriam's eyes got wider.

"Tell me where you hid the letter. Maybe I can get to it before Schaeffer does. Then I'll get you out of here and handle negotiations. I'll see to it that you get what's coming to you." *Yes, I will!*

Miriam's eyes narrowed and her lips compressed into a tight line of resistance. "How do I know that you won't take the letter and blackmail them yourself?"

"I don't need your letter to blackmail them. I've already heard the WorldCorp story from Randy Dillworth."

Miriam put her arms around Holloway. "Get me out of here now. I'll take you to the hiding place."

Holloway shook his head. "That's not smart. As soon as the guards find out that you're gone, they'll call ahead and have people waiting for us in Kansas." Miriam gave him a skeptical look. "That's what I would do if I was in their shoes," Holloway assured her. "I think like they do. That's why you need me." Still, Miriam hesitated. Holloway persisted. "I'll get a red-eye flight to Kansas tonight and pick up the letter. As soon as I have it, I'll call Vaterman and tell him to release you. Come to the Crown Center in Kansas City. We'll celebrate. I'll get the same room we had the first night."

Miriam studied his face for a time. Then she said, "If you're not at Crown Center, I'll find you and cut your heart out, stud." She put out her cigarette and kissed him with passion. Holloway pulled her sarong up around her waist as they fell together onto the bed.

* * *

Ellis Eaton was about to turn in when the doorbell rang. He pulled a robe on over his pajamas and went downstairs. Holloway was waiting. Eaton's face registered surprise, then melted into a warm smile. "Edward. Come in."

"Surprised to see me, Ellis?"

"Frankly, yes. I understand the police are looking for you and I heard that you had left the country."

"I owe you a final report on The Seven and I need some help."

They went to the study. Eaton headed for the chair behind his desk, but Holloway stopped him. "Sit over there on the couch. I always feel upstaged when you're behind the desk."

Eaton smiled and sank into the leathery comfort of the sofa, his hands folded in his lap. Holloway took a chair opposite him.

"So, you've come to tell me about The Seven?" said Eaton.

"Let me give you a hypothetical case, Ellis. There's talk around Washington about a 'self-sustaining, off-the-shelf, covert action capability' being used to support the CIA. Let's say that such an organization exists."

"Pure balderdash!"

"I ran into a fellow named Randolph Dillworth who doesn't think so. He said that Jack Slayton was a secret member of the organization. His job was to identify covert CIA projects that had been disapproved either by the Administration or on Capitol Hill, and make funds available for them. It was a way for the CIA to short-circuit both the President and Congress."

Eaton frowned and said, "That is a wild accusation and, of course, Slayton cannot defend himself."

"I think it's wild, too, because Slayton didn't have access to that kind of information either in the Pentagon or the White House. Still, he got information regularly on covert projects and passed it along to a bank in Geneva for funding. The obvious conclusion is that someone in a position to know passed the projects to Slayton. It would have to be someone at the CIA—like Admiral Schaeffer. Also, it could be someone who sat on the President's Foreign Intelligence Board, or the covert action approval committee, or someone who advised the President on national security matters—someone like you, Ellis.

"Slayton was your protégé. You brought him to the National Security Council. I checked with the White House personnel office.

"You two shared the WorldCorp secret. I'll bet that if I researched your career carefully, I'd find that you worked for the CIA in Saigon in 1975. You're 'the Embassy Man,' Ellis."

Eaton seemed to relax, the way one does when the burden of a dark secret is finally removed. "So, you've talked to Mr. Dillworth and now you know our secrets. How much did he tell you?"

"Everything."

"Pity." The word was a reminder. "By the way, my condolences concerning the death of your partners. Nasty business, drugs."

Holloway's anger blazed. "Don't push your luck, Ellis."

Eaton looked at his hands and back at Holloway. "All the same, my condolences are sincere. Violence and power make for a rather difficult combination in Admiral Schaeffer. I assure you that if I had been in the decision loop on that operation, it would not have happened. I had the greatest respect for Mrs. Goodwin—and for you."

"I don't want your respect. I want Schaeffer."

Eaton looked down at his hands again and said nothing.

"Who else was in on the hit?"

"Edward, it won't do any good to—"

"Who else?" Holloway's hand moved quickly and Eaton found himself looking into the barrel of the Smith and Wesson hammerless. "And stop calling me 'Edward.' "

Eaton cleared this throat. "Trung and Schaeffer's driver, Pinchot."

"But the hit was Schaeffer's idea?"

"Yes."

Holloway shook his head slowly. "You people. No matter which one of you I talk to, the really bad stuff was always somebody else's idea."

To Eaton's relief, Holloway lowered the gun. "I want two things from WorldCorp, The Seven, or whatever the hell you call yourselves. I want Schaeffer and I want to know what the plan was for framing the President for the Iran-Contra scandal."

Unruffled by Holloway's belligerent mood, Eaton said, "Let me handle the easy one first. We made no specific plans to implicate the President, in spite of what Dillworth may have told you. It was a conceptual discussion, a 'what if' exercise."

"Jack Slayton didn't seem to think so."

"Slayton had his own agenda. All of us want to be remembered for something. His consuming passion was to be seen and remembered as a civil servant dedicated to the security of this country. Not a monumental ambition, to be sure, but there you are.

"Leaving the White House in disgrace was a devastating experience for Slayton. As the Iran-Contra operation began to unravel, he was tortured by the thought that he would be remembered—if at all—as simply a casualty of the scandal. So, Slayton embellished the 'plot' for his own purposes. Such a dramatic revelation would have gotten him a sympathetic hearing at the White House and given him leverage to negotiate a pardon or plea bargain at the expense of the other Committee members. In his own eyes, at least, exposing a plot to frame the President would have restored a portion of his tattered reputation."

"Why did you drag me into this after your people killed Slayton?"

"That was not my idea. I told you the truth when I said that the President asked for you by name. Slayton's untimely death and his allegations of a plot against the President upset the First Lady. The President wanted someone competent and discreet to conduct the inquiry. He remembered you. I assumed that you would make your inquiries, find nothing, and that would be the end of it. Unfortunately, Ackerman was sloppy when he terminated Slayton. You found the capsule and Slayton's letter warning the President about us. We were sloppy and you were at your best." Eaton stood up. "'Mind if I get a drink?" Holloway waved the gun toward the whiskey cabinet and Eaton poured himself a Perrier. "Something for you?"

"Get on with it," Holloway commanded.

Eaton went back to the couch. "Where was I? Oh, yes. You went to the White House with Slayton's letter. At that point I felt the damage was controllable. I saw no reason to tell Schaeffer or the others about your inquiry. Schaeffer would have had you killed immediately." Parenthetically, he added, "Schaeffer tends to see violence as the answer to most people problems. However, your death would have only reenforced concern at the White House, and my objective was to give the President and the First Lady a sense of security. I tried to keep you occupied with those worthless Tower Commission documents, but Miriam Slayton sent you off to Geneva.

"When Colonel Can came out of the woodwork, the thing spun out of control. You," Eaton smiled, "were out of control." He took a sip of sparkling water. "When you got hold of the military records and linked Schaeffer to our little group, the admiral took action without consulting the Committee." Eaton paused and gave Holloway a look that might have been admiration. "By the way, how did you get those military records?"

"I have my sources."

"Yes. I would expect that of you." Eaton crossed his legs and removed a speck of lint from his bathrobe. "Now, as to the matter of

Admiral Schaeffer, I can appreciate your desire to avenge the loss of your friends. However, I want you to set your feelings aside for a minute and think like an intelligence professional. View Schaeffer from that perspective. The man is a unique national asset. He is at the nexus of sensitive intelligence requirements and capabilities. He knows where the gaps are in the intelligence community and what can and cannot be accomplished through official channels. When a worthwhile project cannot make the official list, Schaeffer can bring WorldCorp's covert assets on line to satisfy the requirement. If something needs to be done, we just do it. There's no red tape, no leaks, and no paper trail for the Monday morning quarterbacks to follow. The Seven Committee has worked for years to get people like Schaeffer into key positions and we have done some very good work for this country. You would be surprised by what we have achieved, the Iran-Contra debacle notwithstanding. You want us to throw all that away because your friends died? What are the consequences for the United States if you kill Schaeffer to satisfy your blood lust?"

Holloway snapped back, "I don't give a damn about the consequences. And don't worry. I'm not going to kill anybody. Schaeffer is your mad dog. You put him down."

Eaton gave Holloway a long, disapproving look. "Why should we do that? In return for your silence? Really, Edward, it's disappointing to see you add your name to the long list of people who have tried to blackmail us—many of whom are dead, I might add."

"Don't get snotty with me, Ellis. You're lucky I don't just blow you away and walk out of here." Holloway forced his temper back in check. "I didn't come here to blackmail you. I'm not as dumb as Miriam Slayton." Eaton's eyebrows went up again. Another surprise from Holloway. "I have something to trade for Schaeffer."

"What could you possibly have of such value?"

"If Miriam publishes Jack Slayton's letter detailing the history of WorldCorp, all of you will go to jail."

"We'll find Slayton's letter," Eaton assured him. "It's just a matter of time."

"But not before I do. I know where it is."

"Is that what you propose to trade for Schaeffer's life?"

"Yes."

"Let me be frank with you. Slayton's revelations could wound us, but not mortally. The intelligence operation in Geneva is being dismantled at this very moment. By the time anyone starts poking around, there will be no trace of The Seven at WorldCorp. If we fall, other like-minded men will simply take our places on the Committee." Eaton sat back comfortably. "And as I said, we will find the infamous 'history' soon, anyway. At that point, Miriam Slayton will, herself, become history."

"Suppose I tell my story to Congress and the Secret Service?"

"I suggest you reconsider that option," cautioned Eaton. "There is the matter of the late Colonel Can whom you shot to death in Geneva. We have the gun with your fingerprints and the location of the colonel's body. Add that to your association with drugs and I think you might have a credibility problem with the authorities. The fact is, you don't have a single card to play. The best you can do is give yourself up to the police and hope to convince them that you had nothing to do with the deaths of your friends."

Eaton paused to let Holloway consider his dilemma, then offered the life preserver. Softening his tone, Eaton said, "There are alternatives. I know that you are a patriot and one of the authentic heroes in the intelligence community. For that I salute you. Why not put your background to use and join us? You could pick your job. That won't bring your friends back, but think of the good you could do. If you don't want to work for us directly, go back to the Company. Schaeffer could find you a worthwhile position. From there, you could keep us abreast of situations in which WorldCorp's covert assets could be employed. Of course, you would be well taken care of when you chose to retire."

"Like Dr. Reid was taken care of?"

"Dr. Reid was naive," said Eaton, dismissing the subject. "Our nation is locked in a struggle for survival. In that war there are only three entities: our soldiers, the enemy, and the innocents. We protect our own, we destroy our enemies, and the innocents have to fend for themselves. Which are you? You must choose."

Holloway was frustrated and angry. "You want choice? Here's your choice. If I don't read Schaeffer's obituary in the *Washington Post* one week from today, I'll kill all of you. Tell that to what's left of your Committee."

* * *

Holloway had no intention of giving them a week to run him down. If Eaton wouldn't bargain, there was another way to handle the problem. He found a pay telephone and called Fort McNair.

"Admiral Schaeffer."

Holloway said, "Just listen. Jack Slayton wrote the history of The Seven before he died and Miriam Slayton has it hidden away. You want to know where it is. I'm going to tell you. It's in the ceiling of her attic in Kansas between the insulation and the roof."

"Who is this?"

"Don't waste time, Admiral. As for Mrs. Slayton, I leave her disposal in your capable bands. Oh, and when you see her, tell her something for me." Holloway gave Schaeffer the message.

"What's in this for you, Holloway?" Who else could it be?

"Satisfaction." Holloway hung up the phone and drove the back roads to Vaterman's as fast as he could.

* * *

Schaeffer dialed a number on the Army post at Fort Leavenworth, Kansas. His party answered. "Phil?. . .Schaeffer here. I want you to go back out to Mission for me and get that document. This time I can tell you where to look. Do it, right now. It's urgent."

* * *

Miriam was stepping out of the shower when they came for her. There were three of them: Schaeffer, Trung and Pinchot. She heard them entering the cottage. Miriam put on her robe and went to the living room. "Did you ever hear of knocking?" she asked, focusing her irritation on Schaeffer. "What do you want?"

"You." Schaeffer nodded. Trung and the Pinchot grabbed Miriam by the arms and forced her into the bedroom. Schaeffer followed, carrying a black leather case. Miriam screamed and fought to free herself. "Don't leave any marks on her," Schaeffer cautioned. The two men pinned her to the bed and Trung clamped a gloved hand over her mouth. Schaeffer put his bag on the nightstand and leaned over the bed. "Listen to me, Miriam. I want information from you. There is no point in struggling. You obviously cannot get away. There is no point in yelling because there are no neighbors to hear you. So, let's make this easy, shall we? Tonight, we recovered Jack's letter from your attic. Now, I need to know if you have any other copies tucked away? Humm?" Trung took his hand away from Miriam's mouth just long enough to permit the escape of an obscenity.

Schaeffer shook his head and tut-tutted. "Very unladylike, Miriam." He zipped open the black bag. "Since you won't cooperate, we'll have to do this the hard way." Schaeffer took out a syringe of clear fluid. "This won't hurt, but it will loosen your tongue. After you tell us about the other copies—if there are any—I have another needle for you. That one will send you on a long, long trip." Pinchot put a knee on Miriam's chest and straightened her arm, exposing the vein.

"I'm sure you're wondering how we found Jack's letter. A friend of yours called and told me where to look. He wanted me to give you this message. He said, 'Once you get past framing the President and a few murders, you've got nothing to lose but the money.'" Miriam's eyes were wide with fear and rage as Schaeffer plunged the needle into her arm. Her mind screamed the last fully conscious thought she would ever have: Hollowaaaay!

Holloway deliberately waited until Schaeffer had stuck the needle into Miriam's vein before he entered the room. He may have waited because it was smart tactics to wait until all three men were fully occupied with Miriam. Or, he may have waited because he wanted Miriam to get a taste of what it might have been like for Dan and Donna before they were shot. When he did enter the bedroom, he slipped in quietly with his gun drawn. Schaeffer was bent over Miriam, injecting the drug. Pinchot was holding her arm, with his knee still on her chest. On the far side of the bed, Trung held Miriam's other arm.

Miriam was the first to see Holloway. She let out a muffled scream and tried to sit up, her eyes wide with hope, but Holloway's impassive face told her there was none. He had not come to rescue. He had come to kill. Trung followed Miriam's stare and was the next to see Holloway. He was the first to reach for his gun and the first to die. His fingers were still clawing at the pistol holster on his belt when Holloway's bullet ripped through his chest. He fell against the nightstand and took the lamp with him to the floor, plunging the room into semi-darkness. Holloway knew that he shouldn't have wasted any more time on Trung but the man was still thrashing around. Holloway fired a second shot that stilled him.

Schaeffer and Pinchot jumped away from the bed and Holloway was late and off target with his next shot. The driver's gun roared and flamed. Impact! Holloway felt like he had been hit in the chest with a baseball bat. There was no pain, but the shock seemed to temporarily disconnect his mind and body. With eerie detachment, his mind recorded and evaluated the event. It told him that he was being thrown up and backwards. The driver must have fired from a crouch, he thought, as he felt his feet lose contact with the floor and his body hurtle back through the doorway into the living room. The gun would be something heavy, a .45, maybe. Where did he hit me? Pain! Holloway felt it when he hit the floor. The entire chest. For a second he lay there flat on his back with the wind knocked out of him. Pinchot's gun roared again and he felt a white-hot stabbing pain eat into his ribs and angle up toward his shoulder blade. He heard himself scream and Miriam hysterical in the background. Schaeffer was yelling, "Get him! Get him!"

It was Pinchot's turn to make a mistake. He charged at Holloway for the kill. Holloway raised his gun with both hands and fired three shots at the driver's onrushing form. Pinchot's head whipped back and his feet seemed to run out from under him as he went crashing to the floor.

In spite of the pain, Holloway drew his legs up to his chest and rolled sideways away from the doorway and out of the line of fire. He dragged himself behind the couch and lay there panting.

Bad show, buckaroo. You're gonna die, if you don't get out of here fast.

Schaeffer called him. "Holloway! You know I've got Miriam. If you don't throw your gun in here to me, I'll shoot her." Silence. "Are you listening, Holloway?"

Holloway was listening, but the pain was too intense for him to speak. If he had been able to say anything, he would have told

Schaeffer to go to hell and take Miriam with him. There was a certain poetic justice in leaving Miriam here at the mercy of her own kind. Holloway summoned as much breath as he could muster and said, "I can wait as long as you can, Schaeffer. You're a dead man."

So much for bluff. He had to get out of there before he bled to death on the living room rug. Holloway shot out the ceiling light, reloaded and crawled backwards across the living room and through the kitchen, until he got to the side door that led to the yard. Holloway had backed out onto the porch and was closing the door when he heard the movement behind him. His intention was to jump sideways, but never made it. His senses registered the flash and impact simultaneously. Once more, he felt his body being lifted and carried. He was thrown forward through the half-closed door, back into the kitchen. Chairs skidded and the table collapsed under his weight. This time, there was no pain when he landed, only the black void.

"I got him, Schaeffer!"

The admiral stepped cautiously into the kitchen and looked at the man standing over Holloway with a silenced revolver. "Well done, Jules, but you certainly took your damned good time."

"I am a financier, not an infantryman," snapped Vaterman. "How did you know that Holloway would be here?"

"He wanted me out here to get even. That's why he told me where Jack's letter was hidden. He knew that once I had it, I would dash over to close out our business with Miriam. Smart man, but predictable. Well, it's done now. Let's clean up the mess. Then, we'll finish with Miriam."

"Don't we have people to take care of this sort of thing?" asked Vaterman.

Schaeffer gave Vaterman a look reserved for the village idiot. "Of course, we do. Just how many more people would you like to have involved in this?"

CHAPTER 20

Sid Mitchell sat at the desk in his work room at home. He had been there for a long time, the words of the detective at the hospital playing over and over in his head: "He's in bad shape."

Holloway had been dumped in Anacostia Park, left for dead. A patrol car found him shortly after 3 a.m. Multiple gunshot wounds. The detective looked at Holloway's near lifeless form in the hospital bed and nodded toward the hall. "Might be a good idea to step outside." Mitchell followed him to a deserted waiting room. "We found your name in his wallet as the person to notify in case of an emergency. Are you family?"

"Friend," said Mitchell, trying to swallow the lump in his throat.

"Do you know that your friend is wanted for questioning in connection with multiple homicides and drug trafficking?"

"Yes. I read the papers."

"If you don't mind my asking, where were you when the hits went down at Holloway's apartment?"

"With the First Lady in New York." Mitchell showed the man his Secret Service credentials.

The detective nodded. "That's a damn good alibi."

"Do I need one?"

"Not especially. When was the last time you saw Mr. Holloway?"

"Before I left for New York. I gave him the key to my house. He waters my plants when I'm out of town."

"You trusted this guy, huh?"

"Yes."

"What about this drug business?"

"I don't believe everything I read in the papers. Do you?"

"Not unless it's about the mayor." The detective broke into convulsive laughter and Mitchell left him to find Holloway's physician.

The doctor had a young-old face that was aging before its time. That must have been one of the occupational hazards of being a surgeon in a city competing for murder capital of the country. "Your friend is in critical condition, Mr. Mitchell. We were able to save the lung. That was a miracle. The rest of him is Swiss cheese. If he makes it through the night, that would be another miracle."

Mitchell sat in the lounge for several hours praying for one. The young-old doctor passed by at dawn and saw him nodding off. "Don't waste your time sitting around here," he said. "Leave your number at the desk and go home. I'll have someone call you if there's any change." He had taken the doctor's advice, but no call had come.

Mitchell took a large envelope from his desk drawer and addressed it to "Chairman, Senate Select Committee on Secret Military Assistance to Iran and the Nicaraguan Opposition, The Capitol, Washington, D.C." He stuffed Holloway's handwritten record of Dillworth's confession into the envelope and sealed it. For several minutes he sat there, wondering what impact the confession would really have.

The Iran-Contra hearing would be one of the biggest media events of the decade, providing priceless public exposure for some congressmen. Jockeying on Capitol Hill for seats on the committees had been keen. Mitchell tried to visualize the hearings. He saw a cast of hundreds, a parade of witnesses flanked by earnest or sarcastic lawyers and backed up by supportive family members. There would be political posturing, righteous indignation, arrogant aloofness, immunity, limited immunity, and all that other damned legal mumbo jumbo. Behind it all, the relentless search for the smoking gun would continue.

Would it mean anything to Joe Six-Pack back in East St. Louis? Or would the man in the street know in his gut that the guilty were going to walk? After the hearings, plea bargains, trials and appeals, would it be Watergate all over again? The bad guys would get pardons and hit the lecture circuit, or go off for a short vacation at the Gentlemen's Rest Home for the Slightly Criminal at Danbury to write their books. After all the legal blue smoke and mirrors, would there be justice for Donna Goodwin and Dan Vogle and Ed Holloway?

Mitchell got angry and went down to the yard to cool off. It was night and the stars were out. He sat at the wooden picnic table on his patio and looked up at them. He didn't consider himself a religious person, but at that moment he wanted badly to know God's views on justice and the law—if there was a God. He sat there until the chill drove him back to his workroom. Mitchell picked up the envelope again, looked at it, and locked it away in his desk. Then he called Joe.

* * *

There was a breeze. It was brisk enough to make the visitor's sandy-gray hair dance about his head and whip his trench coat open at the knees as he walked down the stone path. He was a short, compact man with sharp eyes, a hard jaw, and jutting chin, not a person to be trifled with. He came to the cemetery every Sunday carrying a bouquet of roses. For privacy, he arrived very early or— like today—very late. In spite of himself, he wept during these visits. It was a "weakness" he did not care to put on display for others. As he neared her headstone, the visitor noticed a stranger standing on the hill to his left, overlooking Donna's grave. He wore a dark coat and cap pulled down against the breeze. The visitor laid the roses next to Donna's headstone and stood there for a time, then took out a handkerchief and blew his nose. When he was ready, he walked up the hill to the stranger, hands jammed into his coat pockets. He kept them there when he introduced himself, a signal that he resented the intrusion on his time with Donna. In a tough voice he said, "I'm Joe Grisby." *And I kick ass*, might have been the follow-on implied by his manner.

Mitchell understood now why Grisby had not made a go of it with Donna. She preferred tall guys, a bit laid back, and with a sense of humor. Grisby struck out on all three counts. Maybe just two. Graveyards do nothing to bring out the humor in people.

"Thanks for meeting me," said Mitchell. "Donna and I were good friends." Mitchell could almost feel the hair stand up on Grisby's neck and he hastily added, "It was a sister-brother relationship. She shared personal things with me. She told me you proposed to her."

Mistake!

Grisby looked as if he was about to cut Mitchell's heart out. "Get to the point."

"What would you do if you knew who killed her."

"I'd kill the sons-a-bitches myself." He frowned at Mitchell. "Do you know something that you haven't told the police?"

"I don't have any proof, but I've got hearsay that will knock your socks off."

"Such as?"

"Take a walk with me. I'll tell you a story." They walked along the rows of headstones toward the setting sun. When the story was finished, the two men had returned to the hill overlooking Donna's grave.

"What do you want me to do?" asked Grisby.

"I need some supplies." Mitchell told him what was required and why.

Grisby asked, "Are you sure you know how to use that stuff?"

"Yes," lied Mitchell.

Grisby looked Mitchell up and down, taking his measure, deciding if he was up to what he was proposing. "Meet me here, same time, next week. I'll have it for you." Grisby gave Mitchell another long, hard stare. Then, he looked down the hill at Donna's grave. The wind had blown away all of the roses from the headstone. When Grisby turned back to Mitchell the hardness had vanished from his eyes. He started to say something. Before the words could come, he turned and walked down the stone path back to the cemetery gate.

A week later, Grisby came to the same spot and gave Sid Mitchell a small package.

* * *

Any intelligence officer worth his salt will tell you that, from the standpoint of personal security, patterns can be deadly. However, events in Washington's intelligence community are frequently driven as much by bureaucratic and personal convenience as they are by security considerations. That combination explains why Admiral

Schaeffer went to the Pentagon each Wednesday morning. It was the best time to get appointments with the people he wanted to see. His liaison visit with the Director of Naval Intelligence came first. Afterwards, if he had a particularly juicy morsel of information, he might get a few minutes with the Chief of Naval Operations or his vice—an opportunity for that all-important visibility, without which the careers of otherwise able men often languish. These meetings were always over early and by half past ten Schaeffer was enjoying the personal convenience of changing clothes in the Pentagon Officers' Athletic Club without the press of the lunch hour mob.

Dressed in his black and gold warm-up suit, Schaeffer bounded out of the POAC and jogged along the path to the Arlington Memorial Bridge. Up ahead, a lone runner in a nondescript gray warm-up suit loped toward him. The oncoming runner slowed to a walk a hundred meters from Schaeffer and put a cigarette into his mouth.

Another one of those idiots who runs and smokes, thought Schaeffer. When the admiral was almost face-to-face with the man, he realized that what he had mistaken for a cigarette was a large milkshake straw.

Schaeffer's eyes widened with comprehension. He tried to break his stride and throw up his hands, but it was too late. Sid Mitchell blew a cloud of fine powder into the admiral's face. Schaeffer gasped. His face twisted into a mask of agony. He clawed at his chest in a vain effort to pull away the elephant weight that heart attack victims experience. Mitchell let him fall face down into the dirt before appearing to come to his aid. He rolled Schaeffer over on his back and gave him a futile thirty seconds of cardiac massage for the benefit of any onlookers, but nobody was around to notice and Schaeffer was already dead. Mitchell propped the body against a tree and jogged toward the door of the POAC. Still nobody in sight. He ran past the door and kept going until he reached the Pentagon's south parking lot. Mitchell found the car on the back row with the motor running and a grim Joe Grisby at the wheel.

* * *

Ellis Eaton strode up to the White House Chief of Staff wearing his most engaging smile. "Good morning, Howard."

"Good morning, Ellis." The Chief glanced at his desk calendar. "A little early for your 11:30, aren't you? The President will be in the Cabinet Room with people from The Hill for another ten minutes."

"Then I'm right on time," said Eaton. "I have some rather complicated diagrams to set up." Eaton tapped the leather chart case he was carrying. "It will save the President some time if I lay them out before he arrives."

The Chief was pleased that Eaton might not use all of his allotted time. He needed to squeeze in another visitor in before lunch. "Okay. Do you need an easel?"

"No, thanks. He likes them arranged on the floor."

Eaton's friendly smile faded as he entered the Oval Office. He walked quickly to the desk where the President's personal diary lay closed and began to do what he had practiced for two days with a similar book. He took out a Swiss Army knife, opened it and laid it on the desk. Next to it he placed an address label stuck to wax paper. The label contained eight digits, typed on a White House typewriter. Eaton took the President's diary and stood it upright on the desk as though on a bookshelf. Then he bent the front and rear covers back until the edges touched, creating an opening between the spine of the book and the spine cover. With his free hand, he put one corner of the waxpaper between his teeth and stripped off the mailing label, exposing the sticky backing. Carefully, he inserted the label between the spine of the diary and its cover, pushing it as far down as possible, before attaching it to the spine. A part of the label protruded above the book's spine. Eaton closed the diary and cut away the protruding part of the label even with the tops of the pages. He opened the book again and ran an especially prepared swab over the label to obliterate fingerprints. Satisfied with his handiwork, Eaton returned the diary to its original spot on the desk and pocketed the evidence of his mischief. The process had taken less than thirty seconds.

A few minutes later, the President strode into the Oval Office. "Good morning, Ellis. What's the latest on the Slayton case?"

"I believe I have good news for you. My investigator has completed his labors. We have drawn a complete blank. There is no trace of this mysterious 'Seven' referred to in Jack Slayton's letter.

Frankly, I think Slayton's letter and the information he gave the First Lady were complete fabrications."

The President looked puzzled. "Why would he make up stories like that? It just doesn't make sense."

"I don't like to speculate about people's motives, especially in Washington. However, the man's life was falling apart on all fronts. I believe that he had to invent something to justify his very existence."

"So, there's no conspiracy, no 'Seven' to deal with. What's the next move?"

"There's nothing more to be done. I believe that my usefulness to you in this matter is exhausted."

"Thanks for your efforts, Ellis. All of us will rest easier, now that this thing is settled."

Eaton smiled, "Always a pleasure to serve you, Mr. President."

* * *

They were in the study at Ellis Eaton's Georgetown house. Eaton passed a flute of Dom Perignon to Jules Vaterman, who was saying, "All things considered, we came out of this with few scars. It's not over yet, but I think this Iran-Contra mess was useful for purging our ranks of its more violent elements. Schaeffer, Ackerman, and Trung were a bloodthirsty lot, thugs at heart. Slayton never had the stomach for our covert activities and Dillworth was just poor white trash. They all got pretty much what they deserved. Admit it, Ellis. If they hadn't been charter members, we'd have washed our hands of them long ago."

Eaton said, "I wouldn't judge them too harshly, Jules. WorldCorp lasted quite a long time without a crisis."

"Yes. Well, 'What's past is prologue,'" said Vaterman, dismissing the subject. "Did you take care of that little matter in the Oval Office?"

"Yes." replied Eaton. The number for the Swiss bank account is concealed in the spine of the President's diary. If it appears that any harm will come to us or our enterprises, an anonymous word to the special prosecutor for the Iran-Contra case would produce a subpoena for the diary. That should create enough of a sensation to keep us out of the limelight. How much did you deposit in the account?"

"Two million," said Vaternam.

Eaton winced. "You're awfully generous. Remember what the late Senator Dirksen said: 'A million here, a million there, and pretty soon you're talking about some real money.' "

Vaterman corrected him. "Dirksen said 'billion,' not 'million.' Besides, this is like buying a parachute in case the plane goes down. It's not the time to skimp." He sipped his champagne. "You're sure there is no possibility of the President spotting the account number?"

"None," Eaton assured him. "He would have to tear the back off of the diary. That's not likely to happen by accident, and I hope no one ever has to go looking for it. I detest the idea of implicating the President in our business. Still, I suppose it could become necessary."

"Of course it could. How did you put it in your book? 'We are all soldiers on the battlefield of today's wars, not by choice but by the demands of dark forces which we neither control nor comprehend.' The President is a soldier, too. A reservist, mind you, but a soldier nevertheless. Hopefully, we will not have to call him up. Comfort yourself with that thought, Ellis."

Eaton said an unenthusiastic, "Yes," and looked into his glass for another subject of conversation. "Have you talked to the Vietnamese?"

"I have, and they will be reasonable. We've arranged to aid their tourism industry through private investors, contingent upon their withdrawal from Cambodia. Also, there won't be any Vietnamese intelligence people prowling around for that plane we liberated in 1975. By the way," laughed Vaterman, "I convinced them that their Colonel Can had defected."

"What about the MIA remains?"

"They intend to drag their feet in the MIA talks until relations are normalized between our two countries. I couldn't budge them on that. They'll let a few sets of remains trickle out of Hanoi once in a while, but don't expect any major breakthroughs."

"You know, Jules, this hostage and blackmail business seems to go on forever. Now, we're negotiating for dead hostages."

"A small price to pay, if it keeps the Vietnamese away from WorldCorp. Don't you agree?"

Eaton did not agree, but something more important was on his mind. "Speaking of blackmail, what about this Talbot woman? Will she keep quiet?"

Mention of Jessica Talbot caused Vaterman to frown. "I thought she would. On reflection, I think she views us as a bottomless money pit to finance her political ambitions. As soon as we purge her Geneva files of the WorldCorp material, we should give her the Miriam Slayton treatment."

Eaton made a face. "Distasteful business."

"So is spying, my friend, but it is necessary." Vaterman raised his glass. "Here's to WorldCorp, the stand-alone, off-the-shelf, self-sustaining covert action capability for the United States of America. Let our enemies beware."

"Hear, hear," said Eaton and they drank.

Vaterman smacked his lips in an exaggerated display of delight and put his arm around Eaton. "Now, let's go out and have a little fun. I reserved a table at the Four Seasons."

They went out into the warm Washington evening to eat and drink. By the time the second bottle of wine was opened, Eaton's spirits had lifted and the two men communed with the easy camaraderie of old warriors taking a respite from their secret war on America's enemies. They were two generals displaying the self-assurance that comes with having a fortune in gold under the streets of Geneva to finance their battles.

When they went their separate ways after dinner, Sid Mitchell fell in behind Ellis Eaton and Joe Grisby followed Jules Vaterman.

THE END

Epilogue

In his book, *Decent Interval*, Frank Snepp, the CIA's chief strategy analyst for Vietnam, described the last tragic days of the Republic of (South) Vietnam, the fall of Saigon, and the American evacuation of that city. Snepp reported an agreement between the governments of South Vietnam and the United States to move Saigon's treasury out of the country to prevent its capture by the advancing North Vietnamese Army. He wrote, "[T]he military flight…was to ferry the $220 million in gold that made up Saigon's treasury to the Federal Reserve Bank in New York" for safekeeping. However, plans to *legally* fly the gold out of the country were thwarted by South Vietnam's Economics Minister Hoa. According to Snepp's sources, Hoa was secretly acting on behalf of the communist North Vietnamese regime. (This information was excerpted from *Decent Interval: An Insider's Account of Saigon's Indecent End Told by the CIA's Chief Strategy Analyst in Vietnam,* pp. 423-424.)

* * *

In our story, Jules Vaterman met with Le Kim in May 1987 to lay down the prerequisites for WorldCorp to invest in the Socialist Republic of Vietnam.

In fact, *The Europa World Year Book, Volume II, 2003,* reports that subsequent to that fictitious meeting, the Socialist Republic of Vietnam, took the following actions:

Agreed, in September 1987, "to investigate the fate of 70 [US] soldiers…believed to have been captured alive." (In return "the US Government…agreed to facilitate aid for Viet Nam from US charities and private groups.")

Withdrew its troops from Cambodia in September of 1989.

Established in early 1990, "four independent commercial banks, several joint-venture banks and introduced legislation to permit the operation of foreign banks in Viet Nam."

"Drafted a new constitution guaranteeing the protection of foreign investment" in December 1991.

With these events, the preconditions laid down by Jules Vaterman for WorldCorp investment in Vietnam had been satisfied.

Acknowledgments

While writing and marketing this book I drew on many sources. Here, I acknowledge my debt to those who, knowingly or unknowingly, helped to bring this project to fruition.

I consulted the writings of the following authors to provide authentic backgrounds for my fictional events and characters: Frank Snepp (*Decent Interval: An Insider's Account of Saigon's Indecent End.* NY: Random House, 1977); Senators William Cohen and George Mitchell (*Men of Zeal: A Candid Inside Story of the Iran-Contra Hearings.* NY: Viking, 1988); Shelby L. Stanton (*Vietnam Order of Battle.* Washington, DC: U.S. News Books; 1981) and Stanley Karnow (*Vietnam, A History: The First Complete Account of Vietnam at War.* NY: Viking, 1983). I also studied articles from *Time Magazine* and other news sources. Finally, Dan Poynter was, in absentia, my constant companion and advisor.

Many friends, acquaintances, and strangers provided material and moral support. Jay and Hanna Harris inspired me with their unwavering confidence that this book would be published. Judith Bottiggi, Shirley Gross, Gerri Battle, Rebecca Shivvers, and Karen Ridley read the manuscript and gently pointed out my errors. Former Senator and Secretary of Defense William Cohen also read the manuscript and wrote a generous endorsement. Cathy Tillman and her colleagues in the 'Book-in-a-Box Club' stoked my fire when the flame was burning low. Marcus Wood fed me more information than any human could possibly digest. Colonels Leroy Gross, Mike Herndon, and Butch Jackson, along with Lloyd Newton and Dr. Joan Wilcox, provided aid and comfort beyond any reasonable expectation. Monica Wood gave generously of her time and advice. Colonel H.H. Baker and The Wizard, Oz, unknowingly provided constant inspiration. Other friends, too numerous to name here, constantly asked me about the status of this project and encouraged me to finish it.

Without their knowledge, strangers in the writing life motivated me as I overheard them discussing their successes, failures, and frustrations in airports and other public places. With supernatural timing, they materialized whenever I needed encouragement.

Finally, my wife, Ophelia, permitted me to isolate myself as I wrote. She read and critiqued the manuscript, hissed at my bad guys (and me), and encouraged me to take a year off to finish the book. She was my number one gadfly and cheerleader. In every way, she is also God's gift to an undeserving soul.

In spite of all this help, I frequently ignored advice in pursuit of artistic expression. Therefore, any errors of commission or omission that remain in this work are my responsibility alone.

About the Author

James Scott is a former military officer and no stranger to the territory covered in his novel, *The Iran Contradictions*. He is a native of the Baltimore-Washington, D.C. area and served two tours on the Army Staff. One of those tours involved oversight of military intelligence operations. His other assignments included three years as a paratrooper with the 101st Airborne Division. He served with that organization in various positions from platoon leader to brigade staff officer, and accompanied the Division to Vietnam in 1967. Scott's duties in Vietnam took him from Saigon to the Demilitarized Zone, giving him firsthand knowledge of the settings in his novel. Scott was wounded during the intense combat that accompanied the North Vietnamese Army's Tet Offensive of 1968. Subsequently, Scott served as a battalion commander and traveled extensively in Europe during assignments with the 3rd Infantry Division and with a senior headquarters supporting U.S. Army, Europe/7th (U.S.) Army.

A message to the Reader

Dear Reader, thank you for purchasing this book.
Writing it was a labor of love and pain. I hope you enjoyed
it. If you would like to purchase additional copies
for yourself or another person, please use the
Book Order Form *on the facing page.*
If your purchases are gifts, the publisher will be happy to
include a card with a brief message at no expense to you.
The price is $24.95 (US) plus taxes and shipping.

In combat,
the lives of men and women in our military services
are often characterized by long periods of boredom
punctuated by brief periods of intense violence.
I speak from personal experience when I say that a book is
often a welcomed escape from the stress of armed conflict.
If you would like to provide a copy of this book for one or
more members of our Armed Forces
in a combat area or traveling to or from such an area,
the publisher will select qualified service members
and deliver the book(s) for you at a
15% discount on your purchase.
The price for this gift book is $21.25 (US) plus taxes and
includes a brief message, if you provide one.

If you desire to purchase large quantities,
a more generous discount can be negotiated.
Discounts, message service, and delivery to military service
members are services available only from the publisher.
They are not available in book stores or elsewhere.
I am sure your gift would be much appreciated.

Sincerely,
James A. Scott, Author

AAFTON RESEARCH and MEDIA, INC.
73 Greentree Drive #47, Dover, DE 19904
Phone: 617-407-6619/FAX: 011-496221-1374637
E-mail: AAFTON4201@yahoo.com

Book Order Form

Order by FAX, phone, mail, or e-mail at the above address.

Send __ copies of *The Iran Contradictions,* ISBN: 0-9639250-9-1 to:

Name: _____

Address: _____ City: _____

State: _____ Zip: _____ Telephone: _____

e-mail address: _____

Price: $24.95 U.S./$34.25 Canadian. Add $2.00 for shipping.
Do not send cash. Please make payment by: ___ Check

____ Money order ____ Institutional purchase order or

Credit card: ___ American Express ___ MasterCard ___ VISA

Card number: _____

Name on card: _____

Expiration date: ___/___ Signature _____

___ This is a gift. Send it to the address I have designated.

___ Send my purchase to member(s) of the Armed Forces.

___ I have included a message.

___ Prepare a message of 25 words or less.